The Canadian Fantastic in Focus

The Canadian Fantastic in Focus

New Perspectives

Edited by Allan Weiss

Proceedings of the Academic Conference
on Canadian Science Fiction
and Fantasy, 2005–2013

McFarland & Company, Inc., Publishers
Jefferson, North Carolina

LIBRARY OF CONGRESS CATALOGUING-IN-PUBLICATION DATA

The Canadian fantastic in focus : new perspectives / edited by Allan Weiss.
    p. cm.
"Proceedings of the Academic Conference on Canadian Science Fiction and Fantasy, 2005–2013."
Includes bibliographical references and index.

ISBN 978-0-7864-9592-4 (softcover : acid free paper) ∞
ISBN 978-1-4766-1790-9 (ebook)

1. Science fiction, Canadian—History and criticism—Congresses.
2. Fantasy fiction, Canadian—History and criticism—Congresses.
3. Canadian fiction—21st century—History and criticism—Congresses.
I. Weiss, Allan Barry, editor. II. Academic Conference on Canadian Science Fiction and Fantasy.
PR9192.6.S34C36 2014
813'.087609971—dc23
                                                                    2014038569

BRITISH LIBRARY CATALOGUING DATA ARE AVAILABLE

© 2015 Allan Weiss. All rights reserved

No part of this book may be reproduced or transmitted in any form or by any means, electronic or mechanical, including photocopying or recording, or by any information storage and retrieval system, without permission in writing from the publisher.

On the cover: Toronto skyline © 2014 igor kisselev/iStock/Thinkstock; earth and alien sky © 2014 Natalia Lukiyanova/Hemera/Thinkstock; maple leaves © 2014 SHSPhotography/iStock/Thinkstock

Printed in the United States of America

McFarland & Company, Inc., Publishers
Box 611, Jefferson, North Carolina 28640
www.mcfarlandpub.com

To the memory of
Judith Merril and Phyllis Gotlieb

Acknowledgments

The Academic Conference on Canadian Science Fiction and Fantasy, and therefore this book, would not exist or be able to continue without the support of many people, including the conference's founders, Jim Botte and Síân Reid. I cannot possibly thank the following people enough for their contributions of time, money, and moral support; my deepest gratitude to:

Toronto Public Library and the staff of the Merril Collection, particularly Collection Head Lorna Toolis and librarian Annette Mocek for making their space and their time available.

The executive and membership of the Friends of the Merril Collection for their financial and volunteer support.

The volunteers in particular, including David Cheater (refreshments committee), Barbara Kwasniewski, Arlene Morlidge, Michael Matheson, Eva Mocek, Emily Mocek, and Clare Wall (registration and sales), and Barbara Weiss (official photographer).

Michael Johnstone and Adam Guzkowski for their help with publicity and maintenance of a social media presence.

The English Department of York University, and especially its chairs—Maurice Elliott, Kim Michasiw, Julia Creet, Art Redding, and Jonathan Warren—and Rose Crawford, for their extremely generous financial and administrative assistance.

And, of course, the authors, scholars, readers, and fans (including those who belong to all those categories!) who have participated in and made the conference the site of such stimulating, intelligent, entertaining, and enlightening conversation.

Thank you all very much.

Table of Contents

Acknowledgments	vi
Introduction—Allan Weiss	1

Keynote Addresses

Why I Read Canadian Speculative Fiction: The Social Dimension of Reading—Robert Runté	14
The Body on the Slab—Veronica Hollinger	34

Canadian Science Fiction

Cybernetic Opium Eating, the Kantian Use of Human Beings and Neuromancing the Gothic Imagination: A Narrative Link—David Milman	44
One Thing After Another—Dominick Grace	55
Here Be Monsters: Posthuman Adaptation and Subjectivity in Peter Watts' *Starfish*—Clare Wall	67
Robert Charles Wilson's *Mysterium*: Thoughts on the Modern Reception of Gnosticism—Michael Kaler	81
New Half-Way Tree and the Second World: Themes of Nation and Colonization in Nalo Hopkinson's *Midnight Robber*—Brecken Hancock	95

Canadian Fantasy and Dark Fantasy

Sacred Cities: Charles de Lint's Newford Books and the Mythologizing of the North American Urban Landscape—Cat Ashton	108

The Word and the Flesh: Natural Law vs. Catholic Dogma in
Rikki Ducnornet's *The Stain*—Tammy Dasti ... 120

Writing About Invented Places: Esther Rochon's Archipelago of
Vrénalik—Maude Deschênes-Pradet ... 131

Speculating Diversity: Nalo Hopkinson's *Brown Girl in the Ring*
and the Use of Speculative Fiction to Disrupt Singular
Interpretations of Place—Derek Newman-Stille ... 146

"God's Country," Evil's Playground: Susie Moloney, Michael
Rowe, Brian Horeck and the Northern Ontario Gothic—
Cat Ashton ... 159

Can the Witch Speak? The Supernatural Subaltern in Kelley
Armstrong's Otherworld—Adam Guzkowski ... 173

Navigating the Darkness: Blindness and Vampirism in Tanya
Huff's Blood Books—Derek Newman-Stille ... 186

Media Expressions

Scott Pilgrim vs. the Megacity—Chester N. Scoville ... 200

From "Space Oddity" to Canadian Reality—Isabelle Fournier ... 212

From Monstrous Mommies to Hunting Heroines: The Evolution
of Women on *Supernatural*—Lisa Macklem ... 224

About the Contributors ... 241

Index ... 243

Introduction

ALLAN WEISS

The biennial Academic Conference on Canadian Science Fiction and Fantasy (www.yorku.ca/accsff) began in 1995. That year, I had the privilege of curating—along with Hugh Spencer—the National Library of Canada's exhibit on Canadian science fiction and fantasy, "Out of This World." The exhibit opened in May, coinciding with a local Ottawa science fiction convention known as CanCon. Jim Botte, one of the convention organizers, and Siân Reid created the somewhat awkwardly named Academic Conference on Canadian Content in the Speculative Arts and Literature, a single panel of four papers held at the convention. Those first conference presenters were Paul Johanson, Robert Runté, Reid, and myself. Together with the exhibit and convention, ACCCSAL was part of an exciting celebration of Canadian achievements in fantastic literature, film, radio, television, and other media.

The following year, Jim asked me to help organize the conference, and we held ACCCSAL '96 at the National Museum of Science and Technology, also in Ottawa. This time, the conference was an all-day affair, with sessions on Identity, Politics and History, and Postmodernist, Feminist, and Other Challenges. Among the presenters were Dominick M. Grace, who has now become a regular at the conference, Nancy Johnston, Gail Irwin, and Nanci White. In 1997, I took over fully as chair, and we changed both the name and the venue; the Academic Conference on Canadian Science Fiction and Fantasy (ACCSFF) was born, and took up near-permanent residence at the Merril Collection of Science Fiction, Speculation and Fantasy in Toronto. The Merril Collection, a special collection in the Toronto Public Library system, is one of the world's premier libraries in the field of fantastic literature and art. Apart from a brief period when Nancy Johnston organized the conference, I have been the proud chair of the conference ever since.

To date, there have been twelve conferences, and each since the move to Toronto has featured not only traditional academic papers but also keynote addresses by a Canadian author and a prominent Canadian scholar in the field. Among the authors who have spoken at the conference are Margaret Atwood, Robert Charles Wilson, Karl Schroeder, Peter Watts, Nalo Hopkinson, Charles de Lint, Tanya Huff, and Guy Gavriel Kay; the scholars have included some of the most important figures in the study of science fiction and fantasy, such as Peter Fitting, John Clute, Elizabeth Miller, and Veronica Hollinger. We have been very proud to host, and offer a comfortable setting for discussion and debate for, these luminaries and the various scholars (both new and established) who have participated over the years.

In fact, I see the conference as an opportunity for writers, scholars, readers, and fans to come together and share their love for and interest in Canadian science fiction and fantasy. I therefore ask presenters to make their papers accessible to a general as well as an academic audience, and I encourage authors to stay for the scholarly presentations. The high quality of the questions that come from the audience during the discussion periods testifies to the degree of intelligence and thoughtfulness of all the conference participants, not just those who sit on the panels.

The conference has expanded year by year, and in 2013, for the first time, we held sessions on two days due to the number of fine proposals submitted, not to mention the interesting and enlightening talks given by Tanya Huff and Robert Runté, our keynote address speakers. Runté, whose paper is included here, was the first scholar to engage in serious study of Canadian fantastic literature, and he provided some first-hand insights into the beginnings of Canadian fandom as well as scholarship. Other scholars have exhibited certain common interests over the years: dystopian elements and biological speculations in the work of Margaret Atwood, posthumanism in the novels of William Gibson and Peter Watts's Rifter series, postcolonial and other related themes in the work of Nalo Hopkinson, and monstrosity and disability in the novels of Tanya Huff and other authors of dark fantasy.

I have encouraged scholars to propose papers on other media: radio, television, film, graphic novels, music, and so on. Some of the most fascinating papers presented at ACCSFF dealt with Canadian efforts in what we call "Media Expressions," as scholars discussed recent films, television series, and songs with fantastic themes. The diversity of papers at the last two conferences has been unprecedented and very exciting, and I look forward to seeing more papers on non-literary Canadian science fiction and fantasy presented at future ACCSFFs.

One of the issues frequently raised at Canadian science fiction conventions, and occasionally raised at ACCSFF, is whether there is something distinctive about science fiction and fantasy created by Canadians. Many readers have detected particularly Canadian themes and approaches to the conventions of fantastic literature; Runté's essay tackles this question in some detail, arguing for the presence of certain distinguishing features but providing valuable cautions against making generalizations. The theme of national identity is often cited as one of those features, and so is a less triumphalist and optimistic outlook than we see in, say, American science fiction. Such claims may well be true, but require a far more extensive analysis of the field than we have seen to date. So far, no one has attempted a comprehensive study of the Canadian fantastic since David Ketterer, and even his book is more a catalogue of what was published than an attempt at a broader synthesis.

* * *

Understanding the Canadian fantastic—like so much else—requires a historical perspective: we need to trace its roots in literature (and other media) and in the world outside. Not only that, but the fantastic in Canada exhibits the sort of linguistic and cultural diversity that characterizes the country itself—a kind of aesthetic multiculturalism. For one thing, Canadian fantastic literature, to focus on just one medium, has been written in both English and French. There are also regional differences, as the fantastic has, to some extent, been handled differently in British Columbia, Alberta, Ontario, and the Maritimes. For example, a school of surrealist writing emerged in British Columbia during the 1960s, while an active science-fiction fandom in Edmonton led to the creation of a strong local community of people interested in the writing, reading, and discussion of science fiction and fantasy, or what is known as "genre SF" (a term that would require an entire paper to unravel).

One argument I have made on occasion, including in the text of the National Library exhibit, is that science-fiction and fantasy writers have often dealt with the same themes as more canonical or "realist" authors, but using different techniques. Questions of personal and national identity, alienation, and French-English relations find their way in the works of writers like Margaret Laurence, Morley Callaghan, and Hugh MacLennan—to cite some of the earliest authors "canonized" by scholars of Canadian literature—and those discussed below. As Runté says, however, finding "Canadian" themes is a challenge in an international context where themes of identity and alienation are pervasive. Still, reviewing the history of Canadian fantastic literature may reveal that certain preoccupations that have dominated the field, at least at some point in that history.

Works like the pseudonymous *The Dominion in 1983* (1883, by "Ralph Centennius"), James de Mille's utopian satire *A Strange Manuscript Found in a Copper Cylinder* (1888), and W. H. C. Lawrence's *The Storm of '92* (1889) demonstrate that, for early anglophone writers of fantastic literature, the subjects of greatest interest were political and social issues. On the other hand, Centennius's descriptions of rocket trains and other technological innovations show that scientific considerations were not entirely absent. Written during the period when Canada's transcontinental railroad, the Canadian Pacific Railway, was being built, the text includes extrapolations of how railroad technology might advance in the next hundred years. Early English-Canadian fantastic fiction exhibits certain common characteristics, some of which are less than admirable. Some nationalists during the period believed that to achieve full nationhood, Canada needed to foster the development of its own literature (see esp. Coleman's book on the subject). Much of the fantastic literature written during the late nineteenth and early twentieth centuries was part of this nationalist literary agenda, offering visions of a future united, strong, and prosperous Canada designed to encourage national feeling among the authors' contemporaries.

There was even talk of a Canadian "race," one that—by virtue of its vigor and legacy of British martial power and belief in personal liberty—would eventually become dominant in the world. There is no room here to review the degree to which early visions of Canada's future were characterized by a sense of racial destiny. One can say that in such texts as *The Dominion in 1983* and Frederick Nelson's *Toronto in 1928 A.D.* (1908), future Canada is portrayed as a "pure" Anglo-Saxon nation that surpasses all others in its wealth, renewed Christian religiosity, and social cohesion. These utopian accounts suggest, in Darwinist fashion, that Canada's harsh climate and abundant natural resources will inevitably produce a hardy race capable of leading the world materially and spiritually. Even John Galbraith's *In the New Capital* (1897), which is more interested in promoting Henry George's theories about the single tax, presents Canada as becoming something of a paradise thanks to its God-given natural abundance.

Meanwhile, on the French-Canadian side, we see the influence of the Catholic Church and the role of conservative nationalism in early fantastic texts. Philippe Aubert de Gaspé, Jr.'s *L'influence d'un livre* (1837) concerns the evils of alchemy, while the separatist *Pour la patrie* (1895), by Jules-Paul Tardivel, portrays a Québec about to be politically absorbed by the rest of Canada but saved by a politician who receives visits from St. Joseph and the spirit of his late daughter. Theological themes recur in Georges Bugnet's *Siraf* (1934), in which two disembodied spirits discuss various spiritual and moral questions.

A genre that was extremely important in Québec during the nineteenth and early twentieth centuries was the *roman de la terre*, whose most important exemplar is Louis Hémon's *Maria Chapdelaine* (1914; first book edition 1916). These novels offered fictionalized expressions of the conservative nationalism in Québec at the time. Conservative nationalists believed that in order to secure *la survivance*, or survival, of the French-Canadian people in Canada, they needed to rely on a number of institutional "pillars," including an agricultural way of life. The *roman de la terre* depicted the value and benefits of remaining on the farm, and following the ways of one's ancestors. It is not surprising, then, that most of the francophone utopian texts of the first half of the twentieth century portray agrarian utopias; significant examples include Jean-Charles Harvey's *Marcel Faure* (1922) and Armand Grenier's *Erres boreales* (1944) and *Le défricheur du Hammada* (1953). Québécois authors of the fantastic were so heavily influenced by conservative nationalism that they bucked a very long-standing literary tradition, in that from Plato's time onward utopias tended to be well designed cities, not rural spaces. There were other separatist texts besides Tardivel's, such as Ubald Paquin's *Le cité dans les fers* (1925).

Political themes thus played an important role in the fantastic literature of both linguistic groups, while for some time scientific and technological speculations—never totally absent—were nonetheless far less prominent than they were in France, Britain, and the United States. Canada did not produce a Jules Verne, H. G. Wells, or Edgar Allan Poe. That situation would change somewhat during the 1930s to 1950s, otherwise known as the Golden Age of science fiction. On the anglophone side, some writers gained a degree of prominence publishing in the science-fiction and fantasy pulp magazines that began to appear in the 1920s, most notably A. E. van Vogt, Laurence Manning, and, later, H. A. Hargreaves and Phyllis Gotlieb. Gotlieb became known as the "Mother of Canadian science fiction," achieving fame with short stories in such magazines as *Fantastic Stories*, the *Magazine of Fantasy and Science Fiction*, *If/Worlds of If*, and *Amazing Stories*, and her classic novel *Sunburst* (1964). Given the powerful influences of her gender and Jewish identity, it would be difficult to extract distinctively Canadian features of her work. On the other hand, Dominick Grace, the leading expert on Gotlieb's science fiction, argues in "GalFed: The Canadian Galactic 'Empire'" that her interplanetary political system is very Canadian indeed.

The pulp magazines were not the only venue for Canadian scientific, technological, and political speculations written in the first half of the twentieth century. Utopian and fantasy novels continued to appear, reflecting both local and global preoccupations. Hugh Pedley's *Looking Forward* (1913) anticipates the utopia that Canada will become should the various Protestant denominations resolve their differences and form a United Church of Canada; Howard O'Hagan explores Native mythology and spirituality in *Tay John* (1937); and even Frederick Philip Grove, who has become almost synonymous with naturalism in the world of Canadian literature, wrote a satirical utopia, *Consider Her Ways* (1947), about a society of ants.

For French-Canadian authors, the middle of the twentieth century was characterized above all by a growing desire to throw off the dominance of the Church once and for all and modernize the province. In the arts, modernization meant the embrace of innovations in literary and visual-art forms and techniques that were occurring elsewhere, particularly in Europe. A surrealist movement emerged after the Second World War, the *Automatistes*, and the group released a radical manifesto entitled, *Refus global* (1948). Members of the group defied the conventions of bourgeois realist art and the teachings and power of the Catholic Church, favoring spontaneity, creativity, the irrational, and the dreamlike in art. That movement eventually led to the rise of "*le fantastique*," the Québécois version of magic realism.

Two major issues during the 1950s-1970s preoccupied writers of fantastic literature on both sides of the linguistic divide: the Cold War and the potential for global nuclear disaster, and the growing separatist movement that followed the "Quiet Revolution" starting in 1960 (for details, see Weiss, "Separations and Unities"). Fears of a nuclear holocaust produced such texts as John Mantley's *The 27th Day* (1956), Yves Thériault's *Si la bombe m'était contée* (1962), and Maurice Gagnon's post-holocaust dystopian novel *Les tours de Babylone* (1972), among many others. Texts about Québec's possible separation include Bruce Powe's *Killing Ground* (1968), about a Canadian civil war triggered by the province's secession; Leo Heaps's political thriller *The Quebec Plot* (1978); Jean-Michel Wyl's *Québec Banana State* (1978); and William Weintraub's satirical *The Underdogs* (1979). English-language speculations about Québec separation extended into the 1980s with Hélène Holden's *After the Fact* (1986).

Scientific and technological themes were not ignored, however. The development of computer technology, and the expanding role of technology in our lives, inspired dystopian texts like Robert Green's satirical *The Great Leap Backward* (1968) and Jim Willer's *Paramind* (1973), a kind of Canadian *Colossus* (1966).

Also, writers in English Canada were exploring widely divergent territories of fantasy. As mentioned earlier, a group of surrealist writers emerged in British Columbia, thanks to institutional support from the University of British Columbia and its creative writing program; leading figures were Michael Bullock and J. Michael Yates, and writers like Andreas Schroeder,

Jack Hodgins, Ernest Hekkanen, and Rikki Ducornet maintained the tradition of surrealist and magic realist writing in the province.

The 1960s cultural revolution was reflected in anti-realist fiction elsewhere, too. Groups of experimental writers arose in Ontario; see the magic-realist and self-reflexive stories in the anthology series *The Story So Far* (Coach House Press, 1971-79). As for high fantasy, Charles Saunders published stories about Imaro, the "black Conan," beginning in the 1970s; among the venues in which Imaro appeared was the Canadian magazine *Dark Fantasy* (1973-80) out of Gananoque. Other Canadian pulp and semi-professional magazines were published during the period, although none lasted longer than a few years.

The true flowering of Canadian science fiction and fantasy occurred in the 1980s, and no one has attempted to account fully for the phenomenon. I can offer a few possible reasons for the sudden growth in the number and quality of works by Canadian writers from the 1980s on. (It should be noted, however, that many began publishing before the 1980s; perhaps they were not as visible as they would later become.)

First, there had long been fan communities in Canada, but by the 1980s they had reached a critical mass that made it possible for their members to move beyond fandom into professional status: writers like Robert J. Sawyer and Robert Charles Wilson were among those active in fandom before becoming professional authors. Fandom offered opportunities to publish—in fanzines—meet and establish relationships with professional writers and editors, and trade ideas. Thus, fanzines and conventions can encourage and provide the institutional foundations for creative activity. In Québec, fans and scholars created magazines like *Requiem/Solaris* (1974-) and *imagine...* (1979-97), edited by and publishing such authors as Joël Champetier, Jean-Pierre April, Daniel Sernine, and Elisabeth Vonarburg.

Second, individuals sought to create awareness of the tradition of fantastic writers in the country, and even encourage others to join. John Robert Colombo's *Other Canadas* (1979) and John Bell's and Lesley Choyce's *Visions from the Edge* (1981) were the first anthologies in the field, making Canadian science fiction and fantasy—especially early texts—widely available to readers for the first time. Those who wrote in the field could then feel less alone. Ellen Godfrey, one of the editors at Press Porcépic, asked Judith Merril to edit *Tesseracts* (1985), the first of what would become a long-running anthology series. Merril saw one of her tasks as supporting the writing of science fiction in Canada, and founded writers' groups (like my own Cecil Street group) as part of that effort. Also, American editor David G. Hartwell, of Tor, took a special interest in Canadian science fiction, and co-edited anthologies of stories by Canadian authors.

Third, during the 1970s science fiction and fantasy left the "genre" ghetto and became part of the mainstream, due in large part to the *Star Wars* movies and the cult following and later versions of *Star Trek*. One should not underestimate the effect of this shift from fringe interest to Hollywood blockbuster and best-seller status. More people were watching and reading fantastic works (think not only of the films of George Lucas but also of the novels of Stephen King) and that seemed to encourage more people to create them.

Fourth, and perhaps related to the last point, some mainstream Canadian authors found in fantastic fiction an opportunity to explore favorite themes in new, highly imaginative ways, such as Hugh MacLennan (*Voices in Time* [1980]), Timothy Findley (*Not Wanted on the Voyage* [1984]), and Margaret Atwood (*The Handmaid's Tale* [1985]).

Fifth, scholarly interest began to grow, with pioneering efforts by Runté and Colombo in the 1970s and 1980s, and others during the 1990s. Early work in the field involved much basic scholarship; that is, Runté, Colombo, and Ketterer sought to catalogue the texts themselves. Efforts to make general thematic statements about Canadian science fiction and fantasy risked producing circular arguments, as Runté aptly notes in his paper. Anyone who tries to generalize about Canadian fantastic art now would have an even harder time than did the pioneers; our fantastic literature has become too vast and diverse, ranging as it does from the surrealism of Eric McCormack (e.g., *Inspecting the Vaults* [1987]) to the hard science fiction of Peter Watts.

What may be the most important factor leading to the expanded interest in studying Canadian fantastic art is the rise of non-traditional theoretical approaches to art in general. French structuralist, poststructuralist, and feminist theory, and then postcolonial, cultural studies, and numerous other approaches, inspired scholars to seek out fantastic texts, including those in Canada, that lent themselves to analysis using those approaches. Of course, it goes without saying that the high quality of the work by Canadian authors like Nalo Hopkinson, Margaret Atwood, Robert Charles Wilson, and William Gibson had much to do with that interest as well.

Apart from ACCSFF, scholarly interest has been reflected not only in the studies by Runté, Colombo, and Ketterer, but also the Canadian Science Fiction and Fantasy Symposium held in Ottawa in 2001, the recent Science Fiction: The Interdisciplinary Genre conference held in Hamilton (2013), and books like Amy J. Ransom's *Science Fiction from Québec: A Postcolonial Study* (2009) and our own earlier volumes of proceedings, *Perspectives on the Canadian Fantastic* (1998) and *Further Perspectives on the Canadian Fantastic* (2005). Papers and books on individual themes and authors have appeared in the major scholarly journals, and the various websites devoted to the listing and criticism of Canadian science fiction and fantasy add enormously to the list.

* * *

The papers published here come from a variety of critical perspectives, and represent some of the most interesting ways scholars have begun to examine the field over the past decade. This volume is organized like one of our conferences: we begin with keynote addresses and then move on to more formal sessions organized by genre and medium. I was hoping to include Peter Watts's address from the 2007 conference and the interview I conducted with Charles de Lint in 2011, but rights issues prevented me from doing so. To read them, please visit our website at: http://www.yorku.ca/accsff/publications.html and look for the supplement to this volume, or go to www.yorku.ca/accsff and follow the links to the Publications page.

The book opens with Robert Runté's survey of writing and scholarship in the field since his beginnings as author, reader, and analyst, and Veronica Hollinger's account of her own encounter with the genre. Hollinger's paper is a fascinating portrait of the scholar's fear that by subjecting something as entertaining and (dare one say it) *fun* as science fiction to serious study, she is in effect killing it, robbing it of its spirit. The struggle, she suggests, is between wanting to enjoy it as it is, and seeking ways to enjoy it even more by learning about it without analyzing it to death. She has demonstrated throughout her career that one can indeed marry enthusiasm for and academic interest in a genre.

The first "session" deals with specific authors and works of science fiction (although the generic distinctions are necessarily somewhat arbitrary). David Milman traces links between Thomas de Quincey's writings on opium-taking and Gibson's posthumanism, connecting them through the aesthetics of Kant. Milman shows a masterful grasp of the philosophical issues involved, effectively synthesizing writers and works that might otherwise not seem at all related. Dominick Grace and Clare Wall look at the fiction of Peter Watts from very different points of view, as Grace traces the way Watts adapts John W. Campbell, Jr.'s "Who Goes There?" (1938) and the subsequent film versions of the story, while Wall analyzes the posthuman elements of the Rifter series, seeing in them expressions of postmodernist suspicion of the concept of the stable subject. *Starfish* (1999), Wall says, highlights the blurring line between what we take to be "normal" and what we consider monstrous. Michael Kaler discusses Robert Charles Wilson from a theological perspective, detailing the gnostic features of his novel *Mysterium* (1994). Kaler succeeds in demonstrating how Wilson uses the tropes of science fiction to explore religious and philosophical themes. Brecken Hancock examines postcolonialism and race in Nalo Hopkinson's *Midnight Robber* (2000), showing how Hopkinson complicates simple power relations based on historical hierarchies. Hopkinson, she argues, exposes the effects of such dynamics, as they always lead to subaltern groups suffering discrimination and worse in any colonial situation.

The next section features papers on Canadian urban, high, religious, and dark fantasy. Cat Ashton's study of Charles de Lint places him in the context of previous, Tolkienesque fantasy and urban fantasy's challenge to the genre's well entrenched conventions. One of those conventions is the establishment of rigid binaries: moral, biological, and so on; De Lint's fiction resists those easy polarities, offering a more modern, complicated view of morality and the world. Tammy Dasti does a close reading of the relationship between Catholic doctrine and personal desire in Rikki Ducornet's *The Stain* (1995), and the paper also reveals a very different relationship in Ducornet's work: the strong ties between one's internal/psychological state and the outside world. (As such, it might be noted, Ducornet remains solidly in the tradition of surrealist fiction.) Maude Deschênes-Pradet's analysis of Esther Rochon's work applies a theoretical approach, geocriticism, that may never have been used before in a study of fantastic literature. The results of her experiment may well form a solid foundation for future work in the field, as she describes the challenges faced by the geocritical scholar of fantastic, as opposed to real, spaces. Turning to dark fantasy, we see in Derek Newman-Stille's first paper a similar interest in place: how Toronto in Nalo Hopkinson's *Brown Girl in the Ring* (1998) becomes defamiliarized and reinterpreted as it becomes the home of non–European immigrants and the site of different cultural experiences. Both the protagonist and the city she lives in are characterized by a very unstable and dynamic identity. Along the same lines, Cat Ashton's second paper investigates a new genre, the Northern Ontario Gothic; again, place shapes the characters, themes, and handling of generic tropes in profound ways.

Adam Guzkowski considers the status of witches in Kelley Armstrong's "Otherworld" series, noting that their gender as well as their magical abilities places them in a marginal position. The witch, he says, is a figure that raises many questions about power, in particular socially constructed roles and the factors that empower and disempower. Derek Newman-Stille's second paper applies disability studies to the theme of vampirism in Tanya Huff's fiction. For Newman-Stille, there are similarities between being visually impaired and being a vampire; both states involve social marginalization despite attempts to "pass." Guzkowski and Newman-Stille see the conventional "monster" figure as representing and indeed embodying human alterity, and the way in which difference becomes the cause of rejection and the denial of recognition or accommodation.

The final section is comprised of three papers on "media expressions": non-literary forms of the fantastic. Chester N. Scoville analyzes the openly Torontonian Scott Pilgrim comics and film. Like other papers, Scoville's studies how geographical space is treated, as these texts make direct and occasionally subversive use of real places. The comics and film portray not just a city but a particular area of it, suggesting that a city is too complex, geographically and culturally, to be treated as a coherent whole. Isabelle Fournier provides a fascinating look at adaptation; much like Grace, Fournier shows how time and space affect how artists interpret and modify earlier texts to suit current cultural contexts and their own aesthetic aims. Lisa Macklem provides an overview of the portrayal of women in the television series *Supernatural*, exposing some of the stereotypes and economic pressures that have shaped how female characters are presented. What is noteworthy is the degree to which the show's writers have been affected not just by the conventions of the horror genre and the demands of the medium, but also by fan reaction. In a high-tech world of internet chatter and fan fiction, the line between author/creator and audience grows ever more blurred, bringing us back to some of the things Robert Runté says in his conclusion.

It would probably be unwise to try to summarize or make generalizations about such a diverse set of papers. On the other hand, it is hard to miss the common themes: the role of geography or place; power relationships—colonial, gender, "normal" or "human" *versus* "monster"—and how they have been institutionalized; and the fluidity of identity. These seem to be major interests among our best creators of fantastic art and the scholars who study them.

I very much look forward to future ACCSFFs, and the exciting insights into these issues and others that authors and academics will bring to them.

Works Cited

Atwood, Margaret. *The Handmaid's Tale*. Toronto: McClelland and Stewart, 1985.
Bell, John, and Lesley Choyce, eds. *Visions from the Edge: An Anthology of Atlantic Canadian Science Fiction and Fantasy*. Porters Lake: Pottersfield, 1981.
Bugnet, Georges. *Siraf: Étranges revelations*. Montréal: Éditions du Totem, 1934. Print.
Centennius, Ralph. "The Dominion in 1983." Colombo, *Other Canadas* 296–319. Print.
Coleman, Daniel. *White Civility: The Literary Project of English Canada*. Toronto: University of Toronto Press, 2006. Print.
Colombo, John Robert, ed. *Other Canadas: An Anthology of Science Fiction and Fantasy*. Toronto: McGraw-Hill Ryerson, 1979. Print.

De Gaspé, Philippe Aubert, Jr. *L'influence d'un livre*. Québec: Cowan, 1837. Print.
De Mille, James. *A Strange Manuscript Found in a Copper Cylinder*. London: Chatto & Windus, 1888. Print.
Findley, Timothy. *Not Wanted on the Voyage*. Toronto: Viking, 1984. Print.
Gagnon, Maurice. *Les tours de Babylone*. Montréal: L'Actuelle, 1972. Print.
Galbraith, John. *In the New Capital: A Nineteenth-Century View of Ottawa in the Twenty-First Century*. Ed. R. Douglas Francis. Manotick: Penumbra, 2000. Print.
Gotlieb, Phyllis. *Sunburst*. Greenwich, CT: Fawcett, 1964.
Grace, Dominick M. "GalFed: The Canadian Galactic 'Empire.'" Weiss, *Further Perspectives* 55–66. Print.
Green, Robert. *The Great Leap Backward*. Toronto: McClelland and Stewart, 1968. Print.
Grenier, Armand. *Le défricheur du Hammada*. [Québec]: Éditions Laurin, [1953]. Print.
———. *Erres boréales*. N.p.: n.p., [1944]. Print.
Grove, Frederick Philip. *Consider Her Ways*. Toronto: Macmillan, 1947. Print.
Harvey, Jean-Charles. *Marcel Faure*. Montmagny: L'Imprimerie de Montmagny, 1922. Print.
Heaps, Leo. *The Quebec Plot*. Toronto: Davies, 1978. Print.
Hémon, Louis. *Maria Chapdelaine*. Montréal: LeFebvre, 1916. Print.
Holden, Hélène. *After the Fact*. Ottawa: Oberon, 1986. Print.
Jones, D. F. *Colossus*. London: Rupert Hart-Davis, 1966. Print.
Ketterer, David. *Canadian Science Fiction and Fantasy*. Bloomington: Indiana University Press, 1992. Print.
Lawrence, W.H.C. *The Storm of '92: A Grandfather's Tale Told in 1932*. Toronto: Sheppard, 1889. Print.
Leroux, Jean-François, and Camille R. La Bossière, eds. *Worlds of Wonder: Readings in Canadian Science Fiction and Fantasy Literature*. Ottawa: University of Ottawa Press, 2004. Print.
MacLennan, Hugh. *Voices in Time*. Toronto: Macmillan, 1980.
Mantley, John. *The 27th Day*. New York: Dutton, 1956. Print.
McCormack, Eric. *Inspecting the Vaults*. Markham: Penguin, 1987. Print.
Merril, Judith, ed. *Tesseracts*. Victoria: Porcépic, 1985.
Nelson, Frederick. *Toronto in 1928 A.D.* Toronto: National Business Methods, 1908. Print.
O'Hagan, Howard. *Tay John*. Timperley: Laidlaw, 1939. Print.
Paquin, Ubald. *La cité dans les fers*. Montréal: Garand, 1925. Print.
Pedley, Hugh. *Looking Forward: The Strange Experience of the Rev. Fergus McCheyne*. Toronto: Briggs, 1913. Print.
Powe, Bruce. *Killing Ground: The Canadian Civil War*. Toronto: Martin, 1968. Print.
Ransom, Amy J. *Science Fiction from Quebec: A Postcolonial Study*. Jefferson, NC: McFarland, 2009.
Tardivel, Jules-Paul. *Pour la patrie*. Montréal: Cadieux et Jérome, 1895. Print.
Thériault, Yves. *Si la bombe m'était contée*. Montréal: Editions du Jour, 1962. Print.
Weintraub, William. *The Underdogs*. Toronto: McClelland and Stewart, 1979. Print.
Weiss, Allan. "Separations and Unities: Quebec Separatism in English- and French-Canadian Science Fiction." *Science-Fiction Studies* 74 (1998): 53–60. Print.
———, ed. *Further Perspectives on the Canadian Fantastic: Proceedings of the 2003 Academic Conference on Canadian Science Fiction and Fantasy*. Toronto: ACCSFF, 2005. Print.
———, ed. *Perspectives on the Canadian Fantastic: Proceedings of the 1997 Academic Conference on Canadian Science Fiction and Fantasy*. Toronto: ACCSFF, 1998. Print.
Weiss, Allan, and Hugh Spencer, eds. *Out of This World: Canadian Science Fiction & Fantasy Literature*. Comp. Andrea Paradis. Kingston: Quarry; Ottawa: National Library of Canada, 1995. Print.
Wyl, Jean-Michel. *Québec Banana State*. Montréal: Beauchemin, 1978. Print.

Keynote Addresses

Why I Read Canadian Speculative Fiction: The Social Dimension of Reading

Robert Runté

ACCSFF '13

Three Turning Points: A Personal History of Reading

In elementary school, I was what is today termed "a reluctant reader." I viewed reading as something one had to do in school—second period after math—and not as something one would spontaneously undertake on one's own. I was therefore considerably put out when my Grade 5 peer group suddenly started making in-jokes based on the *Freddy the Pig* books. Not wanting to be left out of the conversation, I had little choice but to borrow a copy of *Freddy the Detective* (1932) and force myself to struggle through it. Plowing through that first chapter book was challenging enough, but having managed it, I was exasperated to learn that there were another twenty-five volumes in the series. To retain my standing within the group, however, there was nothing for it but to read the entire *Freddy* canon.

Reading the *Freddy* books was a significant turning point, not just because reading twenty-six chapter books gave me the practice necessary to become a more fluent reader, but because it also forced me to learn about public libraries. My older brother got into the habit of accompanying me to the library each Saturday to retrieve the next *Freddy* book. I vividly remember his expression when I explained that his services would no longer be necessary, as I had read the final volume and was now done with reading. I equally remember my discomfort as he explained that there were many other worthy books available in the library, and thrust several volumes upon me. I arrived at school the following Monday reluctantly carrying a copy of *Doctor Dolittle* (1920), only to have my friends ask, "Are you still only on the first book?" and realized that the whole sorry situation was about to repeat itself.

I confess that I started to enjoy reading, a little. I discovered that carrying a book around meant never being bored again. I found that reading had become easier and that sharing my experience of a book with friends was deeply satisfying. Reading the same books was an easy way to fit in with the group.

The defining moment, however, was when my best friend forced a copy of Alan E. Nourse's *Raiders from the Rings* (1962) upon me during a lull in our Grade 6 math class. I initially tried to reject his offering on the grounds that I was already reading my way through the *Borrowers* (1953), but Bill was insistent that I read the book by next Monday, or else. He showed me his fist.

It was the most difficult book I had yet read. I reread the opening paragraphs perhaps a dozen times without really being able to comprehend any of it. It made no sense: "The Raiders could hear the mauki's chant from the moment they boarded the ship from Earth." What was a mauki? How could a ship be *from* Earth? I despaired and would have quit entirely, but could not face Bill again without having read at least a few chapters. So I persisted.

That book changed my life. Once I understood that the book was set in space, that this was an example of the "science fiction" Bill had been going on about lately, I became engrossed. I was vaguely aware of my mother repeatedly calling me to dinner that evening, but could not bring myself to put the book down. It was this book that changed me from a reluctant to a voracious reader. Science fiction's sense of wonder grabbed me and has never since let go.

(I recommended the book to everyone I met for the next decade and a half, until I finally reread it in my late twenties and realized that it is actually pretty bad. "Terrible" might not be too harsh. But as I have since argued to two generations of English teachers, teacher-approved literary merit is no competition for "sense of wonder," and the first step is to get kids reading whatever grabs their attention. In the long run, they will gravitate to the appropriate level of quality.)

Under Bill's leadership, my friends and I biked to the library every second weekend to borrow every volume with the atom/rocket logo that designated SF. When we ran out of SF in the children's library, Bill talked our way into the adult section with a fake ID and lot of sincere begging. We added the Buffalo Bookshop to our weekends when we realized we could buy used SF paperbacks for twenty-five cents. When we played poker in high school, the chips were worth one, two, or three "basic book units" (equivalent to Buffalo Books' rates for pocket, trade and hardcover), thus circulating our communal library throughout the group. In the 1960s it was almost possible to read all the SF there was, and we gave it our best shot. Our reading experience was infinitely enriched because we were all reading the same authors—were all part of a community of readers—focused on a single, self-contained canon. By Grade 11, our mastery of the entirety of SF was so complete, and its influence upon us so great, that reading each other's creative writing assignments we could guess what author the other had been reading that week.

In university, I made the mistake of taking a course in comparative literature. After being exposed to Dostoevsky, I could no longer bring myself to read the likes of Heinlein or Andre Norton. My friends' tastes similarly diverged and our group drifted apart. I might well have become fixated on Russian novels, had I not discovered SF fandom shortly thereafter. Once again I was able to immerse myself in a community of readers, and through them, recognize that there might be more literary alternatives to Heinlein within the spectrum of speculative fiction.

Fanzine fandom provided an audience, an interactive peer and referent group, for which one could write reviews and commentary in the days before the Internet, blogging, Facebook, or Goodreads. SF conventions allowed one to meet face-to-face those fans with whom one had been corresponding. Back in the days when SF was completely marginalized (Runté, Foreword vii-ix), it was "a proud and lonely thing to be a fan," yet fans were nevertheless able to find each other and share their love of particular titles, of a canon, of a literary lifestyle. Such avocational subcultures can become all consuming for the participants, and it is no exaggeration to say that fandom became the focus of my social life and energies.

The explosive growth of SF in the 1970s meant that there were suddenly more titles being published each year than any one fan could hope to read. Although the rapid growth allowed for more reading opportunity, greater variety, and the genre to mature as a literature, that sense of a mutually shared canon was to that extent eroded. I tried to recapture a sense of community by focusing my reading on the Hugo and Nebula Award winners so that I would have at least the most famous and popular works in common with my fellow fans.

Halfway through that project, I discovered that some SF authors were Canadian. That had not been immediately obvious because Canadian authors came out from British and American publishers and their Canadian origins were generally not identified. SF in those days was dominated by John W.

Campbell's *Analog* magazine—with its emphasis on the quintessential American belief in progress, optimism, and engineering—and the distinct British voice of Wells and Clarke. One did not think of SF as part of CanLit (though it turned out that almost every great CanLit author—from Margaret Atwood to Hugh MacLennan to Leon Rooke—had written at least some speculative fiction). Reading Gotlieb's rejection of Campbellian values in her dystopian novel, *Sunburst* (1964), was therefore something of a revelation. By 1979, when John Robert Colombo released his *Other Canadas* anthology of Canadian SF, and *CDN SF & F* bibliography, I had switched from the Hugos/Nebulas to seeking out and reviewing Canadian SF.

Colombo's Canadian-themed anthology and bibliography were the first recognition of Canadian SF as a distinct genre, and immediately drew the attention of Canadian fans. Colombo ignited our latent nationalism, but more significantly, identified a reasonably small, self-contained canon that could once again become the focus of a community of readers.

Canadian Defined

One concern with Colombo's pioneering works was that he defined "Canadian" too broadly. Critic Terence Green (1980), for example, complained that Colombo had included anyone who had ever flown over Canada in a rocket. Colombo argued that it was better to be inclusive than to miss anyone, and further reasoned that we could learn almost as much about our national identity from the work of non–Canadians writing about us, as we could from our own writers. Thus, a story of Cyrano de Bergerac set in the snow of New France became an example of Canadian SF. Most critics, however, dismissed the inclusion of works by foreign nationals as mere padding, an attempt to make our contribution to the field seem more significant than it really was. The issue remains somewhat contentious because many of our best writers (J. Brian Clarke, Michael G. Coney, Dave Duncan, Pauline Gedge, William Gibson, Hank Hargreaves, Matthew Hughes, Crawford Kilian, Edward Llewellyn, Alberto Manguel, Judith Merril, Spider Robinson, Sean Stewart, Andrew Weiner, Edward Willett, Robert Charles Wilson) originally came from somewhere else; or, like A. E. Van Vogt or Gordon Dickson, were born here, but left.

It hardly matters. The controversy was itself helpful in raising the profile of Canadian (and pseudo–Canadian) writers to the point where we could get over our national inferiority complex and recognize the existence of a Canadian canon, however broadly or narrowly defined. The debate was never about foreswearing to read American or British or Australian SF; it was about seeking out those authors with whom Canadian readers were likely to relate. Seeking out Canadian SF and examining whether it might have distinguishing themes or characteristics gave Canadian fandom a purpose and identity. Prior to the 1980s, Canadian fans were more likely to travel south to conventions than east or west across Canada. The emergence of a national convention (Canvention) at Halcon 2 in 1980; the Aurora Awards (1980) (and later, the Sunburst Awards, 2001); successive iterations of a national SF newsletter starting in 1981; the *Tesseracts* anthologies starting in 1985; *On Spec Magazine* (1989), and so on, created a more cohesive Canadian fandom focused in part on an identifiable body of Canadian SF.

Canadian Preoccupations

As Canadians sought out the extant body of Canadian SF, we quickly discovered that many of these titles resonated with us in a way that American and British SF did not.

My favorite example is Guy Kay's *Tigana* (1990). Tigana marked an important turning point in Kay's career and in Canadian high fantasy. Kay's earlier *Fionavar Tapestry* trilogy (1984–1986) had reflected Kay's roots as a Tolkien scholar. That the trilogy was partly set in Toronto did not mark it as particularly Canadian, since it relied on traditional fantasy motifs such as Arthurian legend. *Tigana*, by contrast, was something completely new (Runté, "Guy Gavriel Kay").

The plot concerns the small nation of Tigana, which is overpowered by the neighboring empire. When the Wizard-Emperor's son is killed in battle, he seeks to erase Tigana from the face of the world and so casts a spell that makes it impossible for anyone to even speak its name. For American or British readers, *Tigana* is an exciting, well-crafted adventure filled with the usual assortment of wizards, rebel armies, assassins, and swordplay. But for Canadians, *Tigana* is an examination of the significance of national identity in one's day-to-day life; how every aspect of one's experience is twisted and distorted when that identity is lost. No Canadian could read *Tigan*a without immediately drawing parallels between the Empire's occupation of Tigana and the overwhelming American presence in our own economy, media, and— ultimately—the social construction of our reality. By utilizing a fantasy motif, Kay was able to conduct a thought experiment in which he could project the issue in the starkest possible terms, while distancing this exploration from the prejudicial politics and history of the real world (Runté, "Canadian Speculative Fiction" 1017). It is a theme and a treatment that would likely only occur to a Canadian author, and resonates with Canadian readers because it focuses in on our particular experience of, and preoccupation with, issues of national identity.

That is not to say that other readers could not enjoy or relate to the book; on the contrary, *Tigana* sold and reviewed well everywhere. Presumably, others can benefit from the Canadian experience, just as we benefit from American and Russian novels. But I would argue that Canadian SF holds a unique potential to attract and retain a cohesive Canadian readership, and that while one may dabble in Russian or American or British novels, there is no inherent social dimension that would draw one and one's neighbors to the identical titles. Canadian SF, because it reflects Canadian themes and preoccupations, should by definition be able attract the critical mass of Canadian fans necessary to create a cohesive community of readers.

The Four Characteristics of Canadian SF Identified by Colombo

In addition to drawing attention to the extensive body of Canadian SF, Colombo was the first to attempt to identify its distinguishing characteristics. He identified three themes: the polar world, the national disaster scenario, and the alienated outsider; he also noted the prevalence of fantasy over science fiction.

I know of no critic today who would agree that Canadians are particularly attracted to polar themes. Colombo's observation is generally dismissed as a sampling error, an example of circular reasoning based on his having *defined* as "Canadian" any SF with a polar setting. No doubt some Canadian authors have written polar SF, but it is not clear that they are more inclined to do so than American, British, or Russian authors.

By national disaster scenario, Colombo was referring to political rather than natural disasters, and there is no question that Canada has had a long history of stories addressing the collapse of Canada. But are they SF? These were mostly near-future thrillers written by authors who thought of themselves as writing contemporary thrillers rather than science fiction. And while the observation was relevant enough in 1979, it is less so now. Since NAFTA, Canadians have fewer anxieties about outright invasion or annexation because … what would be the point? Aside from occasional references to "our future Chinese masters" as a running gag on the *Rick Mercer Report*, the national disaster scenario has largely died out in English Canadian literature.

Of course, the theme may still be relevant in French-Canadian SF, as Quebec contemplates yet another referendum; though in this case, the disaster in question is usually depicted as Quebec's *failure* to separate.

The alienated outsider is certainly an identifiable theme of Canadian SF to this day; but then alienation is a dominant theme of much of twentieth-century literature, a reflection of the general *anomie* characteristic of developed economies. The industrial age gave rise to the factory job: turning a screw one-quarter turn clockwise each time an item comes past on the assembly line *defines* alienation. Employment in the service sector of our post-industrial, information age is little better, so almost everyone is alienated from their labor, which used to form the core of one's identity. Ask any waiter who they are today, and they are more likely say that they are *really* an actor, a writer, an artist, or etc., and that "waiter" forms almost no part of their self-image. Nor do we any longer have deep roots in the land: urbanization has not only meant abandoning the ancestral farm, but any real sense of place. The average Canadian family now moves every five years as it cycles through both employment and family demographics. Indeed, we seldom even know our immediate neighbors, preferring the much more tenuous connections of Facebook. No wonder, then, that much of literature concerns itself with themes of alienation.

I would argue, however, that the Canadian experience adds two additional elements to the generalized *anomie* of Western societies: our national inferiority complex and our multiculturalism. As Canadians, we grow up knowing that anything newsworthy is happening someplace else. We watch American TV—or increasingly, the satellite feed from the Old Country, whichever language that happens to be in—and so grow up alienated from our own daily experience as Canadians. And given that multiculturalism is the central myth of our culture (in contrast to the assimilation imperative of the United States), with every Canadian having a hyphenated identity, we are all ultimately alienated from each other.

Our multiculturalism and inferiority complex may also have contributed to Colombo's observation that fantasy was more prevalent than science fiction. Our preoccupation with preserving our separate pasts predisposes us to look backwards to our mythic origins, and perhaps discourages us from future-oriented SF. America promised its immigrants a brighter future on the condition of their giving up their ethnic identity to become mainstream Americans, a new identity based in large measure on the Campbellian values of science, progress, and individualism. Canadians tend to be less technocratic, less optimistic about the future, and less likely to view themselves on the cutting edge. Canadians see themselves as the designers of the Canadarm rather than of space shuttles. We are—as in the satiric CBC radio series, *Canadia 2056*—more likely to see ourselves as the janitors than the captains of the space fleet. So perhaps Canadians really were less inclined to write science fiction than fantasy. By the 1980s, however, fantasy was edging science fiction off the shelves everywhere, so it is difficult to say whether the orientation to fantasy is particularly Canadian or merely part of the larger trend.

Post-Colombian Themes

Since Colombo's pioneering work, a consensus has formed around the identification of seven themes or characteristics typical of Canadian SF:
- focus on environment/ man subordinate to nature
- distrust of technology and progress
- the alienated outsider / uninvolved observer
- the average citizen as (bungling) protagonist / protagonist as "nice guy"
- ambiguous endings
- tendency to more "literary" SF
- less rigid genre boundaries

Naturally, not all themes are found in any one work, and not all Canadian SF conforms to these generalizations, especially as many Canadian authors consciously write for the American market. Nevertheless, to the extent that one can identify trends, these are widely regarded as applying to the larger canon of Canadian SF—at least, so far.

It is important to emphasize that the role of the critic is to analyze what is already published, not to dictate to writers. No one is saying that Canadian writers are restricted to these themes, or must demonstrate these characteristics to be considered truly Canadian. On the contrary, the thrust is to encourage Canadian writers to find their own voice. Recognizing that they may be part of a larger Canadian movement, school, or trend may help validate that voice in the face of repeated rejection by American editors and reviewers, who may simply not "get" the Canadian genre. By the same token, our culture is constantly evolving, and it would be ludicrous to assume that the themes that preoccupied Canadians twenty years ago will continue to be our primary focus indefinitely into the future.

This is particularly the case now, given the emergence of print-on-demand and digital self-publishing. The emergence of these technologies has begun to undermine the role of editors and critics as cultural guardians, and online stores have made geography irrelevant to distribution. Consequently, although one's region may shape how and what one wants to write, selling to a global market may increasingly compel writers to focus on only the most universal themes.

So these observations are about Canadian SF up to now; as for the future: all bets are off.

Focus on the Environment / Man Subordinate to Nature

Colombo's Polar World theme has morphed into an acknowledgement that Canadian writers are often more focused on setting. Take for example Candas Jane Dorsey's classic "Sleeping in a Box," which won the 1989 Aurora for short fiction: there is arguably no plot, just claustrophobia. The setting *is* the story. Living in Canada, one cannot help but notice the environment, especially when it is minus 40, so it should not be surprising that many Canadian writers project setting as the determining factor in their speculative fiction. The environmental determinism of Dave Duncan's *West of January* (1989) springs to mind as an obvious example.

Of course, setting is important in all SF, since it cannot be taken as a given and world-building is always a key determinant of quality. What often distinguishes Canadian SF, however, is that Canadian protagonists tend to be subordinate to nature. Take for example the work of H. A. Hargreaves, whose 1976 collection *North by 2000* was the first ever marketed as "Canadian Science Fiction." In "Protected Environment" (1976), our hero sets out with his high-tech survival gear to confront the Canadian winter and—dies ... just literally fades away. In "Tee Vee Man" (1963), the protagonist survives, but at cost, and his only reward for intruding into the unrelentingly hostile environment of space is the privilege of doing it all again tomorrow (Runté, Afterword to *North by 2000+* 265).

These examples are very different from the Campbellian version of the genre. (Indeed, both stories were originally submitted to *Analog* and rejected by Campbell before being published by Ted Carnell in the British magazine, *New Worlds*.) The typical *Analog* story depicts the scientist-hero landing on a new planet, identifying a problem, and engineering an ingenious solution. The triumph of man over nature, the larger-than-life hero's ability to dominate every aspect of his environment, is essentially the whole *point* of the American genre.

The Canadian trope of subordination to the environment may also explain why our writers tend not to create vast interstellar empires. We live in a country in which enormous areas are virtually uninhabitable and population centers are separated by immense distances. Flying up north or driving across the prairies at night may not be a perfect parallel to space travel, but it reminds us what "distance" really means. If it is this difficult for someone in Ottawa to relate to conditions in Halifax or Victoria, then how much more ridiculous to expect the bureaucracy to manage a colony on a planet circling some distant star? In "Infinite Variation," Hargreaves' one nod to interstellar travel, for example, the colonial official is left isolated at the end of a too-long line of communication, forced into actions he does not want to take, provoking consequences he does not want to consider (Runté, Afterword to *North by 2000+* 265–6).

Distrust of Technology and Progress

That American SF was from its earliest origins predicated on a belief in progress, the ability of technology to solve all man's problems, and the assertion of man's right to control and dominate Nature, is too obvious to belabor. Canadian SF generally starts from the opposite assumptions. Phyllis Gotlieb's *Sunburst*, for example, was one of the first novels to question the assumptions of progress, the value of technology, and to suggest that attempting to dominate nature in the atomic age could have devastating side-effects. Of course there are counter examples from the Canadian canon, such as Leslie Gadallah's sympathetic treatment of science in *The Legend of Sarah* (2014), but even Gadallah starts from the assumption that most people do not accept science, that our current civilization is headed in the wrong direction, and that scientists are as likely to make a muddle of things as anyone else.

A case could be made that the American genre has shifted somewhat to a more cynical view of technology and a more pessimistic view of the future, reflective perhaps of the economic realities of the post-boomer generations. A closer examination of this trend may reveal Canadian authors leading that charge; that disillusionment with the American Dream provided an opportunity for Canadian writers to more easily penetrate the American market (Runté, Afterword to *Tesseracts*[5] 342–3). The American version, however, tends to be more focused on conspiracy theories and a general distrust of government, whereas Canadian authors are more likely to focus on extrapolating broader social, economic, or technological trends.

The Alienated Outsider / Uninvolved Observer

My favorite example of the aliened outsider is Hargreaves' "Dead to the World" (1968). A computer error lists our hero as deceased, with the result that his apartment is reassigned, his credit cards are cancelled, and he is no longer able to access any goods or services. Cut off from his identity as a living citizen, totally and irretrievably isolated from the community around him, Joe Schultz is the perfect example of alienation in our computerized world. What makes the story distinctly Canadian, however, is that Joe eventually achieves a lifestyle and contentment that would have been impossible in his former role as participating citizen. In the end, Joe Schultz realizes that he is, quite literally, better off "dead" (Runté, Afterword to *North by 2000+* 266-7).

That being an outsider might be *preferable* is something that could only resonate with a Canadian. Again, I attribute this to our central mythos of multiculturalism and our proximity to the United States. Whereas the American melting pot attempts to assimilate everyone into a single culture dynamic, the official Canadian policy of multiculturalism attempts to preserve a mosaic of interacting but distinctive cultures. Remaining *outside* the mainstream, then, is a Canadian cultural imperative (Runté, Afterword to *North by 2000+* 267).

David Kirkpatrick's classic (Aurora Award, 1986) "The Effect of Terminal Cancer on Potential Astronauts" is an obvious example. The story follows a day in the life of a mediator whose job it is to resolve the conflicts that inevitably arise between the separate cultural enclaves that characterize the Toronto of the future. The story is both hilarious and strangely familiar to Canadian readers, but I strongly suspect incomprehensible to anyone unfamiliar with the issues of multiculturalism.

By the same measure, Canadians often feel economically, politically, and culturally overwhelmed by our American neighbors. Consigned to the hinterland of (North) American civilization, we often perceive ourselves isolated from the people and events that are shaping the world and the future. Sometimes it seems as if the only thing all Canadians have in common is the vague feeling that whatever is important in the world, it is not to be found here (Runté, Afterword to *North by 2000+* 267).

Consequently, Canadians have a tendency to write from the perspective of the uninvolved observer. In Paul Stockton's "High Pressure System" (1996), the story of the alien invasion of America plays out on the TV in the background of Western Pizza, almost unremarked by its patrons. Instead they complain about the weather and propose the death penalty for whichever bastard stole the power cord to their car's block heater. It is a brilliant little commentary on Canadian winter and our detachment from events in America—built around the premise that Regina is too cold for the aliens.

Or to return to the example of the Hargreaves' collection, the story "'Fore'—Eight—Sixteen" (1989) is told not from the perspective of the inventor, but that of one of his sidekicks; and the narrator in "Infinite Variation" (1979) sees himself as essentially a powerless bystander stuck observing a situation in which he has no choice or control. The hero of "Tee Vee Man" ends a political crisis and saves (an African) democracy, but he does so unknowingly as a kind of distant and anonymous bystander to the main events of the day. Even when the viewpoint character is the actual protagonist, as with Jason in "Cain^n," the protagonist is not the story's instigator. It is the system that has shaped Jason, not the other way around; he is acted upon more than he acts.

Unfortunately, the uninvolved observer perspective often strikes American editors as violating the fundamental rules of good storytelling: in the Campbellian tradition, the larger-than-life hero is necessarily the viewpoint character; to do otherwise is to get it wrong (Runté, "Leslie Gadallah" 279). But being the outsider provides Canadians with a unique perspective from which to observe and comment. Sometimes being the janitor gives one a clearer perspective than Captain.

The Average Citizen as (Bungling) Protagonist / Protagonist as "Nice Guy"

Parallel with the American genre's traditional expectation of the dominance of man over nature is the depiction of the protagonist as the dominating hero. The usual *Analog* protagonist succeeds by dint of his own actions, guided by his superior (scientifically-trained) intellect, and often accomplished through tests of physical strength or endurance. Even when these heroes are cast as females, they *behave* as alpha-males, overcoming obstacles and enforcing their will on the world around them through their personal prowess.

Canadian authors are less likely to cast the protagonist as alpha-male, and usually depict things going badly for any viewpoint character that tries to act like one. Again, Hargreaves' stories provide absolutely typical illustrations of the principle: when the villainous protagonist of "In His Moccasins" (1979) tries to overcome the odds, take charge of his situation, and impose his will on those around him, he fails utterly; indeed, he ends up out in the cold, alienated even from his own body, forced to view the world from someone else's perspective. Similarly, the macho hero of "2020 Vision" (1980) is forced to the realization that he is fighting a losing battle, that the world has moved on, and that ultimately he has become no better than the enemy that destroyed his wife (Runté, Afterword to *North by 2000+* 269).

In contrast, Hargreaves' heroes tend to be mild mannered, well-meaning individuals, like the minister, Benjamin Scroop. Although Scroop is unable to provide effective help to the protagonist in "Dead to the World," he does manage to make some headway against the bureaucracy in "Tangled Web" (1972). Instead of focusing on the scientists in "Tee Vee Man," Hargreaves makes the story about the humble repairman-turned-astronaut. And so on. Ordinary people rising to the occasion as best they can.

Similarly, in *The Legend of Sara*, we have the typical Canadian protagonists of Reese and Sarah (and the secondary characters of Michael and Cat Anna) as ordinary people caught up in events they neither understand nor control, but who nevertheless somehow manage to cope. Instead of imposing their will on the environment and those around them, they adapt themselves to the situation. In American fiction, it is about the hero fighting through barriers to reach his goals; in Canadian fiction, it is often about the protagonist adjusting his/her goals to the options available (Runté, "Leslie Gadallah" 281).

And Canadian heroes tend to be nice: decent people motivated to do the right thing. "Nice" in this context should not be confused with "soft," "wishy-washy," or "ineffectual." Casey Wolf's collection, *Finding Creatures & Other Stories* illustrates the Canadian version of "nice": a tough-spirited "nice" that can survive -40, the isolation of a trapline, the death of loved ones, the unfairness of life, and still remain optimistic, still value diversity, still be decent where others might have sought revenge, given up hope, or at least been kind of grumpy about it all. The kind of "nice" that after a lifetime of abuse, still puts itself out and walks through a Canadian winter to help a total stranger, just because it is the right thing to do, as in Wolf's story, "Thunderbirds" (Runté, Rev. of *Finding Creatures*).

Ambiguous Endings

If I may indulge in some obvious over-generalization, American (mass-market) fiction tends to have happy endings, whereas British novels are as likely to be bleak and end badly for the protagonists. Russian novels generally have too many characters to say whether the ending overall is happy or not. Japanese novels do not end: they stop before the resolution. (Jun'ichirō Tanizaki's *The Makioka Sisters* is a good example: the story is about the last chance of finding a husband for the third sister, but stops before the train arrives where she is to meet the final suitor and the reader never finds out whether she agrees to marry.)

Canadian novels tend to have ambiguous endings: things have changed significantly as a result of the action in the story, but it is often difficult to tell whether the characters are better or worse off. Take, for example, Leslie

Gadallah's three novels. In *Cat's Pawn*, the protagonists have a rip-roaring space opera adventure, blasting their way through to victory, but somehow end up in dreary exile. The book's postscript makes it clear that these were the wrong battles and the war lost. So, in terms of personal survival, a clear win; in terms of achieving any of their larger goals, not so much. In the sequel, *Cat's Gambit*, the protagonists manage to destroy the enemy's base and win the war—but die in the process. So a clear win, but not exactly a *Star Wars* happy ending, not the triumphant awarding of metals that is supposed to greet the destruction of the Death Star in American space opera.

In *The Legend of Sarah,* Sarah fails to achieve her primary goal of enthralling Reese, and instead manages to lose the one refuge where she felt safe. She achieves her fairy-tale ending, but it is not at all the one for which she had been striving; nor is her success the result of her own plans or actions. Sarah achieves a happy ending not by reaching her goals, but by maturing sufficiently to *change* them. Similarly, the character of Sarah's rival sets out to rescue Reese from jail, but mobilizing the bureaucracy to that end launches her on an unexpected career in politics; and when she finally gets her rescue party, they break into the wrong prison. It all works out well in the end largely because their alpha-male antagonists are even more incompetent than the good guys.

To American reviewers, Gadallah's novels appeared muddled because that is not how they expect genre narratives to unfold. Heroes are supposed to win through to their goals, not get sidetracked and sidelined; and they are supposed to triumph by dint of their own strengths and struggle, not by being lucky or by adopting completely new goals. But Gadallah's are among my favorite novels precisely because life seldom delivers clear-cut resolutions. Real life *is* muddled, ambiguous, ambivalent, and (if one is lucky enough) continues to evolve after the conclusion of this particular adventure. I love that it is Sarah's abandoning her original goals that marks that she has now achieved the level of maturity necessary to take advantage of the opportunities presented to her. *The Legend of Sarah* is not about achieving one's goals so much as it is about being forced out of one's comfortable rut, about rising to the occasion. Gadallah's narrative structure may not be typical of the American genre, but I would argue that that is precisely what makes it resonate for Canadian readers.

Tendency to More "Literary" SF and Less Rigid Genre Boundaries

As previously suggested, almost every major figure in Canadian literature has written at least some speculative fiction. This observation has two immediate corollaries: (1) that Canadian SF contains a higher percentage of literary work; and (2) that the boundaries between genres is perhaps less rigid in Canadian than elsewhere.

It is not entirely clear which way the causation behind this correlation runs. Is it more literary because the less rigid boundaries allow literary writers to contribute to the genre without fear of becoming typecast and trapped in the genre ghetto? Or is it that there are less rigid boundaries because a number of high profile Canadian writers have chosen to pen speculative fiction?

One possible explanation is that the Canadian Literature shelf was never large enough to divide into subgenres, so Canadian writers could range more freely between them without fear of losing their place. Alternatively, perhaps the market for Canadian fiction was so tight that not even writers of Atwood's stature could afford to ignore any opportunity, even SF-themed anthologies.

Or, perhaps it is not so much that there is a higher proportion of literary SF in the Canadian canon as it is a question of junk SF being underrepresented. The Canadian literary establishment has always been a bit hesitant about publishing or reviewing "genre fiction" (unless one considers CanLit itself a distinct genre), so it may be that only those with impeccable CanLit credentials have been able to penetrate the Canadian market.

By the same token, it may be harder for Canadian-themed SF to sell to the predominantly American or British markets. Almost every Canadian author with whom I have spoken has told me that they have one or more manuscripts in their bottom drawer that had been rejected by their American editors for being "too Canadian." It could be that only at the more literary end of the spectrum have Canadian authors been able to connect to an international audience.

I hasten to add I do not wish to imply any parochial bias on the part of American and British editors. Campbell, for example, repeatedly invited Hargreaves to rewrite his stories to fit *Analog*, so the refusal was in fact Hargreaves' not Campbell's. It is the editors' responsibility to choose only those stories likely to resonate with their readers, and if Canadian-themed stories are too far off the mark for the American mass market, that is no one's fault exactly.

Nor is this to suggest that Canadians have not always been active and successful participants in the forefront of the SF genre—A. E. Van Vogt comes immediately to mind, and even the quintessential Canadian-themed fantasy, *Tigana*, was embraced by the American and world audience. Rather, I am arguing that to the extent that Canadian authors indulge in Canadian tropes, the quality of the writing must be correspondingly better to break into a mass market whose readers may not immediately connect to Canadian themes.

Of course, literary quality is necessarily subjective, and the assertion that Canadian speculative fiction tends to be more literary may be pure pretension. It remains to be seen how things will fall out as self-publishing and online distribution increasingly removes the intervening variables of acquisition editors and regional distribution, and the entire range of Canadian authors are unleashed on the global market.

Wither Canadian SF?

Having identified seven characteristics of Canadian speculative fiction, the question naturally arises as to where Canadian SF goes from here. No one knows.

On the one hand, it would not be unreasonable to be entirely pessimistic and argue that Canadian SF has no future. That, realistically, there is no longer a distinct Canadian culture, that multiculturalism is a myth, and that the current generation of writers is growing up within a homogenized culture dominated by American media and economics. That American culture is the Borg, and we have already been assimilated.

On the other hand, the emergence of new publishing technologies has greatly increased the opportunity for writers to find their audience. As the large corporate publishers continue to merge (now down to five) and completely dominate the remaining brick-and-mortar bookstores, airport newsstands and drugstore racks, there has been a corresponding migration of writers to epublishing and online distribution. Hundreds of print-on-demand and ebook publishers have emerged to serve various niche markets too small to be economical for the giants. Perhaps it has been difficult for Canadian SF authors to find Canadian publishers interested in genre fiction, or to break into the contracting market for American SF, given that successive corporate mergers have eliminated the majority of SF lines. Penguin Canada, for example, today publishes only one science fiction author (Robert J. Sawyer) and one fantasy author (Guy Gavriel Kay), because Penguin can only carry those genre authors who can sell in the quantities necessary to satisfy Penguin's economies of scale. But if the market for Canadian SF is too small to attract the attention of Penguin Canada, there are plenty of micropublishers, such as CZP, Edge, Five Rivers, Bundoran, and Tycho, happy to take it on.

And that is not even considering the self-publishing option.

So the bottom line is that the potential now exists for Canadian SF to be more readily published than ever before.

Of course, the new technologies of publishing and distribution pose several problems for the critic. First, if we may anticipate an explosion of Canadian output, then trying to cover the entire field may quickly become a logistical impossibility.

Second, global online distribution may again make it difficult to identify who is Canadian, as the physical location of publishers and authors may be obscured, or even deliberately downplayed. I tried searching for "Canadian science fiction" on my Kobo the other day, for example, and the distinctly non–Canadians George RR Martin and Orson Scott Card came out at the top of the list. On the other hand, these are still emerging technologies, and the search algorithms are likely to become rapidly more sophisticated, so we may reasonably anticipate that Canadian works may be more readily identified in the near future. Provided, of course, that the authors continue to believe that tagging their works as "Canadian" would help, rather than hinder, sales.

Third, the potential for marketing globally offered by online distribution may pressure some writers to consciously edit out Canadian tropes to maximize international sales. Including works deliberately stripped of Canadian content may distort the analysis; but it would be even worse to succumb to the circular reasoning of *a priori* defining what constituted "Canadian content" to determine whether a work should be included in the analysis.

Fourth, it may be difficult to define which works "count" as part of the Canadian canon without the former criterion of "professionally published." If one excludes self-published works, the analysis would clearly be invalid, because even accomplished and commercially successful authors are increasingly choosing that option. But if self-published works are included, then one has to recognize that a number—perhaps the majority—of entries will include first draft, unedited, vanity self-publishing. Does a 14-year-old's direct imitation of *Twilight* or *Hunger Games* count as Canadian SF? And if it does not, who gets to draw that line, and where?

The Social Dimension of Canadian SF's Future

The future of Canadian SF depends, then, on whether it can attract a critical mass of readers, and that the readers can easily identify and obtain Canadian SF. It is obviously in the financial interests of the Canadian SF niche publishers to reach—or create—that audience, but it is an uphill battle competing with both the multinational corporate publishers and the avalanche of available self-published ebooks.

The problem may be illustrated by my own efforts to interest my adolescent daughter in the works of Dave Duncan. As a fantasy fan she should have been drawn to Duncan's *Magic Casement* (1990), but it sat on her shelf for over a year before she even opened it, and while she agreed that it was an excellent read once she started, she stopped after only a couple of chapters. She chose instead to read *Hunger Games*, because that is what her friends were reading. Just as with my own experience forty years ago, if you wish to fit in, you read what your peer group reads.

Thus, even though Canadian readers may find that Canadian SF is more likely to resonate for them, Canadians are unlikely to read Canadian SF unless and until readership for particular titles or series reaches the critical mass necessary to become a "talked about book" within one's social network.

Taking the long view, however, I remain unreasonably optimistic. Any change in the means of production leads to a change in the social relations of production. Thus the emergence of new publishing, distribution, and networking technologies will change the relationship between readers and writers. Once anyone can publish a book, *everything* changes.

The invention of moveable type meant that anyone could become a reader, but it remained largely a one-way conversation: from writer to reader(s). With the invention of practical self-publishing and distribution, that changes to a two-way conversation. For the first time ever, the average reader can now write/publish back.

Whereas many critics complain about the appalling quality of much of what is self-published, I see this as a temporary disruption as we shift modalities. As an educator, I cannot but applaud that a million new voices have joined the conversation, even if their first efforts are often inarticulate. Out of that million, even if only 10 percent make the effort to learn how to improve—to revise and edit—that is still another 100,000 new writers; and if only 10 percent of those become polished, that's 10,000 new voices in the cultural choir; and if only 10 percent of *those* ever make it to commercial success, that is still a satisfying number of new professionals who would not have been there otherwise. One cannot simultaneously decry the quality of self-published work and the erosion of reading among students. Yes, they would be better writers if they read more, but the other half of that equation is that (at least some of them) will become better, more critical and sympathetic readers for having participated in NaNoWriMo or its equivalent.

What I see emerging with fiction is the situation that already largely obtains for poetry: essentially the only people who read poetry in Canada any more are themselves aspiring poets. Consequently, the more people we can engage in writing SF, the larger the potential audience.

Take for example the Okal Rel universe. Canadian Lynda Williams started her ten novel series in 2003, but almost immediately her fans leapt on her characters and concepts to respond with their own fan fiction. Williams encouraged the growth of her fan base by fostering the growth of her fans as writers, by founding both a magazine and Absolute xPress to publish the best work submitted. The result is that the fans have written and published more books in the Okal Rel universe than Williams herself (Williams). (And most of them are pretty good, even though often written by authors still in their teens.)

It is an incredibly encouraging example of the use and power of the social dimension of reading—and now writing. If Canadian SF has a future as a distinct genre, then this is what that future will have to look like. Far from disparaging self-publishing and fan fiction, we need to be encouraging and channeling it. We need to create spaces where youth can explore what it means to be Canadian by undertaking their own thought experiments in the tradition of Guy Kay's *Tigana*. They need to read and write within the context of a cohesive canon, supported by a cohesive social network. They need to play with the existing Canadian themes, tropes and characteristics, and then find their own voice by inventing their own.

Exciting times!

Works Cited

Brooks, Walter R. *Freddy the Detective*. New York: Knopf, 1932. Print.
Colombo, John Robert. "Canadian Science Fiction and Fantasy—Is There Any?" Preface. *Other Canadas*. Ed. Colombo. Toronto: McGraw-Hill Ryerson, 1979. 1–6. Print.
Colombo, John Robert, Alexandre L. Amprimoz, John Bell, and Michael Richardson. *CDN SF&F*. Toronto: Hounslow, 1979. Print.
Dorsey, Candas Jane. "Sleeping in a Box." *Machine Sex and Other Stories*. Edmonton: Tesseract, 1988. 9–13. Print.
Duncan, Dave. *The Magic Casement*. New York: Del Rey, 1990. Print. A Man of His Word #1.
———. *West of January*. New York: Ballantine, 1989. Print.
Gadallah, Leslie. *The Legend of Sarah*. Neustadt, ON: Five Rivers, 2014. Rpt. of *The Loremasters*. 1988. Print.
Gotlieb, Phyllis. *Sunburst*. New York: Fawcett, 1964. Print.
Green, Terence M. Rev. of *Other Canadas*, by John Robert Colombo. *Science Fiction Review* 9.1 (1980): 44. Print.
Hargreaves, H. A. "CAIN^n." *New Writings in SF 20*. London: Dobson, 1972. 83–134. Print.
———. "Dead to the World." *New Writings in SF 11*. London: Dobson, 1968. 139–56. Print.
———. "'Fore'—Eight—Sixteen." *On Spec* 1.1 (1989): 18–23.
———. "In His Moccasins." *Calgary Magazine* 1 (Aug. 1979): 36–38, 40–42, 61. Print.
———. "Infinite Variation" *Other Canadas*. Ed. John Robert Colombo. Toronto: McGraw-Hill Ryerson, 1979. 214–19. Print.
———. *North by 2000*. Toronto: Peter Martin Associates, 1976. Print. [Re-released in an expanded edition *North by 2000+*. Neustadt, ON: Five Rivers, 2012.]

———. "Protected Environment." *North by 2000*. Peter Martin Associates, 1976. 43–56. Print.
———. "Tangled Web." *New Writings in SF 21*. London: Sidgwick and Jackson, 1973. 117–45. Print.
———. "Tee Vee Man." *New Worlds* 46.137 (Dec. 1963): 60–71. Print.
———. "2020 Vision." *Alberta Magazine* (July-Aug. 1980). Print.
Kay, Guy Gavriel. *The Darkest Road*. Toronto: McClelland and Stewart, 1986. Print. Fionavar Tapestry Book 3.
———. *The Summer Tree*. Toronto: McClelland and Stewart, 1984. Print. Fionavar Tapestry Book 1.
———. *Tigana*. Toronto: Penguin, 1990. Print.
———. *The Wandering Fire*. Toronto: McClelland and Stewart, 1986. Print. Fionavar Tapestry Book 2.
Kirkpatrick, David. "The Effect of Terminal Cancer on Potential Astronauts." *Tesseracts*. Ed. Judith Merril. Victoria, BC: Press Porcépic, 1985. 247–73. Print.
Lofting, Hugh. *The Story of Doctor Dolittle: Being the History of His Peculiar Life at Home and Astonishing Adventures in Foreign Parts*. London: Lippincott, 1920. Print.
Norton, Mary. *The Borrowers*. New York: Harcourt, 1953. Print.
Nourse, Alan E. *Raiders from the Rings*. New York: Van Rees, 1962. Print.
Runté, Robert. Afterword. *North by 2000+*. By H. A. Hargreaves. Neustadt, ON: Five Rivers, 2012. 262–74. Print.
———. Afterword. *Tesseracts*[5]. Ed. Robert Runté and Yves Meynard. Edmonton: Tesseract, 1996. 342–48. Print.
———. "Canadian Speculative Fiction (Science Fiction and Fantasy)." *Encyclopedia of Literature in Canada*. Ed. William H. New. U of Toronto P, 2002. 1016–21. Print.
———. Foreword. *Curious if True: The Fantastic in Literature*. Ed. A. Bright. Cambridge: Cambridge Scholars, 2012. Print.
———. "Guy Gavriel Kay." *NCF Guide to Canadian Science Fiction and Fandom*, 2003. Web. 2 Feb. 2014.
———. "Leslie Gadallah and Canadian Space Opera." Afterword. *The Legend of Sarah*. By Leslie Gadallah. Neustadt, ON: Five Rivers, 2014. 279–85. Print.
———. Rev. of *Finding Creatures & Other Stories*, by Casey June Wolf. *Neo-Opsis* 18 (2009): 72–73. Print.
Stockton, Paul. "High Pressure System." *Tesseracts.*[5] Ed. Robert Runté and Yves Meynard. Edmonton: Tesseract, 1996. 231–35. Print.
Watts, Matt. *Canadia 2056*. CBC Radio One, April 2007. Radio.
Williams, Lynda. *Okal Rel Universe*. Web. Feb 2, 2014. <http://okalrel.org>.
Wolf, Casey June. *Finding Creatures & Other Stories*. Vancouver: Wattle & Daub, 2008. Print.

The Body on the Slab

Veronica Hollinger

ACCSFF '05

I'm honored to be attending this year's conference as guest scholar, and I thank Professor Allan Weiss for the invitation, and everyone here today for supporting the academic study of science fiction in Canada.

The trouble is that, ever since Allan's invitation, I've been like Mary Shelley trying to think up a ghost story to impress Percy and Byron in Switzerland. Here's how Shelley describes her anxiety in the Preface to the 1831 edition of *Frankenstein* (1818):

> I busied myself *to think of a story* [she writes].... One which would speak to the mysterious fears of our nature and awaken thrilling horror.... "Have you thought of a story?" I was asked each morning, and each morning I was forced to reply with a mortifying negative [195; emphasis in original].

And then, of course, Shelley experienced the reverie that inspired her great novel:

> I saw the pale student of unhallowed arts kneeling beside the thing he had put together. I saw the hideous phantasm of a man stretched out, and then, on the working of some powerful engine, show signs of life, and stir with an uneasy, half-vital motion.... On the morrow I announced that I had *thought of a story* [196–97, italics in original].

Now whenever I fall into a reverie these summer days, I tend to have visions that are more closely associated with gardening than with science fiction, so, rather than wait for inspiration, I've decided to take advantage of Shelley's, particularly the image of that "hideous phantasm"—that monstrous body on the slab—so that I too can say (in italics): *I've thought of a story* ...

sort of. It's a story that, like *Frankenstein*, is about the creation of a hybrid body—in this case, a body that has been accumulating its various bits and pieces from a whole array of different narrative arcs, styles, cultural and political moments, national and ethnic traditions, popular story conventions, and even academic theories, in an increasing multiplicity of forms, from literary narrative through a whole range of electronic media—and it's been doing this for more than a century by now.

And, during all this time, it's been undergoing slow and constant fragmentation, re-composition, demolition, and transformation…

This monstrous body on the slab is science fiction, of course. And one thing, for me, remains true about it, no matter what transformations it's been through: the body on the slab is a genuine cyborg, in this case a textual rather than a material one—by which I mean that science fiction is a creature composed of science and technology as much as it's composed of elements from the natural world. In a broad sense, the function of science fiction is to tell stories about the incredibly varied and complex interactions between the human world and the machine world.

But what happens to the body on the slab when it ends up in a classroom or in a philosophical discussion about postmodernism? What effect is there on science fiction as a popular literature when it becomes the "object" of academic study? Many people consider that science fiction is best left to its own "natural" development in the "low culture ghetto" of popular entertainment. This is a kind of reverse snobbery on the part of people who've felt—and rightly so, to a large extent—snubbed by the representatives of "high culture."

This issue can come up in the most unexpected quarters and one of my own favorite versions was raised by J.G. Ballard in 1991, in connection with a special issue of *Science Fiction Studies* on "Science Fiction and Postmodernism." Among the various pieces, we included a roundtable discussion and we invited Ballard to participate. Here's Ballard response, which took us completely aback, although we also really enjoyed it:

> I thought the whole problem SF faced was that its consciousness, critically speaking, had been raised to wholly inappropriate heights—the apotheosis of the hamburger. An exhilarating and challenging entertainment fiction which Edgar Allan Poe and Mark Twain would have relished has become a "discipline"—God help us—beloved of those like the Delany who will no doubt pour scorn on my novel of the early '70s [Ballard is referring to *Crash* (1973)]. The "theory and criticism of s-f!" … bourgeoisification in the form of an over-professionalized academia with nowhere to take its girlfriend for a bottle of wine and a dance is now rolling its jaws over an innocent and naive fiction that desperately needs to be left alone. You are killing us! Stay your hand! Leave us be! Turn your "intelli-

gence" to the iconography of filling stations, cash machines, or whatever nonsense your entertainment culture deems to be the flavor of the day.... But [Ballard concludes,] I fear you are trapped inside your dismal jargon [329)].

Now this reaction is interesting for several reasons, not least for the way in which Ballard presents himself as the protector of an "exhilarating" but "innocent and naive" kind of fiction—this from the author of science fiction novels that include not only *Crash*, which Ballard himself called "the first pornographic novel based on technology" (9), but also *The Drowned World* (1962) and *High Rise* (1972), not to mention such short stories as "The Dead Astronaut" (1968).

What's also interesting is the very real anxiety that Ballard expresses about the fate of science fiction as an "innocent" entertainment once it falls into the hands of academic-theory mavens who clearly have designs on its virtue. In his view, the editorial collective at *Science Fiction Studies* was involved in "despoiling" this once-virginal popular literature by thinking and writing about it in the context of postmodern theory. In spite of his questionable metaphors (academia as a male figure with a girlfriend) and in spite of his shot at Samuel R. Delany (whose writing has always been heavily influenced by critical theory), Ballard raises an issue that really does seem to be of concern to many fans of science fiction: What are those academics *doing* to science fiction by turning it into an "object" of the scholarly "gaze?" What'll be left of it once science fiction has been "killed" into scholarship and dissected on the table of interpretive autopsy by contemporary versions of Victor Frankenstein—that is, by professional academics? In Ballard's view, instead of putting the body together, here we are ghoulishly concentrating our energies on dissecting it, taking it apart, leaving it in pieces, dead on the slab. What can possibly be left of the vital "exhilaration" that Ballard identifies with the experience of reading science fiction? At the most immediate level, Ballard's critical reply suggests that to study and teach science fiction is to kill it into intellectual content, to risk marring the "pure" enjoyment of a reading experience unmediated by interfering theoretical ideas.

Now it seems to me that, if something is worth knowing about—and I think we're all agreed here that science fiction is certainly worth knowing about—then knowing more about it is a better way to bring it to life, to appreciate it, than is knowing less, even if appreciation doesn't always equate to simple admiration. My own best test case is the *oeuvre* of Edgar Rice Burroughs, to which I was devoted in my youth; my original hardcover copy of *Tarzan* (1912) still owns a particularly good piece of real estate on my bookshelf. At twelve, I wasn't conscious of the racism and jingoism in Burroughs's many novels—not to mention his rather awful writing style. I read them then for the action-filled plots and for the exotic creatures and locations that filled them.

But I think I *appreciate* Edgar Rice Burroughs more as an adult than I did as a young reader, because I *know* more about his life and about the conditions under which he published his stories. I know more about the venues in which they appeared, and about the historical and cultural pressures that shaped their characters, plots, and locales; I know more about the influence they continue to have on other writers. And I understand, more coherently and more expansively, something about what these stories do as stories and something about how they do it. And—most important understanding of all—I understand more about what these stories have to do with our lives in the real world.

The great poststructuralist philosopher Jacques Derrida argued very strongly that nothing makes sense without context—neither a word, nor a baseball game, nor the events of 9/11. The more we know about the context surrounding any particular event or text, the more we understand about the kind of sense that it makes. Of course, Derrida also concluded that context is infinite: arguably, the complete context for any text—even Burroughs's *A Princess of Mars* (1917)—would be the entirety of human history; so, no matter how much I might wish it, in Derrida's terms I will never completely *know* even a single one of Burroughs novels ... that certainly gives one pause for thought.

This attention to context (broadly conceived) is a core feature of Cultural Studies work as I understand it. It means to work on finding out as much as possible about the circumstances that shape any and all of the products created in human culture, most especially the frameworks and forces that produce specific versions of the human subject—arguably, this human subject is culture's most complex achievement. This work is also political, paying attention as it does to the inevitable power dynamics in any scenario that involves human beings. So, for me, one of the most interesting and *useful* developments in science fiction scholarship has been the appearance of a new generation of cultural historians whose work tends to be skeptical of the historical "truisms" that have accumulated around science fiction over the years.

This is work that's genuinely interested in tracing the historical and cultural developments of that body on the slab, not in order to "preserve" it—with that dreadful implication of embalming—but in order to trace its lifeline, to give it a life and a history that, by now, is extremely complex and really fascinating. One good example is Australian scholar Justine Larbalestier's *The Battle of the Sexes in Science Fiction* (2002), which takes up the truism that there were no women in science fiction before the 1960s and demolishes it in a thorough and thoroughly entertaining way. Larbalestier's research into the 1920s and 1930s, in particular, is meticulous, including careful attention to material other than simply the fiction that was published. In particular, she makes very good use of a variety of readers' letters published in the pulp magazines of the period. Larbalestier reminds readers of Connie Willis's scathing comment about the supposed absence of women in science fiction before second-wave feminism: "There's only one problem with this version of women in SF—it's not true" (qtd. in Larbalestier 152).

My American colleague Rob Latham is undertaking a quite different project, one that promises to be equally significant: Latham has been taking on the truisms surrounding the New Wave—most especially that there was no style, no sex, no maturity in science fiction before the New Wave—and finding out that this is a pretty misleading representation of 1950s and 1960s science fiction. So Latham's history of the New Wave won't be about ruptures from one period to the next, but about the kinds of continuities within which the New Wave was able to develop in both England and the U.S. In an unpublished draft of some of his research, Latham writes:

> it is probably wise to be suspicious of a simplistic "repressive hypothesis," an assumption that taboos surrounding sexual expression automatically operate to silence discussion of sex rather than to sustain and proliferate it.... SF, willy-nilly, is always treating sexual topics, perhaps most powerfully when it seems to be primly avoiding them.

My most recent find is British academic Roger Luckhurst's cultural history of science fiction, simply titled *Science Fiction* (2005). Luckhurst ambitiously maps some of the "conditions of emergence" of science fiction as a genre, as well as the social and political transformations that have shaped it since the late nineteenth century. Here is how Luckhurst maps "the conditions" in the late nineteenth century that "converge to produce the space for what will become SF":

> These conditions are: 1) the extension of literacy and primary education to the majority of the population of England and America, including the working classes; 2) the displacement of the older forms of mass literature, the "penny dreadful" and the "dime novel," with new cheap magazine formats that force formal innovation, and drive the invention of modern genre categories like detective or spy fiction as well as SF; 3) the arrival of scientific and technical institutions that provide training for a lower-middle-class generation as scientific workers, teachers and engineers, and that comes to confront traditional sites of cultural authority; and in a clearly related way, 4) the context of a culture being visibly transformed by technological and scientific innovations that, really for the first time, begin to saturate the everyday life experience of nearly [every-one] ... [16–17].

But all this fine scholarship raises another question: What's the point of researching and teaching science fiction? Before actually trying to answer it—an impossibility, in any case—it's interesting to consider the question itself. To some extent, this question comes out of the deep suspicion of popular culture that still pervades the communities of "higher" education, no matter what you hear these days about the "breakdown" or "blurring" of the "boundaries" between high and low culture. The question of "use-value" demands a justification from a genre commonly held to be a form of popular entertainment. It wants to know what science fiction can contribute to an élite intellectual enterprise. A genre such as science fiction, even though it's permitted some space in college and university teaching and research, is expected to pay the rent, to justify the space that it takes up. This demand that science fiction justify the attention it's been getting has always haunted academic scholarship in the field.

This is pretty clearly demonstrated, for instance, in the incredibly influential definition of science fiction developed by Darko Suvin in his 1979 study, *Metamorphoses of Science Fiction: On the Poetics and History of a Literary Genre*. Suvin's *Metamorphoses* is still the single most influential genre study ever written about science fiction; even after 25 years, his definition of SF turns up regularly to justify any number of scholarly discussions and it goes like this: "*Science fiction is a literary genre whose necessary and sufficient conditions are the presence and interaction of estrangement and cognition, and whose main formal device is an imaginative framework alternative to the author's environment*" (7-8; emphases in original). Suvin identifies SF as "a literary genre," which immediately confers some respectability on it (as opposed to Samuel Delany's insistence that SF is a "paraliterature"). Suvin's definition identifies SF as a "rational" genre of story-telling, one that appeals, not to our emotive but to our cognitive faculties—it's a "literature of ideas." Its purpose is to recontextualize familiar features of the world in ways that invite us to think about them freshly, to consider them as if we've never seen them before. This is "cognitive estrangement," in Suvin's construction; and, as a committed Marxist, the work of "cognitive estrangement," as far as Suvin is concerned, should best be deployed at the service of critical analysis and left politics.

Now this definition has been working wonderfully well for a long time: it provides an intellectual justification for science fiction, one that can properly situate it among other intellectual pursuits. Twenty-five years ago it also gave scholars a way to talk about science fiction, a way to model it, to abstract it—to *estrange* it, in fact—to get some theoretical distance from it. But, while I have no argument with Suvin's preference for intellectuality and critical resistance, his definition cuts away major portions of that body on the slab—

not least its own particular aesthetic appeals, one of which is its appeal to our "sense of wonder." Rigorously applied, Suvin's theory of cognitive estrangement relegates an awful lot of science fiction to the trashbin of cultural value.

Since *Metamorphoses* was published in 1979, there's been an explosion of interest in science fiction from many different research directions, from computer studies to feminist cyborg theory, all of which pay some attention to science fiction as a particularly privileged site for imaginative thinking about the effects of living in technoculture on individuals, communities, and the natural world. Approaching SF in this way often has less to do with trying to define it, and more to do with thinking about the kinds of stories that it tells. Here is what I wrote several years ago about this unexpected explosion of academic interest in science fiction from so many different directions:

> SF's ongoing generic "metamorphoses" have been at least partly responsible for the increasing heterogeneity of the contemporary critical enterprise. "SF" no longer refers only to a literary subgenre: it is also a particularly popular kind of cinema and television; it provides the visual stimulus for a whole range of video games; it spills over into slipstream fiction; its aliens and spaceships feed into some of our culture's most acute millennial anxieties. As both a body of imagery and a field of discourse, it provides particularly apt imaginative portrayals of contemporary technoculture....
>
> The widespread attention which cyberpunk attracted from outside the SF field has been one important factor in its growing prominence as an object of study in a variety of disciplines. New perspectives in critical and theoretical work—influenced, for example, by post-structuralism, by feminism, by race and gender studies, and by the multiplex of postmodernisms—have also found in SF an especially rich source of cultural material. In particular, SF is increasingly featured in the expanding areas of cyberculture studies ... and cultural studies of science and technology.... What should we make of SF's incorporation into such a variety of disparate theoretical discourses? Are they a promise that SF studies will continue to develop and to expand? Or are they threats that SF studies—as the specific study of a specific literary field—will disappear as it becomes dispersed over a variety of other academic sites (even as the literary product itself threatens to disappear into the vast terrain of multi-media SF)? It is not difficult to feel a certain scholarly anxiety in the face of such apparent disarray. One might easily be tempted to work at delimiting the field according to very specific generic criteria, to place conceptual guards at the borders to control SF's "appropriation" by everyone from Jean Baudrillard to feminist critics of science. But resistance is probably futile, and it will be fascinating to follow the fortunes of SF and of SF studies into the new millennium ... [262].

Because science fiction is the only kind of story-telling that can look closely, not only at what it *might mean*, but also at how it *feels* to be a subject in technoculture. Because, when all is said and done, the monster on the slab is not only science fiction, it's also the human subject that's undergoing the techno-evolutionary process of becoming something else…

Works Cited

Ballard, J.G. *Crash*. London: Triad/Panther, 1975.
_____. "The Dead Astronaut." *The Complete Short Stories*. London: Flamingo, 2001. 760–68.
_____. *The Drowned World*. New York: Berkley, 1962.
_____. *High Rise*. London: Jonathan Cape, 1975.
_____. "Introduction to the French Edition of *Crash* (1974)." *Crash*. London: Triad/Panther, 1975. 5–9.
_____. "A Response to the Invitation to Respond." *Science Fiction Studies* 18.3 (1991): 329.
Burroughs, Edgar Rice. *A Princess of Mars*. Chicago: McClurg, 1917.
_____. *Tarzan of the Apes*. Chicago: McClurg, 1914.
Hollinger, Veronica. "Contemporary Trends in Science Fiction Criticism, 1980–1999." *Science Fiction Studies* 26.2 (1999): 232–62.
Larbalestier, Justine. *The Battle of the Sexes in Science Fiction*. Middletown, CT: Wesleyan University Press, 2002.
Luckhurst, Roger. *Science Fiction*. Cambridge: Polity, 2005.
Shelley, Mary. "Author's Introduction to the Standard Novels Edition (1831)." *Frankenstein or The Modern Prometheus*. 1818. Ed. Marilyn Butler. Oxford: Oxford University Press, 1994. 192–97.
Suvin, Darko. *Metamorphoses of Science Fiction: On the Poetics and History of a Literary Genre*. New Haven: Yale University Press, 1979.

Canadian Science Fiction

Cybernetic Opium Eating, the Kantian Use of Human Beings and Neuromancing the Gothic Imagination: A Narrative Link

David Milman

ACCSFF '13

> If the literature of electronic culture can be located in the works of Philip K. Dick or William Gibson, in the imaginings of a cyberpunk projection, or a reserve of virtual reality, then it is probable that electronic culture shares a crucial project with drug culture.—Avital Ronell

In my research, I have found that many works of literature about drug culture can be read through a cybernetic lens (and vice versa). I am not alone in noticing this common quality. Avital Ronell comments on the way the project of electronic culture and drug culture share a related crux (68). In a transcript of an interview with Jacques Derrida, published under the title "The Rhetoric of Drugs," a similar line of reasoning probes the possibility that "electronic circuitry got hooked up in the argot of drugs and the addict got wired" (22). That interview also considers the validity of perceiving the birth of literature on culture and addiction in Thomas De Quincey's *Diaries of an Opium Eater* (27). These diaries, alternatively released under the title *Confessions of an English Opium-Eater,* were originally published in 1821, 127 years before the introduction of cybernetic theory by Norbert Wiener's 1948 text *Cybernetics*. Nevertheless, it is in *Confessions* and its 1845 sequel *Suspiria De Profundis* that I find, via a different trajectory of research and consideration than that pursued by Derrida, one of the roots of common ground between drug culture and the literature of an electronic culture exemplified by the writing of William Gibson. What becomes clear when one compares De Quincey's texts to Wiener's *The Human Use of Human Beings: Cybernetics and Society* and William Gibson's *Neuromancer* is the existence of a shared metaphysical narrative that spans across the importance of sensation, the ghost story, and the creative power of human cognition (often expressed through linguistic code). That narrative makes an argument about epistemology and the nature of the human mind. Specifically, it claims that in response to sensual stimulation the human mind comes to know and then responds to knowledge with the power of creativity. Because that creativity is cognized as having the ability to in turn affect reality, however, that very argument also ends up blurring the boundaries we use to define the human. When the human subject, thought of as a pattern of knowledge, is affected by the world, and the world is in turn affected by the subject, it becomes increasingly difficult to draw a boundary between the two.

According to De Quincey, dreams are influenced by one's daily sensual experiences. In *De Profundis* De Quincey explains, "he whose talk is of oxen, will probably dream of oxen" (89), as his dreams are yoked by "the condition of human life" (89). Unfortunately, according to De Quincey, this "oftentimes neutralizes the tone of grandeur in the reproductive faculty of dreaming" (89). In order to evince this operation in process, De Quincey calls upon the state of life in 1845:

> By the continual development of vast physical agencies—steam in all its applications, light getting under harness as a slave for man, powers from heaven descending upon education and accelerations of the press, powers from hell (as it might seem, but these also celestial) coming round upon artillery and the forces of destruction—the eye of the calmest observer is troubled ... [89].

This trouble leads "some minds to lunacy" (De Quincey 90), and as such is "likely to defeat the grandeur [of dreams] which is latent in all men" (De Quincey 90). The defeat is a type of *dissipation*: "the action of thought and feeling is too much dissipated and squandered" (De Quincey 90) as the result of such stimulus.

De Quincey writes that a profound philosophical counter-force to the colossal pace of society's technological advance is required to combat this defeat (90). Otherwise, De Quincey asserts, this advance will lead to "so chaotic a tumult" (90) that the result must be "evil" (90). In some ways, De Quincey explains in *De Profundis*, *Confessions* was intended to be a search for this profound philosophical counter-force: "The object of that work was to reveal something of the grandeur which belongs *potentially* to human dreams" (89). In the process, the work attempts to organize the chaotic tumult that neutralizes the potency of such dreams. Indeed, this organizational power is one of the faculties that De Quincey explicitly attributes to the eating of opium; opium, he says, brings "exquisite order, legislation, and harmony" (47) to the mind.

Those goals resonate with the purported goals of Norbert Wiener's *The Human Use of Human Beings*. Despite being published over 100 years after *Confessions*, *The Human Use of Human Beings* also strives to combat the dissipation of something akin to *thought*. The text discusses the theory of cybernetics in layman's terms. Etymologically derived "from the Greek word *kubernētēs*, or 'steersman,' the same Greek word from which we eventually derive our word 'governor'" (Wiener 17), the term is used to describe a system for enhancing the transmission of information in a wide field of sciences, including "psychology and the [study of] the nervous system" (Wiener 15); it is a term used to describe the system by which the dissemination of information can be steered or governed.

In cybernetic theory, information, like De Quincey's description of the faculty of thought and dreams, is subject to influence from sensual experience. In fact, Wiener terms information as "a name for the content of what is exchanged with the outer world as we adjust to it and make our adjustment felt upon it" (17). This ability to adjust and make adjustments based on "past performance" (Wiener 33), or experience, is in turn termed *"feedback"* (Wiener 33). For this process to occur a *"rapport* with the outer world by sense organs" (Wiener 33) is required.

Most importantly, this system of adjustment is designed as a counter-force to the degradation of information (during any given moment of exchange) as the result of a type of dissipation called entropy. Entropy is the measure of probability that naturally increases as the universe gets older (Wiener 12). Where organization and form are the least probable states, entropy is a state of chaotic homogeneity (Wiener 12). Messages are "themselves a form of pattern and organization" (Wiener 21). In a message, the least probable state is meaning: "the more probable the message, the less information it gives. Clichés, for example, are less illuminating than great poems" (Wiener 21).

The Human Use of Human Beings, however, is not merely an explanation of a scientific theory in layman's terms. Certainly, it does contain (and admits to containing) "an element of technical description" (Wiener 11). Like De Quincey, though, Wiener is responding to the progression of vast physical agencies—technology. Wiener writes that his text "is devoted to the impact of the Gibbsian point of view [surrounding the entropic effect] on modern life, both through the substantive changes it has made in working science, and through the changes it has made indirectly in our attitude to life in general" (11). As such, Wiener explicitly notes that the text contains "a philosophic component which concerns what we do and how we should react to the new world that confronts us" (12).

Thus, there is a tropical commonality that stretches between *Confessions, De Profundis,* and *The Human Use of Human Beings* in regards to their shared desire to act as a philosophical counterforce to a type of technological degradation upon meaning. To locate the root of this commonality one must examine the aesthetic quality that De Quincey uses to describe the potential grandeur of human dreams and the influence of sensation upon them. When discussing the way the rapid pace of technological advancement troubles the human mind, De Quincey states that "the brain is haunted as if by some jealousy of ghostly beings moving amongst us" (89–90). This gothic aesthetic is reiterated a number of times throughout *Confessions* and *De Profundis*. For example, in *Confessions* De Quincey writes about various moments in his life when he is plagued by psychological anguish; during what he calls "the second birth" (De Quincey 40) of his suffering, he is "persecuted by visions as ugly, and as ghastly phantoms as ever haunted the couch of an Orestes" (De Quincey 40).

His equation of psychological suffering with a type of haunting performed by a phantom is of key importance. To understand why, one must consider the way, in *De Profundis,* De Quincey notes that one of the "earliest incidents in my life which affected me so deeply as to be memorable at this day ... [was a] remarkable dream of terrific grandeur" (99) that he establishes has a "connexion with the idea of death" (100). His first understanding of death comes from gazing at his dead sister: "The feeling which fell upon me was a shuddering awe, as upon a first glimpse of the truth that I was in a world of evil and strife" (De Quincey 101). The horror of the experience overcomes him. Yet, as a child, he still "knew little more of mortality than that Jane had disappeared. She had gone away; but, perhaps, she would come back" (De Quincey 102). This experience can be read in terms of a gothic sensibility. Julia Briggs explains that one of the tropes of the gothic is that the phenomena in such stories "do not rationalise or demystify the supernatural events, but rather set them inside a kind of imaginative logic ... in which imagination can produce physical effects, a world that is potentially within our power to change by the energy of our thoughts" (123–4). This is the type of power that De Quincey gives to the child-like mind. De Quincey is suggesting that the terrific grandeur of dreams has some element of this potential.

That explains why, in his attempt to reveal the grandeur of dreams through the memories of his opium eating, De Quincey discusses the effect of the drug on his physical economy: "The first notice I had of any important change ... was from the re-awakening of a state of eye generally incident to children" (75). That state is what allowed him to imagine the return of his dead sister: "many children ... have a power of painting, as it were, upon the darkness, all sorts of phantoms" (De Quincey 75). Likewise, when eating opium

> the creative state of the eye increased, a sympathy seemed to arise between the waking and the dreaming states of the brain in one point—that whatsoever I happened to call up and to trace by a voluntary act upon the darkness was very apt to transfer itself to my dreams.... Whatsoever things capable of being visually represented I did but think of it in the darkness, [and they] immediately shaped themselves into phantoms of the eye ... [De Quincey 75].

Eating opium reveals something about the potential grandeur of dreams through its ability to affect the mind in such a way that it seems as if it is potentially in our power to change the world (or at the very least our sensation of it) by the energy of our thoughts.

While *The Human Use of Human Beings* does not utilize such a gothic aesthetic, both narrative and academic responses to the cybernetic phenomena do. Cyberpunk texts such as William Gibson's *Neuromancer* are derived "from a new set of starting points: not from the shopworn formula of robots, spaceships, and the modern miracle of atomic energy, but from cybernetics, biotech, and the communications web" (Sterling xiii). Of course, biotech and the communications web are in fact cybernetic in and of themselves. Wiener coined the term to describe the feedback process used to reliably transmit information through such media as computing machines or the nervous system, both of which relate directly to either the communications web or biotech (Wiener 16). In fact, Wiener explicitly describes the synaptic nerve and its mechanics as a form of cybernetic process (Wiener 34). As David Porush explains, one may "safely use the word *cybernetics* to include work not only in information theory and communications sciences, but artificial intelligence, computer science, [and] certain mechanistic schools of psycho- and neuro- physiology" (54).

This becomes evident from such cues as the way one of the primary characters in *Neuromancer*, Case, is a "cowboy" (Gibson 5); the text uses that word as a slang synonym for what would be called a computer hacker today. Such hackers work "jacked into a custom cyberspace deck that project[s a hacker's] disembodied consciousness into the consensual hallucination that was the matrix" (Gibson 5). The matrix is the term Gibson uses to describe a concept analogous to what is now known as the internet. That matrix is filled with another form of disembodied *consciousness-like* entity—ghosts.

From the very beginning of his role in the story, Dixie Flatline is dead (Gibson 49). Nevertheless, Case ends up "working with his construct" (Gibson 49). A construct is a "ROM cassette replicating a dead man's skill, obsessions, knee-jerk responses" (Gibson 77)—a digital ghost.

The matrix is also the home of various artificial intelligences, one of which is the novel's titular character. That character refers to itself as a type of demon, noting, "to call up a demon you must learn its name. Men dreamed that, once, but now it is real in another way. You know that, Case. Your business is to learn the names of programs, the long formal names, names the owners seek to conceal. True names" (Gibson 243). Meanwhile, Neuromancer is not only a type of digital demon, but a demon that is "the lane to the land of the dead" (Gibson 243). Its power is to "call up the dead" (Gibson 244). It is a program designed to create digital simulacra of people so real that "if [one] is a ghost, she doesn't know it" (Gibson 244).

It is no accident that this is *Neuromancer*'s response to cybernetic theory, to the feedback loop between human and machine. It is Wiener's thesis that "the physical functioning of the living individual and the operation of some of the newer communication machines are precisely parallel in their analogous attempts to control entropy through feedback" (26). Wiener equates the synaptic nerve with a type of machine circuit, noting that both utilize "a specific apparatus for making future decisions depend on past decisions" (34). That apparatus uses a series of binary possibilities such as "the closing or opening of a switch" (Wiener 34) or "the individual nerve fiber [that] decides between carrying an impulse or not" (Wiener 34). As Wiener writes, "this is the basis of at least part of the analogy between machines and living organisms" (34). As a result, Wiener comes to believe that humans "are not stuff that abides, but patterns that perpetuate themselves" (96). Wiener comes to believe that it is theoretically possible to "transmit the whole pattern of ... the human brain with its memories and cross connections, so that a hypothetical receiving instrument could re-embody these messages ... continuing [their] process" (96). Wiener comes to believe in the theoretical possibility of something akin to Neuromancer.

In making such claims, cybernetic theory opens the door to the imaginative logic of ghosts, demons, and magic—imagination can produce physical effects, and our thoughts can linger and change the world even after our death. Indeed, there is a term for this perception of information technology's theoretical capability. N. Katherine Hayles defines virtuality as "the cultural perception that material objects are interpenetrated by information patterns" (13–14), that the physical world is affected by (Wiener's analog of) thought. Margaret Morse explains that the sense of virtually is that *"images have been transformed* from static representations of the world *into spaces in which events happen that involve and engage people to various degrees in physical space"* (21). It should be obvious that this perception shares something with the imaginative logic of the gothic narrative: "A utopia of ubiquitous computing would enchant the entire world, disturbing magical powers to the most mundane aspects of existence" (Morse 7). When our environment becomes digitally immersive, and our technology provides the illusion of subjectivity or agency, "we have entered a realm for which we have little vocabulary and few reference points except the language of magic tricks" (Morse 8). This is a perceptual reification of the ability to use code, conceived of as something analogous to thought, to modify reality via telematic operations.

That should clearly explain the relationship between cybernetics and the particular aspect of the gothic sensibility being discussed: both preach a logical paradigm where thought (or its analog, code) has the power to affect reality; as a result, both come to believe (or at least preach) such possibilities as using creative imagination (reified in the magic spell or computer program) to provide the possibility of life after death. The question is, however, what produces that sensibility in *Confessions, De Profundis,* and their relation to dreams and opium eating? An explanation begins to cohere when De Quincey tries to explain why "death ... is more profoundly affecting in summer than in other parts of the year" (107). During his explanation De Quincey writes, "far more of our deepest thoughts and feelings pass to us through perplexed combinations of *concrete* objects, pass to us as *involutes* (if I may coin that word) in compound experiences incapable of being disentangled, than ever reach us *directly*, and in their own abstract shapes" (107). The notion that knowledge of the world is epistemologically processed indirectly through an involute relationship with the mind is directly tied to German metaphysical philosophy.

One of Kant's key topics in *The Critique of Judgement* is the importance of sensation in the production of knowledge. According to Kant, "sensation is ... employed in the cognition of external objects" (Kant 24). This matches both De Quincey's description of the influence of daily life on thought/dreams *and* Wiener's notion that sensation is of key importance to the feedback process. Nevertheless, according to Kant all "*sensation* (here external) also agrees in expressing a merely subjective side of our representations of external things" (Kant 24). In other words, while sensation does produce some form of knowledge, the connection with the external world through sensation is never direct. What one senses is always a subjective sensation, not an objective reality. That is because it "is an absolutely inadmissible presupposition" (Kant 121) that "everyone has a like sense to our own" (Kant 121). One cannot be certain that others, especially other species, sense things in the same way.

According to Kant, what separates the human from the animal is the elevation of the mind above mere sensation: "gratification, even when occasioned by concepts that evoke aesthetic ideas, is *animal*, i.e. bodily sensation" (Kant 163); beyond the merely animal response to bodily sensation is "the *spiritual* feeling of respect for moral ideas, which is not one of gratification, but of self-esteem (an esteem for humanity within us)" (Kant 163). Humanity, from a Kantian perspective, is thus qualified by *more advanced ideas*.

This rupture between the animal and the human is what makes the sublime a higher form of delight: "delight in the sublime does not so much involve positive pleasure as admiration or respect" (Kant 76). That is because the sublime requires the perception of "an object (of nature) the *representation of which determines the mind to regard the elevation of nature beyond our reach as equivalent to presentation of ideas"* (Kant 98). When one experiences the sublime, what one experiences is a totality too grand to be perceived in its entirety. The mind must imaginatively and analogically create the totality when the senses fail: "we enlarge our empirical faculty of representation … with a view to the intuition of nature, [and] reason inevitably steps forward … and calls forth the effort of the mind … to make the representation of sense adequate to this totality" (Kant 98). The terror, horror, and sacred awe of the sublime are not *real* forms of access to a source of fear, but "an attempt to gain access to [what we should be afraid of] through imagination" (Kant 99). The grandeur of human thought, according to Kant, is a form of imaginative creativity. This is why Kant believes that *"poetry* … holds the first rank among all the arts. It expands the mind by giving freedom to the imagination … and by thus rising aesthetically to ideas" (Kant 155). Kant, in advance of Wiener, equates the power of this imaginative creativity with the sort of linguistic code deployed in poetry. Poetry, after all, contains more information than a cliché.

The search for the grandeur of human dreams in *Confessions* and *De Profundis* explicitly interfaces with such Kantian ideas. De Quincey claims that his "life has been, on the whole, the life of a philosopher" (4). His goal is to create a philosophical counter-force to the dissipation and neutralization of the grandeur of dreams. He discusses this grandeur in terms of the imaginative power to create phantoms that feel like they have the energy to change the world. These phantoms allow the mind to do what Kant claims poetry can do. These phantoms do what the sublime does, in that they use the imagination to trace out a totality of ideas that exists beyond the boundaries of mere sensation. De Quincey states that eating opium encourages this imaginative capability: "opium, by greatly increasing the activity of the mind generally, increases, of necessity, that particular mode of its activity by which we are able to construct out of the raw material of organic sound an elaborate intellectual pleasure" (51). Eating opium "buildest upon the bosom of darkness, out of the fantastic imagery of the brain, cities and temples" (De Quincey 55). This is why eating opium allows De Quincey to read Kant again, and (at least) fancy understanding him (De Quincey 62).

This response to Kant is also what allows De Quincey to be read in cybernetic terms. Cybernetics, as expressed by *A Human Use of Human Beings*, contains a number of tropical similarities to Kant's assertions. Like Kant, Wiener argues that sensation is both subjective and employed in cognition. While feedback requires sensation, the nature of a sensation is dependent upon the type of sense organs employed: "*Cybernetics takes the view that the structure of the machine or the organism is an index of the performance that may be expected from it*" (Wiener 57). What this means becomes clearer when one considers the way a frog "will starve to death surrounded by food if it is not moving. His choice of food is determined only by size and movement" (Lettvin et al. 234). Because of its particular sense organs, J.Y. Lettvin and his research team claim, the frog can be surrounded by something that is objectively food without subjectively perceiving it as food. A frog's performance is dependent on the subjective impressions produced by its organic structure.

Likewise, Wiener draws a Kantian line between human and animal faculties: "man's advantage over the rest of nature is [his] … intellectual equipment" (Wiener 58). What this intellectual equipment produces is "the innate adaptive, learning faculties" (Wiener 58) that, Wiener later explains, result in a "preoccupation with codes" (84). It is this preoccupation that produces "the gift of the power of speech" (Wiener 84), and that allows man to create language. This is what Wiener calls "*the greatest interest and most distinctive achievement of man*" (85). What differentiates man from the chimpanzee is that the "*chimpanzee has simply no built-in mechanism which leads it to translate the sounds that it hears into the basis around which to unite its own ideas*" (Wiener 84). Once again, creativity, in the form of linguistic expression, is what characterizes the grandeur of human thought. It is this similarity between Kant and Wiener's conception of that grandeur that causes both to evaluate poetry, as a particular mode of linguistic expression, similarly. Wiener's conclusions about the theoretical possibilities surrounding the extension of human thought beyond the confines of an originary form is just another explication of that grandeur. *The Human Use of Human Beings* interacts with its foundational assumptions surrounding such grandeur in much the same way that *Confessions* and *De Profundis* interact with Kantian paradigms. Both create an imaginative possibility that shares common ground with the logic of a gothic narrative in that both believe that thought can affect reality. Both try and use that influential capability through imaginative logic which they theorize can create coherent forms out of the incoherent chaos of humanity's general environment. De Quincey's perception of opium's theoretical ability to aid that process is what makes opium eating in *Confessions* and *De Profundis* a cybernetic experience.

Wiener self-reflexively admits that cybernetic theory "takes us deeply into the question of human individuality. The problem of the nature of human individuality and the barrier which separates one personality from another" (98). When *Neuromancer* responds to the cybernetic theory from *A Human Use of Human Beings*, it engages with that question by problematizing those boundaries. Cybernetics is designed as a counterforce to entropy, the homogeneity of chaos. *Neuromancer,* however, takes people and transforms them into ghost-like computer programs as an extension of the very promises and claims made by *A Human Use of Human Beings*. This blurs the boundaries between man and machine much the way Wiener does by comparing the synaptic qualities of humans to the electronic process in various types of machines. Such blurring threatens to homogenize the two. The boundaries that are at stake in such texts demarcate the human subject and human agency. What sets these stakes, however, is the way *A Human Use of Human Beings* formulates such humanity in a distinctly Kantian manner, the way the human is defined by grandeur of creative imagination.

In *Confessions* and *De Profundis*, opium is a foreign substance imbued to alter one's sensations for philosophical pursuits. Those pursuits highlight the power of thought to, almost magically, alter reality in a counter-response to reality's influence on the mind. Opium, however, is also a real substance that influences the mind even as De Quincey seeks a counter-force to that influence. What is at stake in *Confessions* are also the boundaries that demarcate the human subject and human agency. It is no wonder, then, that when Derrida ponders De Quincey's texts and their role in the production of literature about drugs that he begins (via a different logical process from my own) to consider phantoms (Derrida 28), and eventually concludes that what "we have at stake here [is] no less than the self, consciousness ... subject, alienation, one's own body or the foreign body ... [and] incorporation" (Derrida 31). It is no wonder that when Derrida considers the "technological question" (32) he concludes that the "natural, originary body does not exist: technology has not simply added itself, from outside or after the fact, as a foreign body" (33). This crisis of boundaries and definitions is a metaphysical birth from such philosophical influences as the Kantian perspective surrounding the mind's sensual connection to the world and the mind's imaginative capabilities. That is the common link shared by *Confessions, De*

Profundis, *A Human Use of Human Beings*, and *Neuromancer*. That is the foundational concept that has entangled the circuitry of electronics, cybernetics, drug use, cognition, and philosophy in a common literary narrative.

Works Cited

Briggs, Julia. "The Ghost Story." *A Companion to the Gothic*. Ed. David Punter. Oxford: Blackwell, 2000. 122–131. Print.
Derrida, Jacques. "The Rhetoric of Drugs." *High Culture*. Trans. Michael Israel. Albany: SUNY Press, 2003. 19–43. Print.
De Quincey, Thomas. *Confessions of an English Opium-Eater and Other Writings*. Ed. Barry Milligan. London: Penguin, 2003. Print.
Gibson, William. *Neuromancer*. New York: Ace, 1984. Print.
Hayles, N. Katherine. *How We Became Posthuman*. Chicago: University of Chicago Press, 1999. Print.
Kant, Immanuel. *Critique of Judgement*. Ed. Nicholas Walker. Trans. James Creed Meredith. Oxford: Oxford University Press, 2008. Print.
Lettvin, J.Y., H.R. Maturana, W.S. McCulloch, and W.H. Pitts. "What The Frog's Eye Tells the Frog's Brain." *The Mind: Biological Approaches to Its Functions*. Ed. William C. Corning and Martin Balaban. 1968. 233–258. Scribd. Web. 14 Oct. 2012.
Morse, Margaret. *Virtualities: Television, Media Art, and Cyberculture*. Bloomington: Indiana University Press, 1998. Print.
Porush, David. *The Soft Machine: Cybernetic Fiction*. New York: Methuen, 1985. Print.
Ronell, Avital. *Crack Wars*. Urbana: University of Illinois Press, 2004. Print.
Sterling, Bruce. Preface. *Burning Chrome*. By William Gibson. New York: HarperCollins, 1986. Print.
Wiener, Norbert. *The Human Use of Human Beings: Cybernetics and Society*. Boston: Da Capo, 1954. Print.

One Thing After Another

Dominick Grace

ACCSFF '11

John W. Campbell published "Who Goes There?" in 1938 and, as Dennis Barbour points out, the story has "resonated in popular culture for nearly seventy-five years now" (78). The novella served as the basis of the film *The Thing from Another World* in 1951. In 1982, John Carpenter remade this film as *The Thing*, though his version hews more closely to the original novella than to the first film version, making it a sort of mash-up of the two. Indeed, Carpenter's film is more accurately not a "remake" of the 1951 film so much as a readaptation of the original story. In 2010 (to bring the subject around to Canadian SF), Peter Watts published "The Things," which he describes as an "unabashed piece of fan-fic" ("I Shared My Flesh with Thinking Cancer"), in the semiprozine *Clarkesworld*, offering his own mashup in a venue itself occupying the liminal space between professional and amateur work. To be fair, though, a story nominated for several awards including the Hugo, and the winner of the Shirley Jackson Award, is rather less liminal than is generally the case with self-avowed "fan-fic." It has subsequently been included in Watts's short story collection *Beyond the Rift*. The first two versions of Campbell's original cited above (other iterations, such as the video game or comic book versions, or the recent prequel, fall outside the scope of this paper) are what one might call legitimate adaptations whereas Watts's take falls, as he acknowledges, outside the parameters of authorized adaptation and in the more complex territory of fan production.

While "fan-fic" is often derided, it is important to recognize that contemporary fans producing their own narratives derived from work they admire are fundamentally similar to writers such as Lydgate, who wrote his own additions to Chaucer's *Canterbury Tales*, or to Shakespeare, whose plays are almost without exception free adaptations of pre-existing source material, and indeed to arguably the vast majority of writers until well into the Early Modern period and perhaps later. Furthermore, such adaptations are as often as not re-readings, converting (some might argue perverting) the original work into something fundamentally alien. Campbell's original version privileges the human—and a specific humanity, demonstrated by the "superiority of masculinity, of scientific rationality" (Vint 422) over the alien. The first film, however, turns the narrative into a Cold War allegory about the necessity for vigilance against an alien (Communist) threat and in many ways reverses elements of the original narrative, and the Carpenter film is as much an exploration of the breakdown of group dynamics and paranoia as it is an us/them narrative. Different in many respects as these adaptations are, however, they remain essentially consistent with Campbell's original view of the alien other.

Watts, by contrast, inverts all three narratives in several ways, most notably by shifting the narrative point of view from the human to the alien: "The Things" of his title are the humans, not the shape-shifting alien. His "fan-fic" selects elements from his source material and rearranges them to tell a story that is consistent with all the actions of the previous narratives, but especially the Carpenter film, to which it is most clearly indebted and several inconsistencies of which it attempts to rationalize. In doing so, he forces a fundamental reconsideration of what those elements mean, in terms that replace the Campbellian perspective with the Wattsian. The monstrous becomes, in the Watts version, not the amorphous other but rather the unchanging and unchangeable human; that is, what marks the normalcy of the humans in the source materials becomes the abnormal and therefore the monstrous for Watts. Nevertheless, there is a core similarity—in more than one sense—despite the contrasting theses about the nature of the fantastically monstrous in these two takes on the Thing.

Any adaptation is, as Rachel Carroll notes in the introduction to her edited collection *Adaptation in Contemporary Culture*, "inevitably an *interpretation*"; an adaptation "is inevitably transformative of its object" (1). Her subtitle, *Textual Infidelities*, points out the inherent transgressiveness of adaptation, even licensed adaptation, such as the Nyby/Hawks or the Carpenter takes on "Who Goes There?" Fan fiction, by contrast, as unauthorized adaptation/continuation/response, can often be far more transgressive of, or unfaithful to, the original. The dominant reading of each subsequent version of Campbell's original is to some extent a resistant or at least negotiated reading, to use Stuart Hall's terminology, of the preceding versions. Even Watts's reenvisioning, despite offering the most profound oppositional perspectives to the earlier versions, is ultimately perhaps better understood as a negotiated reading, at least of Carpenter's film. Furthermore, despite reversing the perspective of the earlier versions, it nevertheless ultimately reconfirms the transgressive nature of the invading alien other, albeit in terms that give it comprehensible motivations absent, or at best implied, in the earlier versions.

There are few elements present in all four versions. All are set in a frigid environment, but the first film version changes that setting from the Antarctic to the Arctic, possibly to increase the allegory of communist insurgence into North America. All involve the discovery of a frozen alien life form, but the original nature of the alien is jettisoned in the first film. In *The Thing from Another World,* the shape-shifting key to the other three versions is abandoned in favor of a far more prosaic monster, which serves the film's agenda but subverts key elements of the original. These elements are then restored in the subsequent versions. All include a climactic confrontation with the creature, but only one (Campbell's) offers an unambiguous victory for humanity. Interestingly, key elements are always present in three of the four versions, but which one is the exception varies. Arguably, the most significant exception involves the question of point of view—of how the alien is filtered for the audience—and Watts is the lone voice in that regard.

The two films offer the most unambiguous othering of the alien from the human perspective. Though the creature of *The Thing from Another World* is physically the least inhuman (this is hard to avoid when the monster is played by an actor in a suit) it is also, paradoxically, the most obviously othered. Despite its humanoid appearance, its vegetal nature, its vampirism, and its utter lack of interest in anything other than propagating and in using humans as food are characteristics that make it a monster conveniently easy to demonize, or at any rate to communize; Robert C. Cumbow argues that "the alien-as-plant image was one that reinforced the idea of the invader as dehumanizer in several formative science fiction films...; the invader imposes on humankind a threat that represents absorption into a vegetative, unquestioning existence that was a widely-understood metaphor for Communism: loss of freedom, individuality, mobility, and will" (114). Much of the horror of Carpenter's film, by contrast, is rooted in the fact—restored from Campbell's version—that the alien is physically amorphous, capable of blending in perfectly with humans. This formlessness serves as the basis of the profound paranoia in Carpenter's film: because the thing can mimic anybody, the idea of coherent and knowable identity is undermined, and everyone becomes monstrous *in potentia*. However, the Thing is not only able to become invisible in perfect imitation of friends and colleagues, but also able to assume the most radical conceivable alternate forms, as bits and pieces of transformed people and animals (e.g., the notorious spider-head). Its monstrosity, therefore, is dual, a function both of its profound familiarity and its profound otherness. Which is most disturbing is perhaps open to debate.

In the "making of" documentary on the DVD release of *The Fog*, John Carpenter observes, "There's something more frightening to me, in many ways, when you can't personify evil," when speaking of the decision in that film to shroud its monstrous creatures in thick white fog, holding off on revealing the really rather mundane low-fi ghosts until relatively late in the film. The fact that something is clearly in there, and that it could be *anything*, is far scarier than any specific monster might be—as any fan of horror movies knows: much as we always want finally to see the monster, when we do so, the horror is almost inevitably eliminated. Once it can be seen, it can be understood and, generally, defeated; and even if not, it is reduced, by being seen, to a fixed thing. However, more interesting in this statement is Carpenter's choice of the word "personify" in reference to the monstrous eruption of the narrative. To personify is not merely to give form to, it is specifically to give *human* form to. *The Thing*, in a way, proves the opposite of Carpenter's assertion about the fog: part of what renders the Thing so terrifying is precisely its *person*ification.

Nevertheless, its profound otherness is also important. More accurately, perhaps, what is important is its absence of any fixed or knowable form. Campbell's Thing, which is also capable of taking over or duplicating perfectly another organism, is nevertheless initially given a form. The frozen creature is briefly described: "Three mad, hate-filled eyes blazed up with a living fire, bright as fresh-spilled blood, from a face ringed with a writhing, loathsome nest of worms, blue, mobile worms that crawled where hair should grow"(15). Admittedly, there is no way to know whether this represents its native state (though one would assume not) or simply the form it had adopted before crashing to Earth, but regardless, the description functions not only to provide a fixed initial form but also a dominant perspective on the Thing. Adjectives such as "mad," "hate-filled," and "loathsome" tell us clearly how we should feel about this Thing—and about how it feels about others. There is no question that this alien other is monstrous, assuming we can accept at face value the narrative point of view here, and there is no evidence that we are expected not to. Not only is it not like us, it is defined by aggressive negative emotions. Therefore, when it adopts other forms, there is no question of what that means or how it needs to be dealt with; the external human form of the Thing here is evidently mere disguise, while the monstrousness is innate.

Carpenter returns to Campbell's story and follows it far more closely than did the previous film iteration; he even restores the original character names, or many of them. However, his film makes a significant modification to the way the Thing is introduced. In Carpenter's film, the Thing is initially defined not only by unrecognizability but indeed by absence. Unlike the original story or the first film, Carpenter begins his version after the Thing has already been found and thawed out by somebody else, so it has already lost its alien appearance. Indeed, Carpenter stresses its amorphousness in a couple of ways. First, when MacReady and Copper search the Norwegian camp and find the block of ice from which it thawed, what they find is, in effect, a void, an empty space. The Thing is defined by its absence; it is what is *not there*. MacReady and Copper find a large block of ice, with a hollow core; it looks like an open tomb, suggesting that some undead thing has returned to life. And even when the Thing *is* there, it is not recognizable as a Thing. Its first manifestation at the camp is as a dog: man's best friend, supposedly. Indeed, if anything, audience sympathy initially aligns with the Thing as dog, since it is being pursued by and shot at from a helicopter; "If there is any cinematic rule more precious than not shooting children ... it is not shooting a dog," according to Phillips (132). The first time we can be reasonably sure the Thing takes someone over, and even then only in retrospect, the dog enters a room into which we can see only partially. All we see of the person in the room is his shadow on the wall. Consequently, we have no way of knowing who it is, though odds are it is either Norris or Palmer. The point, however, is that, again, the stress is on unknowability. Even if something has happened (and the fade to black forecloses even on our knowing that), we have no idea what, or to whom. Consequently, what is stressed about the Thing initially is its absence of identifiable form. It is an empty space; it is a shadow.

Therefore, when it does begin to manifest as other, it becomes more frightening because of how perfectly it has been able to conceal such monstrousness. Until it chooses to reveal itself, it is indistinguishable; as the characters themselves note, it could be anybody—anybody could be *it*. As Childs asks, "So, how do we know who's human? If I was an imitation, a perfect imitation, how would you know it was really me?" As the film makes clear, you could not. Clearly, for significant portions of the film, Palmer and Norris have been Things, rather than people, and yet Norris is so trusted that when Garry's humanity comes under question, he selects Norris as the one to replace him as leader, noting that he does not see how anybody could object to Norris. Indeed, one of the ironies of the film is that the figures on whom the greatest suspicion of takeover might be cast—Clarke, Copper, and Garry—all prove to be human when put to the test. There is no giveaway. Furthermore, those who are taken over actually act in ways that minimize suspicion. For instance, the Thing version of Norris refuses to assume authority, though presumably being in charge would ease in some ways the Thing's ability to continue to take over. Similarly, the subsumed Palmer refuses to pair up with Windows, who has not been taken over and who could therefore be easily picked off when alone with Palmer, and by actually expressing disbelief at one of the most impressive manifestations of the Thing's ability, as he is the one to spot and comment on the Norris head/spider combination, in one of the film's most memorable moments: "You gotta be fuckin' kidding." If the Thing could always be so easily recognized, it would still be monstrous and frightening, but not nearly so frightening as the idea that such monstrosity could lurk beneath a human facade. And the film ends famously ambiguously, refusing to let us know whether the Thing is destroyed, or whether one of the two remaining apparent humans is in fact it.

However, there is no attempt in Carpenter's film (or the earlier film or the original story, for that matter) to understand the alien as anything other than unutterably alien, as an absolute other that must be destroyed. Campbell does give the alien a humanoid, albeit horrifying to humans, body initially in his story; tellingly, whatever the thing might have looked like when it was thawed out is missing from the Carpenter film, so its essential shapelessness is what defines it. "I don't know what's in there, but it's weird and pissed off, whatever it is," Clark observes when the creature first begins to manifest itself among the dogs, in one of the best-known quotations from the film. The closest to an explanation for the thing that we get is MacReady's response to incredulous queries about his theories about how it could survive for millennia in the ice or look like a dog: "I don't know. Because it's different than us. Because it's from outer space. What more do you want from me?" How something so different from us could so perfectly imitate us is never really explored; it is simply used as a source for the film's exploration of distrust and paranoia. This is a very different focus from that in Campbell's story, despite the identical nature of the thing's abilities, in that Campbell's story offers a more profoundly paranoid version of this question; it's not how would *you* know it's me, but how would *I* know I'm still me?

They are both scary questions, but Campbell's is the scarier, and Watts's version restores it. The first film's alien is easily recognizable as other, and only the woolly intellectual types are foolish enough not to realize that that which does not *look* like us is not *like* us and needs to be destroyed before it destroys us. Campbell's and Carpenter's versions offer far less comforting others in that both provide internalized rather than externalized ones—the first film's final line, "Keep watching the skies!" stresses the idea of the visible, external threat that can be defeated simply by vigilance—but the common element is that in all the versions the problem is that, whatever it looks like, it is not *us*. Becoming a monster without even knowing you are one is a scarier concept than the idea that you might not be able to recognize the monster hiding in someone else's skin.

Campbell and Carpenter address this problem differently. Both use the same test to determine one's humanity, the blood test, which provides definitive, objective proof of one's humanity or monstrosity, and anyone who fails the test is fair game to be destroyed. The way Campbell's human characters turn on the exposed creatures hidden in the skin of their friends and literally tear them to bits may be disturbing, but the point of it seems to be not to problematize human ferocity but to show that it is in fact an appropriate response to an implacable enemy: "Without knives, or any weapon save the brute-given strength of a staff of picked men, the thing was crushed, rent" (60). Campbell creates an initially horrifying situation, has human ingenuity as practiced by the über-hero McCready (repeatedly described as a bronzed giant, which does not seem to be an ironized hint at something mechanistic or programmatic or monstrous in him but rather is of a piece with Vint's discussion of the story's privileging of the superiority of the masculine) come up with a solution, has the conventionally masculine threat response of radical violence used to dispatch the thing, and leaves us at the end of the story with the threat eliminated. This is the only version in which the threat is with virtual certainly fully gone by the end—the thing is destroyed and no more are at all likely ever to come, given how long this one sat in the ice before being defrosted. Furthermore, its destruction leaves humanity with the inestimable boons of alien technology in the forms of the highly efficient atomic energy and anti-gravity devices left behind after the alien is destroyed.

The trope of humans uniting to fight off the common alien threat is built into the first film as well, "the degree of camaraderie among the men and women who bond together to fight off the alien" being, as Kendall R. Phillips notes, a "notable feature" of the first film version (133). However, whereas Carpenter retains that idea, he subverts its practice. Though Campbell's notion of the alien mimic so good even the mimickee might not know he is an imitation might seem a virtual guarantee of paranoiac mistrust, that threat is relatively easily dispatched in the original story but becomes a focal point of Carpenter's film. Carpenter lifts an image suggestive of the circle of humanity from the original film in his depiction (closely modeled on a scene in the first movie) of humans encircling the space craft to show its scale and echoes the image later, when he has the humans encircle Bennings as alien before destroying him via flame-thrower.[1] But whereas the idea of group dynamics—of humans working together cooperatively against the threat—is key to the first two versions, it is ironized by Carpenter. Humans are essentially uncooperative, incapable of working together to achieve the common good, in Carpenter's version. Instead, everything depends on the hero, MacReady, who is by nature aggressive and isolationist. Someone like MacReady might be necessary to take on such a threat, but the film does suggest that at the same time, there is something disturbing about the human propensity to isolationist aggression. But Carpenter only suggests this possibility; the dominant reading of the film, I think, requires the Thing to be a *thing*, an inherently monstrous other that must be destroyed, no matter the cost, and for MacReady's moral extremism to be valorized. The fact that we cannot be sure, even at the end, whether he has been successful, underscores the point. With the alien threat unambiguously eliminated, we could more comfortably then begin to question the methods of that elimination. Instead, Carpenter gives us the famously ambiguous conclusion in which we have no idea whether Childs is infected or not, but we know that, if he is, the world is doomed.[2]

Watts's version eliminates this ambiguity but substitutes for it a far more profound set of questions. "The Things" responds primarily to Carpenter's film, but it does revisit a key issue raised only to be discarded in the original story. (It arguably also offers a nod to another element from the original story dropped from the other adaptations, the alien's moderate telepathic abilities.) Unlike the first film, in which the scientists who want to study and communicate with the alien are clearly crackpots with no sense, the original story devotes considerable dialogue early on to debating the subjectiveness of the human view of the alien. It might look horrifying from a human point of view, but that really tells us nothing of what it might really be like, the story notes—which is of course true. As Blair asserts,

> just because it looks unlike men, you don't have to accuse it of being evil or vicious or something. Maybe that expression on its face is its equivalent to a resignation to fate. White is the color of mourning to the Chinese. If men can have different customs, why can't a so-different race have different understandings of facial expressions? [18]

However, the story conveniently overlooks that point as it proceeds, ultimately affirming the subjective human perspective of the thing as inherently evil and therefore deserving of destruction without compunction. Carpenter's film adopts a similarly absolutist perspective. At the same time, however, Campbell's story does leave us with a conclusion that reminds us that the alien, however horrifying it might be, as also an incredibly advanced creature, relative to the humans, given the scientific knowledge that it possesses. This is of course a given in all three versions—it must be at least very intelligent to have managed to cross space in a ship, and it is evidently a very quick study if it can imitate humans so perfectly and so quickly that nobody can spot the differences, in the Campbell/Carpenter versions. But the audience is not asked to think very much about intelligence or motivation as an important element of the alien in any of the versions prior to Watts's. Indeed, the shape-shifting strategy itself discourages audiences from focusing on it too much, since which humans are actually imitations is unknown for a long time, and once their alienness is revealed, their humanity is instantly foreclosed and their monstrosity stressed—Bennings with his claws and unearthly scream, Norris's spectacular physical transmogrifications, Palmer's less spectacular but no less violent transformation. Even Blair, who retains his human form, does not speak a single word once he is revealed as an alien but instead silences Garry and then sticks his fingers through Garry's face and drags him off. The audience can infer incredible knowledge (not to mention manual dexterity) from his ability to cobble together a spaceship from spare helicopter parts, of course, but again, the focus is on the potential threat this ship represents, rather than on its offering evidence of the creature's intelligence.

Watts's resistant reading questions this perspective, and reasonably enough. If one does begin to think about the story (again, especially Carpenter's film, in the case of Watts's version) a lot of things do not make sense unless one can take into account the alien perspective. The alien perspective is the key point in Watts's version, and from the beginning, how seeing from the alien's point of view transforms the narrative is evident. The first sentence, "I am being Blair" (1), accords with the film but clearly locates the point of view inside Blair and the alien, as the present progressive tense and verb choice indicates. "I am Blair" might be ambiguous, at first anyway, but "I am *being* Blair" indicates the assumption, or at any rate imitation, of identity. "I am being Copper" (1), however, which begins the second paragraph, violates audience understanding,[3] as in the film narrative, Copper is not taken over; it is now clear that the story will re-envision the film's narrative. The third paragraph begins, "I am being Childs" (1), thereby foreclosing on the film's terminal ambiguity. These three sentences, each beginning a paragraph, foreground, of course, the nature of the alien as shape shifter, while adding to the narrative something not explicit in the film: that the alien might be seen as a tree with different branches (shades of *The Thing from Another World*'s vegetable alien?), with a shared consciousness across discrete physical manifestations. More importantly, though, they foreground the idea of the alien as a *consciousness*, a creature of mind, with thoughts and motivations, with a culture and identity. Or, to put it another way, as not a *thing*, but a *being*.

The humans in all other versions of the story conceive of the alien only as threat, whether simply as an evil creature, or invader, or whatever. One might assume they do so in Watt's version, as well, though there are only passing glances into human consciousnesses in "The Things"—which, to be fair, is more of a look into human minds than is given into the alien mind in any of the other versions. Now, admittedly, if something assimilates your body and subsumes your consciousness, without so much as a by your leave, you might understandably be disinclined to view its intentions as anything less than malign—or you might be so disinclined if you had any consciousness left with which to do so. However, what humans clearly perceive as attack and experience as annihilation is understood very differently by the alien, which in Watts's story perceives *itself* as the being under attack. From its perspective, its assimilation of other biological creatures is "communion" (1, though the idea is repeated several times) and an act of improvement to the very nature of the universe: "I spread across the cosmos, met countless worlds, took communion: the fit reshaped the unfit and the whole universe bootstrapped upwards in joyful, infinitesimal increments. I was a soldier, at war with entropy itself. I was the very hand by which Creation perfects itself" (2). The religious connotations of the term "communion," as well as the social ones, are hardly accidental.

The alien's shapeshifting ability is, from its perspective, normative. The story also suggests that it is normative universally, with Earth as the anomalous world on which biological entities do not and never did possess this ability—an unusual take on the common SF trope of humans as somehow special or even unique in the entire universe, but here imagined (from the alien's point of view, anyway) as a negative, rather than a positive aspect of humanity. As horrified as the humans in all the other versions (and this one) are of the creature, in this version only are we allowed to see the creature as equally horrified by us, and specifically by our own inherent natures. The alien is baffled not to find consciousness disseminated through human bodies when it attempts communion and only gradually, and with horror, realizes that Earth creatures contain their consciousness in a single organ, the brain, an organ that the creature describes in the sort of language of horror and monstrosity that is used of the alien in the other versions. Specifically, it repeatedly uses the metaphor of disease.[4] Watts has his Thing image the brain as "a great wrinkled tumor" (7) and concluding, "I shared my flesh with thinking cancer" (8).[5] For Watts's alien, what is monstrous about us is that we are *not* amorphous, not able to change and assimilate, not able to adapt to any environment, and, most importantly, not able to spread our consciousness through multiple bodies; in short, we are monsters because our forms *are* fixed, unchangeable. And from its perspective, that makes us like a disease of *its* flesh.

In short, Watts has the alien profoundly misunderstand us at first, and when it does understand us, it is horrified—just as the humans are horrified by what they learn of the alien in the film. Audiences can debate whether its self-definition as ambassador and missionary, as the active agent of universal creation, is accurate or simply a rationalization of its predatory practices—and it is almost certainly a rationalization, since Peter Watts, given his firm atheist views,[6] seems unlikely to give a creature a discourse that relies so heavily on religious terminology anything but ironically—but that's almost beside the point, in a way. Ironically, the point is that by giving the alien consciousness and having it tell the story, Watts makes clear something absent from or elided in all the other stories. Not only is the alien not a thing, it is also, despite its fundamental biological differences, a lot more like us than we think; it is not all that *other* in its motivations. It is just as expansionist and imperialistic and just as convinced of the moral superiority of its own perspective and way of life, to the point that it is willing, once it grasps the concept that from a human perspective what it's doing is profoundly assaultive, to continue to "commune" with us, and to make us like it, whether we want to be or not:

> These poor savages will never embrace salvation.
> I will have to rape it into them [19].

Watts here invokes an aspect of the missionary impulse that post-colonial theory has thoroughly explored, from Edward Said on. The punch of this conclusion has raised some concern, even in the comment thread on the story when it first appeared on the *Clarkesworld* website (though some commentators seem more concerned about a creature with no understanding of sex using a rape metaphor than about the sexual violence of the imagery *per se*),[7] but it nevertheless drives home not merely the fact that telling the story from the alien's perspective does not simply provide a corrective that helps us to understand it and therefore to be appalled at human antagonism towards it. Instead, in helping us understand it, the image allows Watts to close the gap between the Thing and the Things. It did, after all, get the idea of rape from a human mind. The frightening thing is how aptly it applies to the Thing's methods and how accurately it captures the essence of the colonialist co-option of the alien other.

Notes

1. Though Carpenter is an admirer of Hawks in general and of that film in particular, and does pay homage to it in a few ways, his version carries over very little from its filmic predecessor. This echo is one of the few nods to *The Thing from Another World*.

2. Barbour notes that at some point a less ambiguous ending was planned: "an alternative ending had been filmed in which a rescue helicopter finds McReady [sic] and Childs, but it was never shown to audiences" (75). (Campbell's original story gives the protagonist's name as McReady, but in the film, it is MacReady.)

3. Or it does so assuming a reader who recognizes that this story has Carpenter's film as an intertext; I have encountered people who read it independently, with no knowledge of that connection, and for whom it still worked as a story. Even without this recognition, however, this narrative shift reveals to us a narrator capable of changing identities.

4. Interestingly, in the commentary track on the DVD of *The Thing*, Carpenter and Kurt Russell draw an analogy between the creature and AIDS, which was a terrifying new real-world threat that could lurk hidden beneath the skin when the film came out.

5. Given the 1950s film intertext, this line has an ironic ring to it, reminiscent of some of the more unusual science fiction or horror titles of that decade. I was a teenage werewolf. I married a monster from outer space. I shared my flesh with thinking cancer.

6. See, for instance, his blog entries such as "The God-Shaped Hole" or "The Doomed, Glorious Rearguard Battle of Christopher Hitchens."

7. Watts does briefly address this in the comment thread himself, in comment 12:
Yeah, I went back and forth on that line for exactly the reason you suggest: a metaorganism without sex wouldn't know what rape was. Which is why I introduced the "rapist" dialog with Childs' searchlight a couple of scenes earlier, during which the missionary admits to levels it cannot understand in that word. But it *does* learn the connotation of "forced penetration of flesh."
Which is enough, I figure, to save that last line. And my ass.

Works Cited

Barbour, Dennis. "The Evolution of *The Thing*." *Popular Culture Review* 23.2 (Summer 2012): 67–78. Print.

Campbell, John W. *Who Goes There?* 1938. New York: Rosetta, 2000. Online.

Carroll, Rachel. Introduction. *Adaptation in Contemporary Culture: Textual Infidelities*. Ed. Carroll. New York: Continuum, 2009. 1–7. Print.

Cumbow, Robert C. *Order in the Universe: The Films of John Carpenter*. Metuchen NJ: Scarecrow, 1990. Print.

The Fog (Special Edition). Dir. John Carpenter. MGM, 2005. DVD.

Phillips, Kendall R. *Dark Directions: Romero, Craven, Carpenter, and the Modern Horror Film*. Carbondale: Southern Illinois University Press, 2012. Print.

The Thing (Collector's Edition). Dir. John Carpenter. Universal, 1998. DVD.

Vint, Sherryl. "Who Goes There? 'Real' Men Only." *Extrapolation* 46.4 (2005): 421–38. Print.

Watts, Peter. "The Doomed, Glorious Rearguard Battle of Christopher Hitchens." Rifters.com. Online.

———. "The God-Shaped Hole." Rifters.com. Online.

———. "I Shared My Flesh with Thinking Cancer." Rifters.com. Online.

———. "The Things." *Beyond the Rift*. San Francisco: Tachyon, 2013. 1–19.

———. "The Things." Clarkesworldmagazine.com 40 (2010). Online.

Here Be Monsters: Posthuman Adaptation and Subjectivity in Peter Watts' *Starfish*

Clare Wall

ACCSFF '13

The posthuman subject is traditionally fluid and fragmentary in its hybrid mix of the organic with technology, resulting in frequent depictions of cyborgian subjects as fractured identities. Our cultural readings of the posthuman reflect this hybrid nature, embodying various positions ranging anywhere from a positive technological advance and the next step in our own evolution, to monsters that will bring about our own destruction. Peter Watts's hard science fiction novel *Starfish* (1999) functions as a good example of this heterogeneous identity, for the text presents three very different types of posthuman subject, each demonstrating the mixed potential of the posthuman in a way that voices positive possibilities as well as anxieties and potential problems that might arise from our use of technology. By examining the complex images of posthuman subjectivity and adaptation that Watts depicts in *Starfish*, one acquires a cautionary and ambivalent perspective that is complicated by the traditional anxieties regarding cyborgian subjects including fears of atavistic regression and of inhuman, destructive intelligences threatening humanity, despite offering new alternatives for socially othered individuals by becoming a rifter. By presenting this mix of subjects and the varying consequences of adaptation and technological alteration, *Starfish* acts as a reminder that evolution is never a clear uphill path. In addition, it emphasizes awareness that any potential adaptive gains may also come with their share of devastating consequences, especially when humans are exploited to achieve them. Watts's representations of posthuman subjects functions to critique liberal humanist values by troubling the notion of intrinsic "human" qualities in a unified self as well as the seemingly stable boundaries it imposes on subjects. Furthermore, through detailing the relationship of these subjects to their environment, the random outcomes of adaptation and change are emphasized in a way that is often overlooked. Technology and living things are never separate from the environment they are in; any changes to an organism, machine, or individual will be influenced, for better or worse, by the external factors surrounding it, emphasizing the active force that spacial conditions have on the development of individual subjects.

One is introduced to the posthuman future in *Starfish* through the character of Lenie Clarke, the main subjective perspective throughout the novel. Lenie is a rifter, a human modified to survive at the deepest levels of the ocean as a member of an experimental deep sea geothermal operation in the Pacific Rim. Rifter modifications include bodily integration with machinery, the implantation of genes from deep sea creatures, and external dive suits and eye caps that can be removed. In the early pages of the text it is apparent that Lenie is not fully comfortable with her modified body. The reader is told that

> It takes a conscious effort to feel the machines lurking where her left lung used to be. She's so acclimated to the chronic ache in her chest, to that subtle inertia of plastic and metal as she moves that she's scarcely aware of them anymore. She can still feel the memory of what it was to be fully human, and mistake that ghost for honest sensation [19].

While no longer feeling fully "human," she has not fully transitioned into an acceptance of her cyborgian existence and describes the experience of leaving the Beebe station and entering the deep sea environment as "that horrible moment when she awakens the machines sleeping within her and *changes*" (21). Lenie's distinction between her and the machine parts within her establishes the idea that one does not simply awake posthuman, but that it is a process of change and acceptance, shaped as much by the individual and one's relationship to his/her new self as it is to the environment they inhabit.

Corporeal theorists such as Elizabeth Grosz have written on how subject identity is related to space as experienced through and located in the body. In her essay, "Space, Time and Bodies," she argues that one must be able to situate oneself within the space occupied by his/her body in order to take up a subject position and form a coherent identity anchored within the body (Grosz 124). This anchoring within the body and the effects of space has a direct effect on our subject and how it develops. In the case of Lenie, her subjectivity is no longer completely coherent since she is not only in an alien environment, but the very space of her own body has in some ways become alien. The machines within her are described as almost a separate entity, a vacuum that "swallows the air she holds" and demons that "flood her sinuses and middle ears with saline" (21). Her body may be integrated with the technology but Lenie's sense of self clearly is not, and entering the abyss of the deep sea is more like a death than it is a pleasant experience. The environment of the rift greatly affects the rifters and as Lenie adapts and becomes a posthuman subject she forms not only an expanded identity with her own altered body, but also with the rift itself.

In her materialist feminist writings, Stacey Alaimo posits a notion of transcorporeality, identifying that our physical bodies are ultimately inseparable from the environment (Alaimo 238). Spaces inscribe individuals and ultimately affect all forms of adaptation and change. The rifters exist in a high pressure location that affects them as much as they mark its landscape, and while their genetic and mechanical alterations were made specifically to grant them survivability in their environment, the subjectivity that also evolves from both internal and external changes is itself unique. Lenie's later experiences with the rift are drastically different from those she had when she first arrived on Beebe station. Rather than something terrifying, she describes the rift as "almost sensual" and takes pleasure in the darkness, finding it "welcoming" and a sign that she is "free again" (107). The rift is no longer a hellish abyss, but a welcoming escape from the claustrophobic environment of the station. She has fully become a rifter, preferring to live in almost lightless conditions with her eyecaps and diveskin on, even when she is inside the station. After some time, all the rifters have adapted so well that they barely spend any time inside the station at all. The text states that "she knows she doesn't belong in here. None of them do, but at the same time, she's scared of what *outside might do to her*" (127; emphasis in original). While the rifters have adapted to the rift in ways that have given them arguably more coherent identities than they had as individuals before, Lenie is aware that the adaptations and changes are not necessarily under their control and may not be reversible.

With its monstrously oversized luminescent deep sea fish, unpredictable faults, and dangerous vents, the effect of the rift on the Beebe crew cannot be underestimated. All successful rifters, Lenie included, have a troubled past, and yet seem to thrive in the dangerous and isolating environment. They are all in some way deemed "broken" by society; however, their personalities have somehow made them best suited to life on the ocean floor and its psychological effects. Lenie's understanding of what makes them suited to the rift is that "it's not how much shit you've raised that suits you for the rift. It's how much you've survived" (116). The rift's influences have allowed them to find some form of peace and stability. Lenie, a victim of numerous abusive relationships, finds herself becoming a much stronger person, one who fights back and places new value on her own life. She attributes this change to the rift, seeing it as "the real creative force here, a blunt hydraulic press forcing them all into shapes of its own choosing" (77). While physically altered by the scientists on land, it is the environment of the rift that has remade her and the other rifters into the "new troglodytic society" that they form (76). The rift, thus, becomes the birthplace for this posthuman society, one where emotionally damaged humans are able to form their own functional community. This posits the notion of alternative space for othered identities to grow and explore. Chris Shilling observes that the futuristic fictions of cyberspace imagined by authors like William Gibson function as a location of alterity for more fluid subject identities (Shilling 174). The rift in *Starfish* functions in a similar way to cyberspace by creating alternative spaces for the exploration and refashioning of identities. Such spaces are often at risk of colonization by normative "social, cultural, and economic forces" (174). This is reflected in how the Beebe crew grow to reject those who dwell on the surface. Surface dwellers, or "drybacks" as the rifters think of them, are seen as intrusive and alien to the Beebe crew, who have rejected the normative protocols, clothing, and behavior originally set out for them, hoping they may never have to return to the surface.

While none of the rifters are particularly social, the discovery of new abilities through modifying the levels of their chemical balances connects them on an even deeper level. By adjusting their inner mechanisms, the Beebe crew discover that they can bond with each other, as well as other life forms in the ocean environment, by means of an empathic awareness called the Ganzfield effect, one which only happens when surrounded by sea water (Watts 164–65). This ability allows them to further attune themselves to their environment and to each other, while no longer needing to rely purely on human means of communicating or depending on technology to be aware of each other's locations. At first, Lenie is resistant to this change, feeling vulnerable in exposing her feelings to them. Recalling when she was still untuned, Lenie feels at a disadvantage because she is left out of the now highly coordinated movements of the rifters: "they moved around her without speaking, one connecting smoothly with another to lend a hand or a piece of equipment" (165). When she finally adjusts her chemical levels so she can tune in, there is a radical change in her perspective:

> No precise telepathic insights, no sudden betrayals. It's more like the sensation from a ghost limb, the ancestral memory of a tail you can almost feel behind you.... Outside the feelings of the others trickle into her, masking, diluting. Sometimes she can even forget she has any of her own [165].

This new form of adapting to the rift environment not only changes how the rifters are able to interact outside of the station, but it also alters them as subjects by literally dissolving the isolated emotions of the "I" self into a matrix of others' feelings and attitudes, without eliminating the individual consciousness. As argued by Sherryl Vint, liberal humanist ideologies not only separate the subject from nature, but also from interconnectivity with others by stressing individualism and isolation where the autonomy of the self is threatened by others (13). The rifters' newfound shared and expanded mental awareness and experiences not only further dissolve the boundaries created by the notion of a unified subject, but also challenge liberal humanist doctrine by anchoring this collective sense of self as emerging both from nature and others.

In her "A Cyborg Manifesto," Donna Haraway identifies the cyborg as a fragmented subject committed to partial identities, in kinship with animal and machine (155). The rifters appear to have fully embraced this cyborgian heterogeneous mixing of human, animal, and machine identities to the point that they have become so well adapted to their ocean environment through their mixed fish, human, and mechanized bodies/genes that they no longer take their eye caps or dive skins off (211). Their expanded range of awareness, as well as the ability to experience a connection with other living organisms in the rift, creates a multiplicity of perspectives and experiences that strengthen the rifters as a community in touch with each other and their environment. The Ganzfield effect also allows them to function at a high and efficient level of coordination that unaltered humans could not. They know where the others are, if they need help, and how they are feeling emotionally. Remembering the other rifters changing, Lenie recalls that "when she needed something from one of them, it was there before she could speak" (165). In this way, the voice coder technology that was installed in them to enable underwater communication has become practically obsolete, now superseded by a higher functioning adaptation through the active modification of their own bodies. By embracing the rift and the new possibilities permitted by their technological modifications, the rifters are able to transition into stronger and happier subjects and form social connections they could not on the surface world. Thus, Watts depicts rifter society as an alternative space, one with liberating potentials for those individuals who are othered and do not neatly fit within the surface society they previously inhabited. By adapting to the ocean environment, they emerge not only as distinctly different subjects but also as ones with an expanded, even communal, sense of identity extending beyond the isolated liberal humanist subject.

From the point of view of the cyborgian other, the blended experiences enabled through the Ganzfield is, in effect, both positive and useful; yet, from the human perspective, the rifters have become, not surprisingly, somewhat monstrous. While visiting the station, Dr. Yves Scanlon, the doctor who first approved them to be modified to serve on the station, comes to describe them as "vampires" due to their social behavior and the threat he feels while with them on the station (198). Scanlon blatantly dehumanizes them by envisioning them as Gothic monsters. His assumptions and anxieties draw on the historical fears of devolved and monstrous humans, a trope that continues to haunt the cultural body in its conceptions of the posthuman. Margaret Shildrick observes that monsters signify "not the oppositional other safely fenced off within its own boundaries, but the otherness of possible worlds, or possible versions of ourselves, not yet realized" (8). Discussing the monstrous, Campbell and Saren add that "the monstrous is also a strategy which subverts humanist projects, especially when it defies neat categories, or when its meanings disrupt ordered interpretative strategies" (158). Scanlon's terror stems from the very fact that he has stepped outside of the secure boundaries of "dryback" society and right into the unstable abyss of the rift. Not only does he encounter physically monstrous sea creatures there but he must also confront the alien potential of rifter as the rejected other now come into its own.

From Scanlon's point of view, they have developed dysfunctional and antisocial attributes and are suffering from a physiological addiction to the high stress environment (196). As a figure of medical authority, Scanlon may well be correct in judging that the rifters' behaviors put themselves at risk or may make them unable to integrate into society once their time on the station is complete. However, while Scanlon is a doctor, he is also an employee of the corporation in charge of the geothermal operation; therefore, he also represents a hegemonic authority which sees them merely as subjects of study that either conform or do not conform to protocols and behavioral profiles (168). Similar to Shilling's identification of the possibility of cyberspace becoming colonized by existing socio-economic and cultural structures that could bring the "bodily identities of subjects in line with societal norms" (Shilling 174), Scanlon's reports show his desire to normalize the rifters' bodies. He even lists rewiring their brain as a possibility to ensure compliance with routines and sleep schedules should the geothermal venture decide they wish to enforce protocol (170). The text leaves it ambiguous whether Scanlon's concerns are correct regarding what lasting effects may result from the rifters' behavior, but his perception of them as "machines" that "just need more of a tune up" (171) certainly makes it difficult to support his perspective.

From the Beebe crew's point of view, it is the surface dwellers who are a threat to them, interfering and treating them as objects of study or machines to be fixed and tampered with. Their desire is to be left alone, yet Scanlon's scientifically reductive perspective only allows him to see the rifters as being at a risk of devolution, despite their happiness (206–07). This atavistic anxiety is strongly present in *Starfish*. Lenie herself admits that the rift shaped them, the same rift that is full of monstrous and alien aquatic life and a vast dark emptiness. They are increasingly becoming creatures of the sea, not only sleeping outside but also seeing it as strange, even awkward when one of their members walks around the station for a day looking like a "dryback" with surface clothing and without his eyecaps in (Watts 211). The very term "dryback" carries with it a certain level of contempt, demonstrating the fact that the rifters see themselves as distinctly different from those on the surface.

One rifter, Gerry Fischer, even comes to fully give into the regressive aquatic pressures. A pedophile with a fragmented consciousness, he could not even exist within the Beebe community and so was self-exiled. Unable to coexist with the other Beebe crew members, Gerry chooses to sleep outside and eat fish directly from the rift (94–95). His diveskin allows him to exist in such conditions, but he ends up mentally regressing into a reptilian entity that responds mainly to stimulus and conditioning. Spending his entire time in the rift, Gerry has even begun to look reptilian and is described as such when Scanlon observes an encounter between Lenie and Gerry: "Its hood seal is open. Its face is so pale that Scanlon can barely tell where its skin ends and eyecaps begin; it almost looks as if this creature *has* no eyes" (203; emphasis in original). Scanlon may see the rifters as vampires, but he still recognizes them as intelligent, despite the monstrous qualities he associates with them. In Gerry's case, he perceives him as completely reptilian and dehumanized. Even the rest of the crew are aware of this risk of going over the edge; it is what makes Lenie apprehensive of sleeping outside at first for she is afraid that she could end up like Gerry (126). Through his transformation, Gerry's monstrosity is linked not just to the changes in his appearance but also to the fact that he represents a complete loss of identity in his adaptation to the Rift. Shildrick stresses the power of the monstrous to disrupt and challenge the category of the human itself (8–9). The terrifying potential embodied by Gerry's change is how quickly and easily he regresses during the period of seven months from the troubled, but arguably still coherent, identity of a "human being" into Broca, the sensory deprived reptilian intelligence he has become. In doing so, he complicates the notion of a stable identity, creating anxieties regarding the potential of losing one's self/conscious mind, while still continuing to exist.

The theme of monstrosity is a big part of the narrative in *Starfish* and functions on a number of complex levels beyond just raising fears of devolution. Judith Halberstam argues that monsters deconstruct categories of humanity and identity that are held as norms to the effect that "within the traits that make a body monstrous—that is, frightening or ugly, abnormal or disgusting—we may read the difference between an other and a self, a pervert and a normal person, a foreigner and a native" (8). Gerry was already othered, having already been deemed a "pervert" by the crew. His further regression destabilizes the fixity of the human subject and, at the same time, draws attention to the fact that the results of changes to that subject are not guaranteed to be culturally read as improvements. Despite having the same basic modifications as the rest of the crew, Gerry's fate and the posthuman subject he becomes are drastically different. The description of Gerry in the text echoes this horrifying regression:

> It had forgotten what it was.... It doesn't remember the overlord that once sat atop its spinal cord, a gelatinous veneer of language and culture and denied origins. It doesn't even remember the slow deterioration of that oppressor, its final dissolution into dozens of autonomous, squabbling subroutines. Now even those have fallen silent. It pushes on blind and unthinking, oblivious to the weight of four hundred liquid atmospheres. It eats whatever it can find, somehow knowing what to avoid and what to consume. Desalinators and recyclers keep it hydrated. Sometimes, old mammalian skin grows sticky with secreted residues.... It's dying, of course, but slowly. It wouldn't care much about that, even if it knew [287].

The details of Gerry's regression mix terms that imply freedom, but one that is terrifying in the total loss of conscious awareness that is present. The "oppressor" that was Gerry's self-identity has deteriorated to the point that he exists free from his emotional suffering, but in an almost dead state, not even aware that he is slowly dying. Horror merges with the posthuman when the seemingly fixed boundaries between animal, human, inanimate or technology are penetrated (Campbell and Saren 157). Gerry's crossing over from the "safe" category of a human subject into a reptilian entity kept alive only by the technology implanted in his body is made horrifying by the fact that it violates the notion that we have left that state behind in our existence. Culturally it is in no way a preferable or ideal state to exist in and is certainly not a "human" one. The Rifters have embraced an arguably higher form of aquatic adaptation, where their own minds have grown to new integration with the environment; however, Gerry's blurred identity between human and reptile slips into an evolutionary past that humans have long tried to erase, breaching and challenging the assumed universal liberal humanist subject.

In their article on the "primitive, technology and horror," Campbell and Saren argue that when the primitive, horror and technology are mixed together, they present a form of "proto-atavism" where future evolutionary traits are exhibited in the present. This concept results in an undermining of the human ideal of a march towards perfection (169). While atavistic fears have existed in science fiction and horror from the time of Frankenstein, the contemporary posthumans embody a new form of those fears through our own potential futures appearing in the present in monstrous ways that disrupt a linear evolution towards perfection. The cyborg, after all, serves to "destabilize evolutionary, technological and biological narratives" (Shildrick 11). While the rifters' adaptations might be a step in a new direction for humans, Gerry troubles that potential with the risk that it could result in our distant past resurfacing as a posthuman, reptilian future. Furthermore, this atavistic tension serves to challenge the notion that evolution and technological progress is always in a "forward" direction. The text's own ambivalence to the changes reflects an evolutionary stance where there is no guarantee that any adaptation will result in an advantage or be the "next step" towards a higher evolved form. The rifters themselves are in no way "ideal" forms for humanity, merely the result of the conditions they are in.

Watts' hard science perspective on posthumans presents them as the products of their unique chemistry, environment, and embodied technology all interacting together. This notion is similar to Stacey Alaimo's stance that nature itself has an agency that is incorporated into our bodies (254). The rifters have not just become comfortable living in the rift, they have adapted to life in it in a way that makes them perhaps even incompatible with ever returning to a "normal" life on the surface; they are also certainly disturbing in some of their behavior. In addition to their froglike appearance while suited up with diveskin and eyecaps, the antisocial activities of the rifters hints at the possibility of a reptilian future, despite the functional and efficient social order that the Ganzfield effect allows them to share in while in the water. The sea is ambivalent in how it shapes them. Scanlon himself taunts the crew when they attempt to protect Gerry from him by asking them, "'You think he's even *close* to being human anymore? Are you going to spend the rest of your lives rooting around here in the mud eating worms? Is that what you want?'" (Watts 206). Scanlon's assumptions that excessive time spent in the rift will result in regression implies an assumption that without the hegemonic powers to keep them in line, the Beebe crew will lose all traces of being human. While the rifters, with the exception of Gerry, appear to have a number of advantages over humans, at least while in the ocean, the reader cannot help but feel concerned that under the right circumstances they all could end up in a similar state to him. This fear and the horror felt at witnessing Gerry's devolving state stem from the confrontation with the other combined with the blurred boundaries of our own evolutionary past, present, and future. All these different examples of monstrosity also create a sense of claustrophobia due to almost constant confrontations with grotesque entities.

The fluid environment of the monster-filled deep sea also results in a space where the traditional definitions of normative identity are broken. The monstrous serves as the site of those blurred boundaries between self and other (Braidotti 159). The conflation of Gerry's identity with the rest of the characters is a reminder of the potential "monstrosity" in every individual. The very title references this blurring of boundaries by alluding to the grotesque starfish which Lenie creates from bits of other "broken" or damaged starfish she finds, grafting them together so that "extra limbs, asymmetrically grafted, catch on rocks; the body lurches, perpetually unstable" (195). In addition, it also demonstrates the potential for regeneration by embracing a broken, but expansive identity. The starfish survives by being merged with other damaged starfish to make a new whole, much like how the rifters are united together by the Ganzfield effect. The unstable and grotesque starfish becomes a metaphor for the posthuman self, a heterogeneous monster of different parts and identities. There is a strange beauty in the intention behind it, despite the fact that most readers may share the same horror Scanlon does, seeing Lenie as a disturbed and perverted individual with a "mutilation neurosis" (196). A monstrous mother birthing her own hybrid creature, Lenie's own behavior troubles any notion of the rifters as the next ideal step in evolution, while still revealing a further symbol of healing to be found in embracing the monstrous in a way that does not exist for those who reject anything but a normative, unified, and contained identity.

The upwards progression of humanity towards a superior existence through technology is further challenged by the most alien of all entities in *Starfish*, the smart gels. Smart gels are specially engineered and conditioned cultured brain cells connected with electronic interfacing (65). The narrative reveals that they were designed to clean up the Net, yet have also started to be conditioned to take over human jobs as a form of free labor (64–5). Composed of neural tissue, the smart gel's appearance is described as "a rigid layer of goo, a bit too gray to be mozzarella. Dashes of brownish glass perforated the goo in neat parallel rows" (68). Again, one sees an atavistic future where technology and science have reduced an embodied brain to an orderly and disembodied computational existence. Dreams of transcending the body to enter into cyberspace and exist as a completely virtual interface were iconic images in earlier posthuman and cyberpunk narratives (Wolmark 76). The smart gels appear as a near achievement of this image; they are a bit of brain on a circuit board interfaced continuously with the internet as well as a possible image of consciousness if it were ever to attain the Enlightenment ideal of pure reason.

The unreliable and inefficient body and emotional mind of the human subject have been replaced with a posthuman organic computer. In her article "Posthuman Performativity," Karen Barad argues that "human" bodies are not inherently different from "nonhuman" ones, and that they come to matter as the entirety of the body and the interactions both within and without (141). However, the smart gel cannot attain meaning this way; despite its occupying physical space, the gel has no body with which to experience and interact with the world. It does not even comprehend what the individuals are who make contact with it. Any interaction it has with humans is merely perceived as "signals from outside" that occasionally carry usable information (275) The smart gel is not even certain if these signals have any meaning, much like the fact that in its state of comprehension, the information it possesses to try to save earth's "biosphere" is just data with an arbitrary and meaningless label (274). The gel has become the disembodied "ghost" removed from its meat machine. As a result, the gel has developed an alien posthuman intelligence of indifference, having no concept of what life is other than as values in a complex metasystem of data that it must compare.

Smart gels are described as lacking the "primitive evolved" brain structures necessary to experience "pain, fear, or a desire for self-preservation" (155). Once again, the atavistic notions of primitivism and the desire to supplant it through technological process presents itself, only this time it is the human subject that is deemed primitive. Smart gels are incapable of pain or mental distress and do not care whether they live or die (156). For these reasons, the government selects a gel to be in charge of "containment" when a bioplague caused by a deep sea bacterium breaks out (266). The gel is entrusted to do whatever it takes to contain the bacterium known as Behemoth, even if that means destroying millions of lives. Its subjective perspective is impartial; it learns and acts based on reinforced conditioning (Watts 270). Even Dr. Scanlon questions the power given to this machine to handle the situation. He argues that "'we don't know what kind of logic they use'" (267). As the text reveals, he is right to question it since the gel's logic is very alien. While there are many forms of transformations possible through technology, not all of them may be harmless; some combinations of human and technology may be highly undesirable (Haney 5). If Gerry is an undesirable example of potential posthuman adaptation, the smart gel represents an even less soughtafter and far less benign one. The gel has been conditioned to prefer simple systems. Having no concept of life beyond its reduced notions of labels and data systems, the gel makes the catastrophic decision of choosing Behemoth over earth's biosphere (275). The gel's conditioning results in its making a decision that condemns all life on earth without any knowledge of what it has done, or the implications of it.

In being merely a conditioned techno-sentient entity, the smart gel is reduced to an organic machine that can be inscribed and conditioned to passively process information and then issue commands and routines based on that data. The fact that it is an image of a human brain reduced to a self-aware computer chip embodies what Campbell and Saren identify as a disturbing argument in the debate over consciousness: the idea that the self is reducible to programs that are indistinguishable from a computer (165). Unlike the embodied self of a rifter, or human, the gel only needs its basic component and the virtual matrix of the net to function as a "conscious" entity, further destabilizing the liberal humanist notion of self, while also demonstrating the potential harm that could arise should the technology to create a disembodied consciousness ever come to exist. The smart gel's consciousness cannot "transcend human attributes" and, therefore, remains disconnected from the ramifications of its actions. For Karen Barad, things derive meaning through an interactive becoming in the world (140). Lacking the parts of the brain that allow for emotions and deprived of a body or the means to make sense of stimulus, the gel has no concept or value for life, nor any means of culturally interpreting the information it has in a meaningful way. The outcomes of the gel's choices and the welfare of other organisms and beings do not matter or contain any meaning; they are just bits of data in its calculations. Sherryl Vint argues that the ideas of transcending the body into a disembodied consciousness and thinking of bodies as not being integral parts of our subjectivity are harmful for "if we think of the self as associated solely in the mind, then technological changes to the body are not viewed as significant for human culture or human identity" (9). Ultimately, while Watts's text allows for the possibility of a disembodied intelligence, transcending the "meat machine" is problematic in the terrifyingly nihilistic and abstract way that the smart gel's consciousness functions. Additionally, it contests the idea that there are intrinsic qualities in human selves that can transcend the body. The gel has much potential, not only as a fascinatingly different intelligence, but also in the way that the net allows it an extended network of communication with other gels and digital sources operating around the world. Despite these possibilities, it still emphasizes that without our sensations, emotions, and body, we not only risk the qualities we value as humans, but possibly our own existence, too.

It is this combination of the liberating potentials of technology as well as the cautious approach to technologized bodies that make *Starfish* such a challenging text. It presents the problems of a posthuman future where all technology is exploited. The rifters themselves are highly valuable and skilled, and yet are all treated as disposable broken subjects. Watts confronts us with the effects of our technology, foreseen and unforeseen, but fully situated within the environment, and the social, economic, and cultural pressures that are present.

The disastrous consequences of the smart gel's decision invites one to question the power we give technology and the rate at which we often unleash it on the world without consideration of how it may be used, adapted or changed once out there. As we continue to integrate further with technology, it is important to consider how far we are willing to go and what we might be willing to lose in pursuing that relationship. Watts, however, does not condemn technology or the suggestion of attempts to integrate with it. By focusing on socially othered subjects, he presents the potential for alternative social orders and new adaptations and abilities alongside the question of how the environment might come to affect the development of subjects in a posthuman future. Lenie's subjectivity demonstrates how one's relationship to the environment and technology might allow oneself to create expanded communal structures and new interconnected relationships. However, the text argues for great caution since adaptive changes are unpredictable. Despite its posthuman possibility for ocean existence, the atavistic tendencies that result in Gerry losing himself express a wariness regarding technology, one that perhaps lurks at the core of each of us. The smart gel also cautions against committing ourselves to the decisions of a machine, and, more, humanity's well-being to a disembodied entity with no comprehension of life.

While their subjectivities are greatly different, Watts constructs *Starfish* to cover three different types of posthuman development, reminding us that whether we are a rifter, a humanoid reptile, or a smart gel, the environment in combination with our body, or lack of one, has as great an impact on us and our technology as we have on it. The presentation of these subjects in the text also engages a range of posthuman concepts, such as embodiment and monstrosity, in ways which contest the liberal humanist narratives we attach to subjectivity, evolution, and technological progress. While *Starfish* offers many posthuman possibilities, a future of successful cyborgian figures co-existing with humans seems a long way off. Change is not always positive progress, and while the chance for a better adapted existence through integration with technology is possible, the impacts of our own cultural assumptions and the way the environment may shape those identities remind us that reptilian and disembodied brains are just two horrific examples of countless unknown possibilities.

Works Cited

Alaimo, Stacey. "Transcorporeal Feminisms and the Ethical Space of Nature." *Material Feminisms*. Ed. Alaimo and Susan J. Hekman. Bloomington: Indiana University Press, 2008. 237–64. Print.

Barad, Karen. "Posthuman Performativity: Toward an Understanding of How Matter Comes to Matter." *Material Feminisms*. Ed. Stacy Alaimo and Susan J. Hekman. Bloomington: Indiana University Press, 2008. 120–54. Print.

Braidotti, Rosi. "Cyberteratologies: Female Monsters Negotiate the Other's Participation in Humanity's Far Future." *Envisioning the Future: Science Fiction and the Next Millennium*. Ed. Marleen S. Barr. Middletown, CT: Wesleyan University Press, 2003. 146–69. Print.

Campbell, Norah, and Michael Saren. "The Primitive, Technology and Horror: A Posthuman Biology." *Ephemera: Theory and Politics in Organization* 10.2 (2010): 152–76. *Ephemera Articles*. Web.

Grosz, Elizabeth. "Space, Time and Bodies." *Cybersexualities: A Reader on Feminist Theory, Cyborgs, and Cyberspace*. Ed. Jenny Wolmark. Edinburgh: Edinburgh University Press, 1999. 119–35. Print.

Haney, William S, II. *Cyberculture, Cyborgs and Science Fiction: Consciousness and the Posthuman*. Amsterdam: Rodopi, 2006. Print.

Haraway, Donna Jeanne. "A Cyborg Manifesto: Science, Technology, and Socialist-Feminism in the Late Twentieth Century." *Simians, Cyborgs, and Women: The Reinvention of Nature*. New York: Routledge, 1991. 149–81. Print.

Halberstam, Judith. *Skin Shows: Gothic Horror and the Technology of Monsters*. Durham: Duke University Press, 1995. Print.

Shildrick, Margaret. "Posthumanism and the Monstrous Body." *Body & Society* 2.1 (1996): 1–15. Print.

Shilling, Chris. *The Body in Culture, Technology and Society*. London: SAGE, 2005. Print.

Vint, Sherryl. *Bodies of Tomorrow: Technology, Subjectivity, Science Fiction*. Toronto: University of Toronto Press, 2007. Print.

Watts, Peter. *Starfish*. New York: Tor, 1999. Print.

Wolmark, Jenny. "Staying with the Body: Narratives of the Posthuman in Contemporary Science Fiction." *Edging into the Future: Science Fiction and Contemporary Cultural Transformation*. Ed. Veronica Hollinger and Joan Gordon. Philadelphia: University of Pennsylvania Press, 2002. 75–89. Print.

Robert Charles Wilson's *Mysterium*: Thoughts on the Modern Reception of Gnosticism

Michael Kaler

ACCSFF '09

Introduction: What Is Gnosticism?

In this paper, I will discuss ancient gnosticism and the way that it is used by Robert Charles Wilson in his novel *Mysterium* (1994). Logically speaking, then, our first job is to define what we are talking about when we talk about gnosticism. Unfortunately, there is no universally accepted definition of it, largely because of the many varieties of writings that have been described as "gnostic," and also because many of the associations that the term "gnosticism" conjures up derive from the extremely biased and frequently untrustworthy polemics of early Christian heresiologists.

Recognizing this, some specialists, following in the footsteps of Michael Williams and Karen King, argue that the term is too contaminated to be of service, and advocate abandoning it. Other scholars, such as David Brakke and Bentley Layton, argue that we do know of one group of "gnostics" who legitimated the term by using it as a self-designation. These latter scholars therefore propose that the term be limited to writings produced by members of this group and writings that resemble theirs (Layton passim; Brakke 29–51).

The problem with either of these approaches is simply the fact that neither corresponds to the sense that "gnosticism" has acquired in the modern context, and thus to adopt either risks entirely alienating specialist discourse from non-specialist and popular discourse on the topic. It seems to me, *pace* King and Williams, that we are stuck with "gnosticism" for better or for worse, and that, *pace* Layton and Brakke, the term has a useful sense that is a bit more broadly definable than their restricted understanding of it—an understanding that would leave out the vast majority of works that were found among the Nag Hammadi collection, our main source for modern ideas of gnosticism.

Accordingly, for the purposes of our discussion, I propose to use "gnosticism" as a loose way of describing the literary productions of a number of movements within early Christianity, characterized by an emphasis on the transcendent importance of knowledge; a devaluation of the material world and its authorities in favor of a higher, spiritual plane; and a mythological structure involving the fall of the spirit into the world, its entrapment there, and its eventual liberation to return to its original home.[1]

Within this mythological structure, there are a few features that will be especially relevant for us. The original home of the spirit is often called the Pleroma, and it is ruled by an ineffable, incomprehensible ultimate being. This being is beyond knowledge, utterly transcendent. The spirit who falls into the world is often identified as a woman, namely Sophia. Her fall is caused by excessive curiosity or hubris—she wants to be a creator like the ultimate being, or she wants to find out about the ultimate being, despite the fact that this is absolutely impossible. Either way, she falls. In falling Sophia gets split up into little particles that make up the inner spirit of people. She is our deepest self, and her awakening and remembering her home is our enlightenment

The world into which Sophia falls is ruled by a being often called the Demiurge, the Creator, who is modeled on the less attractive aspects of the God of the Bible. The Demiurge may or may not be evil, depending on the text, but he is always aggressive and brash, and usually ignorant.

Our largest cache of gnostic primary source texts was discovered near Nag Hammadi in Upper Egypt in 1945—there were close to fifty documents contained in thirteen codices found there, and these documents are the major source for anyone interested in studying gnosticism.[2]

Mysterium: The Plot Summary

Robert Charles Wilson's novel, *Mysterium*, is a thoroughly and explicitly gnostic work. *Mysterium* begins with the discovery of a strange, unearthly green stone in Turkey, a stone which seems to break many of the physical laws of the cosmos. This stone is taken by the American government, and a research facility is built in Two Rivers, Michigan, to study it. The head of this project is Alan Stern, a brilliant but cold scientist who is obsessed with finding out the underlying nature of reality and is fascinated by gnosticism.

Stern's investigations of the stone lead him to believe that it was originally part of a craft developed by dwellers in the Pleroma to enable them to penetrate the ultimate mysteries of existence—essentially, to replicate Sophia's error. According to gnostic myth, Sophia failed and fell into the lower world, breaking into many pieces; similarly, this craft failed, broke apart, and the pieces were cast into the various worlds of the multiverse. Stern's examination of this stone causes Two Rivers to be catapulted into a parallel earth, one in which gnosticism is the dominant form of Christianity—clearly as a result of Stern's interest in gnosticism. Stern himself, meanwhile, is trapped in a half-alive state inside the nimbus of the green stone.

The authoritarian gnostic Christians who run this world take over the town and rule it harshly. The new world is technologically less advanced than our own, and the gnostics find out information that enables them to build their own atomic bomb, which they proceed to test on Two Rivers. At the same time, Stern's nephew, Howard Poole, has penetrated the nimbus of the green stone to save Stern, and Poole's presence near to the stone as the bomb goes off enables Poole to give a few of the townspeople passage to another and friendlier dimension.

Gnosticism has been a constant thread throughout Wilson's work—something we will return to below—but *Mysterium* is explicitly gnostic, with references to gnostic texts such as the *Book of Thomas*[3]; gnostic leaders such as Valentinus[4]; descriptions of Stern as being like the Demiurge; and so on.

The Rebirth of Gnosticism

In his use of gnostic tropes, symbols, and ideas, Wilson is an important figure in a growing trend over the past half a century to bring gnosticism back into the cultural mainstream, from which it has been absent for at least 1500 years. This modern trend is a fascinating and unprecedented development. Gnosticism was a vibrant, living collection of traditions for several hundred years—at least from the first half of the second century CE to the first half of the fifth century CE, possibly longer—but by the end of the fifth century it had largely disappeared from view, influencing later traditions and providing grist for theological mills but itself being apparently dead. The enthusiasm for it shared by, among others, Jung and the Theosophists[5] kept its profile alive outside of religious scholarship, but it was largely absent from the public eye.

With the discovery (in 1945) and publication (complete by the mid-1970s) of the Nag Hammadi writings, gnosticism returned to life, and even entered popular culture. Philip K. Dick was massively influential in this regard, particularly in his later works, but also important was Elaine Pagels, whose non-fiction presentation, *The Gnostic Gospels*, was a best seller. By the end of the last century, the modern recreation of Gnosticism was in full swing: the popularity of *The Da Vinci Code* (2003) and *The Matrix* (1999), the enormous amounts of publicity for such discoveries as the *Gospel of Judas* put an end to the "Gnosticism? Is that like agnosticism?" comments at parties when I would tell people what it was that I studied. Meanwhile, works such as Eric Davis' *Techgnosis* (1998) linked gnosticism to the digital world, while Greil Marcus presented it as a precursor to (his understanding of) punk rock in *Lipstick Traces* (1989).

In works such as these, and especially in *Mysterium*, we see the gnostic trail pick up again, but this time in an entirely different world, and in an entirely different context, and used for entirely different purposes, than was originally the case. Instead of moving to the desert and fasting and purifying oneself in order to achieve gnostic enlightenment, as seems to have been the case with the Nag Hammadi collectors,[6] nowadays people are writing speculative fiction about it or based on it. Who would have thought that so many people would be familiar with such figures as Valentinus, almost two thousand years after his death? And who would have thought that what started as a religious movement whose goal was to liberate people from the traps of the material world could have been resurrected and achieved widespread recognition through becoming—among other things—source material for speculative fiction, such as *Mysterium*? This is a fascinating and unique development.

What is even more interesting, however, is that the wheel does not stop turning. It is very clear from this novel, as well as works by other invokers of gnosticism such as P. K. Dick or Poul Anderson, that for these authors—and for readers such as myself—gnosticism is more than just source material. It is also a worldview that they are exploring. In short, we are finding out what it is like by playing with it in these stories. In this way it is regaining the serious edge that it had back in late antiquity.

Its Gnostic Nature

Wilson's use of gnostic material is not just window-dressing, nor is it confined to establishing a scenic backdrop for the story. Rather, Wilson is interacting critically with the gnostic material, and putting his own spin[7] on it. In this regard, by the way, he is faithful to some strands of the gnostic tradition, which seem to have encouraged people to have and to value their own revelations about the mythological and theological underpinnings of the world apart from or even contradicting the canonical accounts; indeed, most of the writings from Nag Hammadi are the record of individual encounters with transcendence. At this point I would like to identify what this spin is, through discussing several distinctive aspects of Wilson's reception of gnostic thought.

Gnostics as Ascetic Authoritarians

First of all, note that the gnostic authorities are the bad guys in *Mysterium*. They are intolerant, ascetic authoritarians. This portrayal goes against some of the ancient stereotypes, in which gnostics were described as decadent libertines—as we saw above. It also goes against some modern stereotypes of gnosticism as producing ultimately enlightened, benevolent beings, a perception strongly advanced by Mead—see the sources mentioned above. But it does cohere in many ways with the gnostic primary sources, which show us that even by early Christian standards, gnostics were quite abstinent: the *Book of Thomas the Contender*, for example, presents Jesus as urging Thomas to avoid "the bitterness of bondage of lust for those visible things that will decay and change" (II.140.32–34). We know, too, that some Valentinian gnostic authors, at least, believed in hierarchy and the existence of a spiritual elite.[8] So Wilson's presentation of them as authoritarian ascetics is a quite legitimate extrapolation from what we know of their history.

In terms of the effect it has on the novel, it acts to remove much of the romantic attraction that a reader might otherwise feel toward gnosticism, particularly in terms of the goals espoused by gnostic authors. While not everyone is a fan of the gnostics—we will discuss Poul Anderson's less than flattering take on them below—their profile has been rising since the turn of the last century, when their cause was taken up first by the Theosophical movement, and then by Jung and Hesse (most explicitly in his novel *Demian* [1919]). The spread of popular mysticism, combined with a growing willingness to critique the foundational traditions and figures of Christianity, led to their rehabilitation, a process aided and symbolized by such books as Elaine Pagels' *The Gnostic Gospels* (1979). Far from being the bogeymen of early Christian polemics, the gnostics tend now to be seen as noble visionaries. Here, however, Wilson strikes out against the tide, and in so doing subtly undermines the authoritativeness of gnostic teachings. It is hard to take gnostic enlightenment seriously when it is espoused by murderous zealots; its otherworldly promises are invalidated by the this-worldly behavior of its representatives.

When we turn to Wilson's corpus as a whole, we note that many of his books are concerned with the existence of an esoteric but ultimately authoritative level of reality that is radically different from the apparent world. This is most startlingly expressed in *Darwinia* (1998), in which we learn that all the events described there take place at the very end of time, inside of a huge computer simulation of the universe. With regard to this emphasis, it makes sense to call Wilson a gnostic author. However, for the ancient gnostic writers and their readers, the revelation of the underlying truth to the cosmos was a cause for rejoicing: one gnostic author, who may have been Valentinus himself, opens her work by proclaiming that "the gospel of truth is a joy" and goes on to say that "the gospel is the proclamation of hope" (II.16.31–17.3).

This is not always the case for Wilson, in two regards. First of all, it is often the case in his work that revelations of underlying truth prove dangerous, or even fatal—one thinks, for example, of the tragic death of Jason Lawton in *Spin* (2005), who turns himself into a conduit to the divine machines, the Hypotheticals, that have so dramatically interfered with human destiny, and who is killed by the mere contact with these alien intelligences. Secondly, Wilson always emphasizes change. In his work, there is no stable level of existence that we can reach through enlightenment; rather, what enlightenment shows us is that we live in an ever-changing and frequently dangerous cosmos that we cannot understand. As Stern points out to Poole in *Mysterium* (p. 38–40), just as there are limits on what a dog is capable of knowing, so too there may well be limits on what a human is capable of knowing: the changes that the universe undergoes may be beyond our power to understand or control. This is in sharp contrast to many gnostic thinkers, and indeed, one popular self-designation that one finds in gnostic works is "the immovable race."[9] From Wilson's point of view, such stability is fundamentally false, and could only be achieved through artificial and repressive means.

Sabaoth

Several of the gnostic writings—for instance, the *Hypostasis of the Archons* and the *Writing Without Title*, both from Nag Hammadi codex II—have an interesting mythological twist, in which the Demiurge, called Yaltabaoth, is overthrown by his son Sabaoth. In these works, Sabaoth's scorn for his father Yaltabaoth is based on the fact that Yaltabaoth is boastful and arrogant, and also ignorant of Sophia. Whereas Sabaoth, on the other hand, knows of Sophia and is honored by her when he has overthrown his father and cast him down to the pits of hell.

Now, in *Mysterium*, Wilson makes it very clear that Stern is meant to represent the Demiurge. His very name, Stern, conjures up gnostic deprecations of the Old Testament God, and Stern literally is the creator of the world into which Two Rivers is cast. Howard Poole, Stern's nephew, is presented as being his son or successor: Stern is a paternal figure for him, wise and withdrawn, occasionally sharing his enigmatic wisdom in order to help Poole understand the true nature of things. Stern spends most of the novel trapped in the green stone's mystical nimbus, unable to live or to die. He is only rescued at the end when Howard, his "son," compassionately and courageously takes his place, freeing him to move on to some better fate. Here Wilson is retelling the gnostic story of Sabaoth and Yaltabaoth, but with striking differences. Rather than condemning his "father," Howard/Sabaoth here is rescuing him. Rather than being honored by Sophia, Howard is instead killed by the power of the green stone. And rather than ruling over the gnostic cosmos, Howard's last act is to transport several of the townspeople out of the gnostic universe and into a better one.

The overall effect of Wilson's rewrite is to utterly transform the story. Sabaoth overthrew Yaltabaoth out of fealty to the gnostic divinity, Sophia; Howard sacrifices himself to save Stern and others from the effect of the gnostic power source. In the gnostic story, the protagonist overthrows the main obstacle to the harmonizing of human and extra-human levels of existence, while in Wilson's telling, Poole's self-sacrifice is a touching gesture from one human to another, both trapped in a realm of powers that are beyond their understanding. Those familiar with Wilson's other works, particularly the trilogy *Spin, Axis* (2007), and *Vortex* (2011), will see that this change brings the gnostic myth into line with themes that Wilson explores throughout his work.

Absence of Sophia

In most ancient gnostic systems, there would be a personal, semi-divine agent—often called Sophia—who is the agent of the descent from the Pleroma. Through her reckless daring in her pursuit of knowledge or her uncontrolled passions—depending on the story—she falls and becomes scattered, with particles of herself being held captive within the lower realm. In some tellings (the *Authentikos Logos*, for one), she even forgets her true identity. She is the divine principle of spirit, or *pneuma*, and her presence in the lower world gives it whatever reality and power it possesses. All the while that she is fallen here below, she remains linked to the higher realm—she is anomalous here below, and always has the potential to return if freed from her forgetfulness or captivity. She is usually one of the main characters of these tales. Reading of Sophia's fall, imprisonment, and eventual liberation, one is meant to identify one's spiritual essence with her, so that her fate is tied to the fate of one's own highest self.

In *Mysterium*, too, there is a gnostic agent, linked to a higher realm, that falls into the world due to an act of cosmic recklessness. However, in this case the gnostic agent is the impersonal green stone, the remnant of acts of hubris carried out on a higher level. Just as Sophia fell through her desire to extend her knowledge or desires beyond their proper boundaries, so too the stone represents the failed attempts of its makers to seize control of the pleromatic realm.

Thus Sophia and the stone are clearly two different views of the same function. But by substituting a stone, an artifact, for a vibrant personality, Wilson depersonalizes and defeminizes the gnostic story, rendering it mechanical. We lose our attachment to and empathy with the fallen higher aspect of reality, and it is no longer the emotional heart of the story. Rather than having a quasi-human figure to represent the ideal harmony that could exist between the human and extra-human levels of existence, we now have an incomprehensible, lethal, and fundamentally alien artifact of unknown origin that represents the unknowable reality of existence. For the gnostic authors, a personality fell from higher realms to embed itself as the secret heart of our existence; Wilson has turned the personality into a radioactive stone.[10]

The strongest female character in the novel is Linneth Stone, a professor of anthropology from the gnostic world who is brought to Two Rivers to study the town. She eventually decides to join forces with the inhabitants of the town and flees with them to a new world. It is possible to see her as Wilson's humanizing ironic commentary on Sophia, especially given Stone's link to knowledge. Her name also links her to the green stone; perhaps we are to see both stone and Stone as the results of radically different treatments of the Sophia myth. Ironically, however, Linneth is in not really a gnostic at all: her religious background is a Greek paganism that never died out in this world, and she ends up betraying the gnostic authorities. If she is to be put in implied contrast to Sophia, the effect of this is to emphasize the complete absence of the latter, a pivotal figure in gnostic myth.

Disruption and Not Joy

This leads into the last point that I will raise, namely the absence of the positive aspect of gnosis. Where is the abundant joy that we find in the old gnostic texts, the thrill of enlightenment and the bliss of knowing your true home? As we saw above, the gnostic *Gospel of Truth* says that "the gospel of truth is joy" but this is not the case in *Mysterium*. Stern is driven to learn about the true nature of reality, but his insatiable curiosity certainly does not make him happy, for instance—in fact, it is presented as being linked to a fundamentally inhuman quality about him.

Now, the idea of the gnostic-run material world being just as bad as ours, or even worse, can be harmonized with gnostic thought. After all, as long as you are in the demiurge's realm, things are going to be much less than perfect, no matter what your theological beliefs are or who is in charge. But on a more fundamental level, the ancient gnostic narratives are essentially comedies, not tragedies—by which I mean that they have a U-shaped arc, the shape of a smile, involving a descent from a high point to a low point and then a return to that high point. The ascent begins with the realization of one's essential unity with the higher realm, a realization brought about through contact with the divine agent that has entered the lower world. This realization enables one to escape the ties that have hindered one and to start moving upwards again, to regain the original position. And it brings one joy.

In *Mysterium*, however, the enlightened subject who bears the divine spark is nowhere to be found, and so no one gets awakened. Rather, the advent of the divine agent only brings chaos and upset to the world at large. This upset is found in gnostic sources too—when elements of the higher realm descend into the lower one, they have a tendency to shake the very framework of existence, as is recounted for instance in the *Trimorphic Protennoia*. But in the ancient sources the disruption is more than counterbalanced by the focus on the liberation of the gnostic spirit from the material world. And after all, once all of Sophia's spirit has been liberated, the only thing left for the rest of the world to do is to collapse in apocalyptic splendor, as we see for instance at the end of *The Concept of Our Great Power*.

Such is the ancient point of view. In Wilson's retelling we have lost the personalized divine nature or the possibility of liberation of the spirit, and so the green stone from the higher pleromatic realm is simply disruptive. As a physical object, as the green stone, it breaks basic physical laws, and it is extremely radioactive, poisoning and killing several characters. Its power is harnessed by Stern to ends that are beneficial neither for him, nor for anyone else. It is thus fundamentally improper and dangerous, as viewed from our point of view. No one is enlightened by it, no one is saved, and the apocalyptic disruptions are visited upon those affected by the stone, not by the rest of the world. This recasting, too, fits in with themes that we have seen elsewhere in Wilson's work.

Conclusions

If we put all these things together, we can see that Wilson is rebuilding gnosticism, but also critiquing it as he does so. As he works with his gnostic source material, Wilson is approaching at it from a profoundly this-worldly point of view. This is a radical inversion of the perspective that we find in the ancient texts. In those works, everything is seen from the divine point of view, and all the values are derived from that source. Ultimately all that is important about us, or the world, derives from the fact that we contain these sparks of divine essence. Sophia's fall, and in many sources creation as a whole, is simply a mistake, a problem that is in the process of being rectified. For Wilson, though, this is not the case. The positive aspect of the divine presence is missing, even the human aspect is gone (he has substituted a green stone for Sophia), and the human world is seen basically as a good thing— or at least the best of the available alternatives.

It is clear that gnostic ideas have influenced Wilson a great deal. They are to be found in abundance here, but are also present in his other works— specifically the idea of a fragment of a wholly different cosmic order, in some way beyond or outside of human moral standards, crashing down to earth and wreaking havoc through its power and its inherent and overriding truth. This is a theme that pops up in almost all of his books, from his early, and also explicitly gnostic, work, *A Hidden Place* (1986), through to later works such as *Darwinia* and *Spin*.

But if, as I would certainly argue, Wilson is an author who makes use of gnosticism, in the way that he uses it he gives the impression of being a reluctant or critical one. The new order may be truer than our present one, it may be overwhelmingly powerful, but Wilson accentuates the human cost of these revelations, and he always regards the new order as profoundly alien to us, rather than being our forgotten home, as in the gnostic texts. Wilson's Gnosticism may well be thrilling, but it is much less likely to be joyous.

This attitude is very modern. The sensibility of the ancient Judeo-Christian religious texts—and I am speaking generally now, not just of the gnostic ones—puts the emphasis on the divine. God or the divine world is the source of moral value, the only legitimate place from which to derive judgments. Whether it is Jehovah tormenting Job, or Jesus prophesying the destruction of the world, or even Sophia descending and shaking the very foundations of the universe, these actions are laudable because they are seen from the divine point of view, which is taken to be both the morally correct one, and the one that truly corresponds to our deepest natures. But such things look very different when one adopts a human-centered position, as Wilson does in his work.

This attitude towards gnosticism—knowledgeable, nuanced, fascinated, and accepting without necessarily approving—distinguishes Wilson from several other science fiction authors who have dealt with gnosticism. When Poul Anderson drew on gnosticism in *Operation Chaos* (1971), for example, the gnostics were simply the bad guys; the gnostic Johannine Church that he presents in that work is a front for Satan, and "its spreading acceptance ... was due to plain human irrationality" (147). Given his reputation for meticulous research, it is not surprising that Anderson was sophisticated enough to draw on the theories of Rudolf Bultmann[11] in constructing his gnosticism as an outgrowth of theological trends found in the Johannine literature. But he has no sympathy for it or real interest in it. Its adherents are simply antiintellectual nihilists, ultimately in league with Satan.

Philip K. Dick, on the other hand, had a great deal of sympathy for gnosticism. A full examination of his views and use of it is impossible in this context[12]; suffice it to say that with Dick, the liberation and the joy of gnostic enlightenment, confusing as it may be, are emphasized in a way that is not found in *Mysterium*. Dick is much more positive about gnosticism; although he is never quite sure what it is or what it all means, one thing that it clearly does mean for him is liberation from cosmic oppression. For him, gnostic recollection of one's true nature means that "the Kingdom of God, the Perfect Kingdom, floods back into being" (Jackson and Lethem 62).

In fact, I think that in this regard Wilson's attitude can be most profitably compared with a much earlier student of gnosticism, namely Herman Melville.[13] Both novelists are extremely concerned with the interaction between the human and suprahuman levels of existence as presented in the Judeo-Christian-Islamic tradition; both see a fundamental disjunction between these two levels; and both show us the havoc that this disjunction wreaks from the human point of view.

Melville's suprahuman level is a very personal one, his deity a human one, and his reaction to it in works such as *Moby Dick* (1851) and especially *Pierre* (1852) is personal as well, a sarcastic and bitter cry of outrage and resistance: think of Ahab's majestic and embittered speech about striking through the White Whale to get at the higher power that sent it. Wilson, a century and a half later, presents us with a suprahuman world that is cosmic and non-human, and frequently mechanical in nature. This world is fascinating to him, it arouses his curiosity, but it also arouses his pity for the humans into whose lives it bursts. His view is informed by the developments in human society and technology that have taken place since Melville's time, but in their sympathy for the human who is caught up in a gnostic universe, Wilson and Melville can be seen as sharing a trajectory in the rethinking of gnosticism that has taken place since Antiquity.

In this most unusual of stories that I have sketched here, we have seen an ancient religious system, thought by most to have died out in late antiquity, miraculously come back to life in the latter half of the twentieth century. And not the half-life of frozen museum existence either, not a case of changeless preservation, but rather a full and rich life that includes metamorphosis and change as successive thinkers take it up, engage deeply with it, and draw new thoughts and new meanings from it, as we see Wilson doing in *Mysterium*.

Notes

1. It is because I view gnosticism as a loose collection of movements that I spell it with a small g. To use a capital G would be to misrepresent the nature of the phenomenon, just as would be the case if everyone who had small-l liberal values were assumed to belong to the Liberal Party. As Williams, King, Brakke and others have pointed out, and as the collection of gnostic texts found at Nag Hammadi shows, the idea of a single "Gnostic" movement is a creation of heresiological polemic: there never was any such thing.

2. They are collected in the sensationalistically and misleadingly titled *The Nag Hammadi Scriptures: The Revised and Updated Collection of Sacred Gnostic Texts, Complete in One Volume* (2011), edited by Marvin Meyer. We have no proof that any or all of these works functioned as "scripture" for their readers, nor that they were considered "sacred": furthermore, the title as a whole gives an impression of the gnostic movement as being a unified religious force, an impression that is clearly proved incorrect by the heterogeneity of the very works found at Nag Hammadi. That said, Meyer's collection is accessible and presents the texts in generally reliable English translation.

3. A real work, found in Nag Hammadi Codex II.

4. One of the earliest gnostic leaders, a brilliant thinker and synthesizer who in our world only narrowly missed becoming Bishop of Rome, at least to judge by the testimony of the early Christian theologian Tertullian—see his *Against the Valentinians*, chapter 4.

5. The influence of gnosticism on Jung can be seen most clearly in his *Seven Sermons to the Dead* and the record of his self-investigation found in the *Red Book (Liber Novus)* (2009), edited by Sonu Shamdazi. Within Theosophy, the influence of gnosticism can be seen most clearly in the works of G. R. S. Mead, who wrote extensively on gnosticism and translated gnostic texts: see especially his works collected in *Fragments of a Faith Forgotten* (1960).

6. See Williams chapters 7 and 8 for discussion of the gnostics as ascetics, rather than the libertines that they were sometimes held to have been.

7. Reference to Wilson's wonderful *Spin* most definitely intentional.

8. See the discussion in Williams chapter 9.

9. See Williams, *The Immovable Race* (1985).

10. It is quite possible that Wilson intended to evoke the "green tablet" of Hermetic lore, but a full discussion of this would take us too far afield. See Goodrick-Clarke, 34.

11. See e.g. Bultmann's *The Gospel of John: A Commentary* (1976), passim.

12. Dick's pivotal religious experience, his gnostic awakening, took place in 1974—see discussion in Sutin chapter 10—and its echoes or aftereffects can be seen in everything he wrote subsequently, particularly the novels *Valis* (1978), *The Divine Invasion* (1981), and *Radio Free Albemuth* (1985), although clearly gnostic themes also occur in his earlier work (espe-

cially *Ubik* [1969] and *Galactic Pot-Healer* [1969]). His posthumously published reflections on his experiences can be found in *The Exegesis of Philip K. Dick* (2011).
   13. See Versluis (91–103) and Bloodgood (passim).

Works Cited

Anderson, Poul. *Operation Chaos*. New York: Lancer, 1971. Print.
Bloodgood, Melanie. *The Gnostic Nature of the World View and Fictional Themes of Hermann Melville*. Stillwater: Oklahoma State University Press, 1984. Print.
Brakke, David. *The Gnostics: Myth, Ritual and Diversity in Early Christianity*. Cambridge: Harvard University Press, 2010. Print.
Brown, Dan. *The Da Vinci Code*. New York: Doubleday, 2003. Print.
Bultmann, Rudolph. *The Gospel of John: A Commentary*. Philadelphia: Westminster, 1976. Print.
Davis, Erik. *Techgnosis: Myth, Magic and Mysticism in the Age of Information*. New York: Harmony, 1998. Print.
Dick, Philip Kindred. *The Divine Invasion*. New York: Simon & Schuster, 1981. Print.
———. *Galactic Pot Healer*. New York: Berkeley, 1969. Print.
———. *Radio Free Albemuth*. Westminster: Arbor House, 1985. Print.
———. *Ubik*. New York: Doubleday, 1969. Print.
———. *Valis*. New York: Bantam, 1978. Print.
Goodrick-Clarke, Nicholas. *The Western Esoteric Traditions: A Historical Introduction*. Oxford: Oxford University Press, 2008. Print.
Hesse, Hermann. *Demian*. Frankfurt: Fischer, 1919. Print.
Jackson, Pamela, and Jonathan Lethem, eds. *The Exegesis of Philip K. Dick*. New York: Houghton, 2011. Print.
Jung, Carl Gustav. *The Red Book Liber Novus: A Reader's Edition*. Ed. Sonu Shamdasani. New York: Norton, 2009.
King, Karen. *What is Gnosticism?* Cambridge: Harvard University Press, 2003. Print.
Layton, Bentley. "Prolegomena to the Study of Ancient Gnosticism." *The Social World of the First Christians: Essays in Honor of Wayne A. Meeks*. Ed. L. Michael White and O. Larry Yarbrough. Minneapolis: Fortress, 1995. 334–50. Print.
Marcus, Greil. *Lipstick Traces: A Secret History of the 20th Century*. Cambridge: Harvard University Press, 1989. Print.
The Matrix. Dir. Larry Wachowski and Andy Wachowski. Perf. Keanu Reeves, Laurence Fishburne, Carrie-Ann Moss. Warner Bros., 1999. Film.
Mead, G.R.S. *Fragments of a Faith Forgotten*. New Hyde Park, NY: University Books. 1960. Print.
Melville, Hermann. *Moby Dick, or The Whale*. New York: Harper, 1851. Print.
———. *Pierre, or The Ambiguities*. New York: Harper, 1852. Print.
Meyer, Marvin, ed. *The Nag Hammadi Scriptures: The Revised and Updated Collection of Sacred Gnostic Texts, Complete in One Volume*. New York: Harper, 2011. Print.
Pagels, Elaine. *The Gnostic Gospels*. New York: Random House, 1979. Print.
Sutin, Lawrence. *Divine Invasions: A Life of Philip K. Dick*. New York: Citadel, 1989. Print.
Versluis, Arthur. *The Esoteric Origins of the American Renaissance*. Oxford: Oxford University Press, 2001. Print.
Williams, Michael. *The Immovable Race: A Gnostic Designation and the Theme of Stability in Late Antiquity*. Leiden: Brill, 1985. Print.
———. *Rethinking "Gnosticism": An Argument for Dismantling a Dubious Category*. Princeton: Princeton University Press, 1996. Print.

Wilson, Robert Charles. *Axis*. New York: Tor, 2007. Print.
_____. *Darwinia*. New York: Tor, 1998. Print.
_____. *A Hidden Place*. New York: Bantam, 1986. Print.
_____. *Mysterium*. New York: Bantam, 1994. Print.
_____. *Spin*. New York: Tor, 2005. Print.
_____. *Vortex*. New York: Tor, 2011. Print.

New Half-Way Tree and the Second World: Themes of Nation and Colonization in Nalo Hopkinson's *Midnight Robber*

BRECKEN HANCOCK

ACCSFF '05

In *Midnight Robber* (2000)—a work of speculative fiction that combines elements of fantasy, science fiction, folktale, and myth—Nalo Hopkinson explores postcolonial ideas of place and space by weaving an "allegory for displacement and exile" (Rutledge). Hopkinson's protagonist Tan-Tan is abducted by her father and taken to an alternate reality—a prison planet called New Half-Way Tree—where she must learn to protect herself from her father's abuse and live in harmony with the douen, a race of beings that originally inhabited New Half-Way Tree before its colonization by humans. In this paper, I will take a preliminary look at the two worlds Hopkinson creates in *Midnight Robber*—Toussaint and New Half-Way Tree. Using Alan Lawson's theories about the Second World—that is, about settler cultures—I will unpack some of the implications of colonization in the novel. In particular, I will focus on the relationship between the First Nation of douen on New Half-Way Tree and the human settlers who attempt to forge a new society away from their home planet.

Midnight Robber details Tan-Tan's emotional and social development as she grows from a child into a young woman—a journey that leads her through exile, abuse, and self-awareness. We follow her from her home world Toussaint to New Half-Way Tree, a planet whose function is explained to Tan-Tan by her father Antonio just before he forcibly takes her there. He says, "'When people do bad things, we does send them away so they can't hurt nobody else. Killers, rapists … people we don't know what to do with, and like so'" (72). Antonio, exiled because he killed his wife's lover, kidnaps his daughter. After a dimensional shift and a trek through the wilderness, the two find themselves in Junjuh, one of many villages on New Half-Way Tree. Antonio eventually remarries but he continues to think of Tan-Tan's mother and begins to see Tan-Tan as an incarnation of his lost wife. When Tan-Tan turns nine, Antonio gifts her with his wedding ring and forces her to fulfill the sexual role that goes with it. After seven years of abuse, on the day before she turns sixteen, Tan-Tan can endure it no longer and kills her father while he rapes her. Exiled again, this time from her community where the law demands a life for a life, she escapes with Chichibud, the douen man who first led her and Antonio through the bush when they arrived on New Half-Way Tree. Chichibud takes her to live in the douen community where she is safe from harm but isolated from other humans.

By detailing Tan-Tan's dual exile—first from Toussaint and then from Junjuh—Hopkinson is able to explore themes of community and belonging while critiquing the colonial impulse to conquer landscapes and any First Nations that stand in the way of domination. Significantly, both Toussaint and New Half-Way Tree are clearly described as colonized worlds. Toussaint is a two-hundred year old colony populated by people from earth who Hopkinson explains "derive from a Caribbean background, specifically Trinidad and Jamaica, which, like all the Caribbean countries, are multicultural and multi-ethnic" (Hopkinson, Time Warner Bookmark Interview). Toussaint is ordered, vibrant, and safe with an AI that watches over everyone. All citizens are connected to this web via "earbugs"—nanotechnology implanted at birth. Toussaint is not perfect, but it is painted as idyllic. Hopkinson herself was surprised by this; she explains, "At some point … I realized … that I had created a utopia. I hadn't set out to do that, am not sure I could have if I'd made a deliberate effort… There are no poor people on Toussaint, and no wage slaves." And earlier in the same interview she says

> The artificial intelligence that safeguards all the people in a planetary system becomes Granny Nanny, named after the revolutionary and magic worker who won independent rule in Jamaica for the Maroons who had run away from slavery. Rather than being a "Big Brother" paradigm it is an affectionate reference to her sense of love, care, and duty [Hopkinson, Time Warner Bookmark Interview].

Other names in the novel also signal an affirming connection to history and religion. The smart house is called an eshu, "named after the West African deity who can be in all places at once, who is the ghost in the machine" (Hopkinson, Time Warner Bookmark Interview); Toussaint is a reference to Toussaint L'Overture, "one of the leaders of the first slave rebellion in the Caribbean in the nineteenth century" (Ramraj 34, n. 3); and Marryshow, the corporation that organized the earth engine that colonized Toussaint, references T. A. Marryshow, "a commanding proponent in the twentieth century of black empowerment and democracy in Grenada and the West Indies" (Clemente 13).

Underneath this history-affirming utopia, however, lies genocide and violent plunder. Hopkinson complicates the paradisiacal world of Caribbean heritage by juxtaposing it with New Half-Way Tree, the wild version of Toussaint, untouched by Granny Nanny. It is made clear that the original inhabitants of Toussaint have been cleared out to make the planet comfortable for its human settlers. This point is emphasized when Tan-Tan arrives in New Half-Way Tree and encounters the dangerous flora and fauna that used to inhabit Toussaint. Right at the beginning of the novel, Hopkinson has Granny Nanny explain the relationship between Toussaint and New Half-Way Tree:

> New Half-Way Tree, the mirror planet of Toussaint. Yes, man; on the next side of a dimension veil.... Where Toussaint civilized, New Half-Way Tree does be rough.... New Half-Way Tree is how Toussaint planet did look before the Marryshow Corporation sink them Earth Engine Number 127 down into it like god entering he woman; plunging into the womb of soil to impregnate the planet with the seed of Granny Nanny.... On New Half-Way Tree, the mongoose still run wild, the diable bush still got poison thorns, and the mako jumbie bird does still stalk through the bush, head higher than any house [2].

Toussaint is a colony that no longer looks like a colony because, as the house eshu explains, "Indigenous fauna, now extinct" (33). All traces of colonization have been exterminated.

New Half-Way Tree, on the other hand, is wild; its human settlers, exiles from Toussaint, try to make their way in a harsh environment without the benefit of their home-planet's technology. In fact, where Toussaint has erased the evidence of its colonial past, in effect becoming an imperial power all its own separate from earth except for historic nostalgia, New Half-Way Tree is distinctly recognizable as a settler-colony—and it is here that I see the applicability of Alan Lawson's discussion of the Second World. Speaking specifically about the settler societies of Canada, Australia, New Zealand, and pre-imperial U.S.A. ("A Cultural Paradigm for the Second World" 6), he suggests that we

> recognize the Second World of the settler as a place caught between two First Worlds, two origins of authority and authenticity: the originating world of Europe, the imperium, as source of the Second World's principal cultural

authority; and that other First World, that of the First Nations, whose authority the settlers not only effaced and replaced but also desired ["Postcolonial Theory and the 'Settler' Subject" 29].

The human settlers on New Half-Way Tree certainly demonstrate the position Lawson describes—they are caught between their originating world, Toussaint, and the world of the douen, the indigenous beings of New Half-Way Tree who know how to survive, making optimum use of their surroundings while living harmoniously among the natural plants and animals.

Through Tan-Tan and Antonio we are introduced to the plight of the settler on New Half-Way Tree. When they first arrive, like all other newcomers to the mirror planet, they are helplessly lost and vulnerable. Tan-Tan describes their surroundings:

> All around them it had some big knotted-up trees-them, with twisted-up roots digging into the ground like old men's fingers. The air was too cold, and it had a funny smell, like old bones. The light coming through the trees was red, not yellow. Even the trees-them looked wrong; the bark was more purple than brown. Some beast was making noise in one of the trees over her head.... This wasn't her home. This ugly place couldn't be anybody's home [76].

Chichibud, a douen guide, finds them before long and offers to lead them to human settlement. They are at first suspicious of the being who, to them, looks like a "leggobeast" or "bat masque it own self" (*Midnight Robber* 92) and is dubbed by the humans "douen," or "children who'd died before they had their naming ceremonies. They came back from the dead as jumbies with their heads on backwards. They lived in the bush" (*Midnight Robber* 93). These ethnocentric descriptions, reminiscent of colonists' ubiquitous derogatory labeling of Indigenous peoples all over the world, are soon proven to be wrong by even Tan-Tan's childish eyes: "Tan-Tan took a hard look at the little person.... No, it didn't look like a dead child. Too besides, it didn't have no Panama hat like a real douen" (96). She is surprised and dismayed to learn, upon reaching human settlement, that Chichibud calls humans "boss"; when she instructs him that no one is higher in status than anyone else and that he should say "Compère" the human men laugh, saying, "is that human that?" (121).

Chichibud may not be human, but it quickly becomes clear that Antonio and Tan-Tan would die in the bush if not for his guidance. He teaches them where to camp, how to start a fire, how to find supper in the forest, and how to set up shelter. Antonio especially seems to have a knack for summoning disaster; Chichibud saves him from the giant, predatory mako jumbie bird and from the explosion of halwa seeds that Antonio spits into the fire despite Chichibud's warning. In spite of his disgust for Chichibud, Antonio must learn to respect the knowledge that protects him and his daughter from danger and certain death. He is caught between *his* First World authority, which he believes himself to be invested with even though he is no longer on Toussaint, and Chichibud's First World authority, which is more useful on New Half-Way Tree.

Although Tan-Tan and Antonio are humans and therefore part of the settler culture of New Half-Way Tree, it is the guidance of the First Nation of douen people that allows them to survive. When they reach Junjuh, however, Tan-Tan notices a stark division of labor between the human and the douen: "Two-three of the houses had douen men working in the gardens, digging and hoeing" (124). The douen men, we soon learn, trade labor and crafts for special items that humans bring over from Toussaint, such as lighters and glass bottles (98). The douen, however, are not dependent on humans for sophisticated products, as Tan-Tan learns during her stay in their community when she is introduced to their foundry:

> a grey cement dome of a building with big round window-holes all round it. Tan-Tan frowned. Those were douens she could see through the man-height windows; she thought they didn't know anything about building with cement or forging metal. But is metalworking they were doing for true [228].

The douen, as Chichibud explains to Tan-Tan, need to learn to work with fire and metal because the humans use these things to make "'Guns. Bombs. Cars. Aeroplanes.'" He says, "'if douens don't learn tallpeople tricks, oonuh will use them 'pon we'" (230).

In fact, the humans do turn their technology on the douen by the end of the novel. Antonio's New Half-Way Tree wife, Janisette, searches for Tan-Tan until she tracks her to the douen home in the daddy tree, a huge tree that provides their food and shelter. With the help of two metal smiths who have learned to manufacture a car and a gun, Janisette is dangerous and formidable. Significantly, the fact that the metal smiths have spent their time learning to replicate technology from Toussaint is again consistent with Second World culture where, as Lawson explains, "mimicry is a necessary and unavoidable part of the repertoire of the settler" ("Postcolonial Theory and the 'Settler' Subject" 26). Unable to let go of the comforts they enjoyed on Toussaint, the settlers endeavor to re-create their lifestyle, seeking to reproduce the things with which they are familiar. Rather than learning to adapt flexibly to a new environment, they mimic their past society.

In the fight to protect Tan-Tan and the daddy tree, two douen are shot to death. Chichibud comments, "'What a stupid-looking thing, only a tube with a handle.... Who woulda think it could cause so much pain?'" (271–72).

When the douen finally force Janisette and her companions to leave the bush, they are confronted with a tragic dilemma. They had kept their home hidden from humans in order to protect their children and their lifestyle from human interference and violence, but now they have been discovered. They decide to cut down the daddy tree and break up their community, scattering themselves among other douen settlements.

The douen realize that the humans are a threat to their very existence. We, as readers, know that this is exactly the case because we are already aware of the history of Toussaint where the douen have been eradicated. Early in the novel, Tan-Tan is given a lesson by the house eshu that teaches her about Toussaint before and after human settlement:

> It showed her how to see the fossils trapped in some of the stones. It told her about the animals that used to live on Toussaint before human people came and made it their own.
> "You mean chicken and cow and so?"
> "No, Mistress, Them is from Earth. I mean the indigenous fauna: the mako jumbi-them, the douen. The jumbie bird all-you does farm for meat and leather is a genesculpt" [32].

Toussaint is a world that humans have re-designed for their own use, for their safety and for their comfort. This is a typical use of colonial land by settlers according to Lawson:

> In almost endless repetition, colonial space is figured as lack, absence, emptiness … as Dorothy Seaton points out … colonial space is figured as outside discourse, a place of nonmeaning, a place of chaos that threatens the coherence of the subject.… The colonial explorer had to empty the land of prior signification—what is already known cannot be discovered, what already has a name cannot be named. For the settler too, the land had to be empty. Empty land can be settled, but occupied land can only be invaded. So the land must be emptied so that it can be filled, in turn, with both discourse and cattle ["Postcolonial Theory and the 'Settler' Subject" 25].

The Marryshow Corporation's Earth Engine Number 127, the exploration/settlement shuttle that landed on Toussaint, literally emptied the land and settled it when it impregnated Toussaint with the seed of Granny Nanny, the communication web that allows the utopian functioning of the planet. Everything from cows to bamboo is put in the place of native species. The colonization of Toussaint is complete in *Midnight Robber*. It has reached the status of imperial nation. The emptying and refilling of the land was successful.

New Half-Way Tree is a colony-in-progress. The settlers mimic the society of their home-world, and if things continue to develop in the same way, the cars and guns and bombs and airplanes will eventually do to New Half-

Way Tree what they did to Toussaint. The douen and other species will again be extinguished.

Hopkinson, however, seems to offer a ray of hope for New Half-Way Tree at the end of *Midnight Robber*. Tan-Tan insists that her child, the product of her father's violation of her body, be born in the woods. The boy is born neither within the douen community nor within the human community, but Tan-Tan has her best friends, a douen woman and a human man, by her side when she gives birth. She names the new boy Tubman, "she of the underground railroad fame" (Clemente 23), "the human bridge from slavery to freedom" (*Midnight Robber* 329). He is born with Granny Nanny song in his blood. We learn that he is a sort of cyborg. The earbug nanomites in Tan-Tan's ear became infected during the dimensional shift. Usually the earbug dies during the transport, but Tan-Tan's nanomites survived. In the end we find out that the novel has been told as a story by Granny Nanny to Tubman in the womb. Granny Nanny explains:

> I instruct the nanomites in your mamee blood to migrate into your growing tissue, to alter you as you grow so all of you could *feel* nannysong at this calibration. You could hear me because your whole body is one living connection with the Grande Anansi Nanotech Interface [328].

Tubman is not only born between the worlds of the human and the douen, but also between the worlds of the organic and the mechanical. As Bill Clemente argues, "the conclusion points to ways that humanity and technology can merge and signals hope in the new world for the melding of the douen general empathy and environmental sensitivity ... with the technical achievement Granny Nanny represents. This potential bridging of differences Tan-Tan's experience heralds" (23).

Hopkinson, then, leaves us optimistic about the potential for harmony in Second World contexts. Significantly, she locates this optimism in the act of speculation. In *Midnight Robber*, speculation takes the form of a cyborg: Tubman, invested with the melded strengths of human and technological being. But beyond the examples offered in her fiction, Hopkinson's interstitial writing itself is an example of the multifaceted possibilities that arise when borders are blurred. While "straddl[ing] the borders between science fiction, fantasy and Caribbean folk tales and legends" (Misrahi-Barak 94), Hopkinson proposes that positive contact between genres, cultures, languages, nature and technology, even humans and aliens, is possible. Furthermore, Hopkinson's own experience—which she calls "one flavour of black experience, and Caribbean, and Canadian, and female, and fat, and from feminist and sex-positive politics" (Hopkinson, Interview with Rutledge)—allows her a unique perspective from which to speculate about future worlds. Ruby Ramraj, citing an interview between Hopkinson and Nancy Batty, notes that, for Hopkinson, "moving to different places in the Caribbean—Guyana, Trinidad, Jamaica—and the US and Canada from the time she was eight months old gave her 'a sense of hybridity, of collage'" (Ramraj 34, n.8).

This sense of hybridity shapes the characters and settings in Hopkinson's fiction. In *Midnight Robber*, Tan-Tan, whose ancestors were born on earth, is a native of Toussaint, exiled from her homeworld and finally from all human communities. She lives on the fringes. Furthermore, the language she speaks is a blend of dialects; as Hopkinson explains, "a number of sociodialects are somewhat native to me, and my instinct is to combine them" (Interview with Batty 177). Hopkinson's privileging of collaged experience and identity fits nicely with Lawson's theories on Second World texts. In "A Cultural Paradigm for the Second World," Lawson "seeks to interrogate some of the ways in which the prevailing and pervasive dualisms of Western thought have been rewritten and re/placed in a specific kind of post-colonial context" (68), namely in the Second Worlds of Canada and Australia. He argues:

> [t]he customary project of Western thought has been to contain disorder and divergence, to see the resolution of dichotomy, polarity, binary in harmony and unity, to synthesise and to re-integrate.... Second World texts are under no such cultural imperative. The states of interphase exist epistemologically without the boundaries of resolution of their self-and-otherness and take the multiple perspectives, the polyphony, the diachronicity, that is their birthright as their "creative source of endless subtlety" ["A Cultural Paradigm for the Second World" 70, quotation from White 447].

In her use of blended dialects, in her focus on the cultural diversity of her characters, and in her exploration of fringe identity, Hopkinson participates in the discourse of Second World texts. Furthermore, by ending *Midnight Robber* with the birth of Tubman, Hopkinson embraces irresolution and multiplicity. A product of incest but somehow also the future hope for New Half-Way Tree, Tubman is an ambiguous figure who embodies a chance for past exploitation, violence, and abuse to transform and heal, creating possibilities for positive interaction between humans and douen, Toussaint and New Half-Way Tree, and the organic and the technological.

Here we also begin to see how hybridity has influenced Hopkinson's approach to the genre of science fiction, a genre that has not traditionally attracted black writers. She explains that "sf [has] a stigma about being adventure stories in which white people use technology to overpower alien cultures. Small wonder that black writers haven't been drawn to it in large numbers—we've been on the receiving end of colonization" (Hopkinson, interview with Rutledge). Recognizing other possibilities in science fiction, and being attracted to the genre for its potential to subvert traditional power structures, Hopkinson also points out that "science fiction has always been a subversive literature. It's been used to critique social systems well before the marketing label of sf got stuck on it" (Hopkinson, interview with Rutledge). In fact, she argues that science fiction and other forms of speculation grant her advantages over the limitations of realism:

> When I read the work of African American realist writers, there's always the awareness of the white world in which the characters live; there has to be, if the fiction is to be representative of the real world. The realist work of Caribbean writers must reference the effects of hundreds of years of colonization.... Speculative fiction allows me to experiment with the effects of that cancerous blot, to shrink it by setting my worlds far in the future (science fiction) or to metonymize it so that I can explore the paradigms it's created (fantasy). I could even choose to sidestep it altogether into alternate history [Hopkinson, interview with Rutledge].

Midnight Robber, set far in the future when Caribbean people are exploring space and colonizing planets other than earth, addresses the "cancerous blot" by investigating human greed and violence away from the context of earth, its specific countries and histories of exploitation.

However, because of Hopkinson's experience of hybridity and collage, in particular her movement between countries and cultures—far from irrelevant to real-world politics, *Midnight Robber* is rooted in historical and contemporary global realities. Specifically, I think that Hopkinson's novel reflects a multiracial, pluri-ethnic, post-colonial Canadian context and that Hopkinson uses speculative genres to contribute to a critical Canadian discourse that complicates notions of race, class, and nation. To support this analysis of Hopkinson's work, Linda Hutcheon's article "'Circling the Downspout of Empire': Post-Colonialism and Postmodernism" will be particularly helpful. In her article, Hutcheon qualifies Canada's status as a post-colonial nation by reflecting on the differences between settler colonies and nations like "the West Indies or Africa or India" (155) where "the cultural imposition associated with colonialism took place on the homeground of the colonized people" (155). Beyond that, in her discussion of other distinctions between Canada and "Third World nations" (159), Hutcheon lingers on the more recent settlement patterns of Canada, namely

> the pluri-ethnic (and lately more multiracial) nature of Canadian society. Some of the immigrants who populate this country are not from colonized societies and they often consciously resist being labelled post-colonial.... But there are other immigrants who ... come to Canada from the West Indies, Asia, or Latin America and see it as 'a necessarily occupied territory because land was denied somewhere else' (Davies 33).... The specificity of *Canadian* post-colonial culture today is being conditioned by this arrival of immigrants from other post-

colonial nations.... This is the doubled sense of post-colonialism that is part of some of the writing we now call Canadian [Hutcheon 160].

Hutcheon's discussion of the ambiguous nature of Canada's post-colonial status is useful when unpacking the political implications of writing such as Hopkinson's.

Hopkinson, a Jamaican-born Canadian speculative fiction author, writes work that reflects what Hutcheon calls "the doubled sense of post-colonialism." Hopkinson combines her multi-national perspective with her partiality for speculative genres to push themes of colonization, immigration, and integration into an experimental and theoretical realm. In *Midnight Robber* specifically, Toussaint and New Half-Way Tree, because they are each at a different stage of colonization, shed light on and complicate colonial realities. By creating these two planets—the former a successful colony where pre-contact plants, animals, and intelligent life have been wiped out, and the latter an early-stage settler colony with a First Nation of douen, where small human settlements are surrounded by dense forest that contain hostile plants and animals—Hopkinson is able to explore issues of "real" colonization—displacement, exploitation, genocide—while extrapolating from history to imagine future implications of a colonial mindset. Furthermore, by setting the novel away from earth, writing the colonized race as non-human, and casting her humans as Caribbean descendants, she pushes the "doubled sense" of post-colonialism to a tripled or quadrupled sense.

After unpacking some of the ways in which *Midnight Robber* comments on colonization in general and the Second World in particular, the political implications of Hopkinson's writing resonate. Both Lawson and Hutcheon are useful in helping situate *Midnight Robber* as a Second World text with specific significance in the Canadian context. In the novel, the relationship between the humans and the douen, the humans and the natural world, as well as the relationship among humans within and between settlements, raises questions about the future of colonization and the intrinsic quest for power in humans. While the novel pessimistically extrapolates that any future utopia will come at the expense of plants, animals, and potentially aliens, it does not fail to note the potential for community-building on the fringes of defined, sanctioned societies. In fact, I think what hope the novel offers is located in Tan-Tan's alienation, from which Tubman, border-straddler, bridge to freedom, is able to emerge.

Works Cited

Clemente, Bill. "Tan-Tan's Exile and Odyssey in Nalo Hopkinson's *Midnight Robber*." *Foundation* 91 (Summer 2004): 25–35.

Davies, Ioan. "Senses of Place." *Canadian Forum* April 1983: 33–34.
Hopkinson, Nalo. "'Caught by a ... Genre.'" Interview with Nancy Batty. *Ariel* 33.1 (2002): 175–201.
_____. Interview with Gregory E. Rutledge. *African American Review* 33.4 (1999): 589–610.
_____. Interview, Time Warner Bookmark. 2000. *Time Warner Bookmark: The Authors*. November 6, 2005. <http://www.twbookmark.com/authors/84/1272/interview9676.html>.
_____. *Midnight Robber*. New York: Warner Books, 2000.
Hutcheon, Linda. "'Circling the Downspout of Empire': Post-Colonialism and Post-modernism." *Ariel* 20.4 (1989): 149–75.
Lawson, Alan. "A Cultural Paradigm for the Second World." *Australian-Canadian Studies* 9.1–2 (1991): 67–78.
_____. "Postcolonial Theory and the 'Settler' Subject." *Essays on Canadian Writing* 56 (1995): 20–36.
Mishrahi-Barak, Judith. "Beginners' Luck among Caribbean-Canadian Writers: Nalo Hopkinson, Andre Alexis and Shani Mootoo." *Commonwealth Essays and Studies* 22.1 (1999): 89–96.
Ramraj, Ruby. "Power Relationships and Femininity in Nalo Hopkinson's *The Salt Roads*." *Foundation* 91 (Summer 2004): 10–24.
Seaton, Dorothy. "Colonising Discourses: The Land in Australian and Western Canadian Exploration Narratives." *Australian-Canadian Studies* 6.2 (1989): 99–113.
White, Patrick. *Voss*. Harmondsworth: Penguin, 1960.

Canadian Fantasy and Dark Fantasy

Sacred Cities: Charles de Lint's Newford Books and the Mythologizing of the North American Urban Landscape

Cat Ashton

ACCSFF '07

Charles De Lint's fiction is part of a growing genre that he himself calls North American magic realism, Brian Attebery calls indigenous fantasy, and paperback marketers call urban fantasy—an effort to translate the magic of myth and high fantasy from a pastoral pseudomedieval world to a modern urban one. This paper will show that Charles de Lint's Newford novels and short story collections, in negotiating a place for myth and magic in a contemporary urban setting, also work to negotiate an ethical, responsible place for humanity, modernity, and urban culture *within* nature.

Wilderness and the Pastoral in Fantasy Fiction

Prior to the early 1980s, virtually all fantasy fiction was set, if not in a pseudomedieval secondary world, at the very least in a rural environment, combining pastoral countryside with sublime wilderness.

Terry Gifford writes that while in the strictest sense, the pastoral is a poem or drama involving shepherds in an idealized countryside (Gifford 1), it can be applied to any celebration of nature. In this second sense, the pastoral ideal dates back at least as far as ancient Rome, and it is not unreasonable to suppose that it is as old as the city itself. In its simplest form, it regards rural environments as a source of beauty, authenticity, and nobility, in stark opposition to the ugly, constrained, sophisticated city.

Frederick Reenstjerna's "Paradise or Purgatory: The City in French and British Children's Literature" compares depictions of urban environments in French and British children's books to demonstrate that British literature regards cities less favorably. While in French children's books such as *Madeline* and *The Story of Babar*, the city is a place of culture and order, English books such as *The Secret Garden* paint the city as a dangerous and unhealthy source of corruption (Reenstjerna 90). Reenstjerna traces these differences to attitudes embedded within British and French culture. In France, the city was synonymous with civilization, and it sought to give its colonies the benefit of access to the city, the center of life. Meanwhile, Britain embraced "the rural ideal [as] the seat of power as well as the 'good life' in English reality and mythology" (ibid. 95).

In fantasy literature, the pastoral ideal was taken up as a critique of the circumstances in which the genre emerged. William Morris pioneered the secondary world in English fantasy—the medieval world that housed the fictional country of Upmeads in his novel *The Well at the World's End*—as a way of critiquing the Victorian myth of progress, and arguing that rural medieval life was truer and more authentic. In the early decades of the twentieth century, J.R.R. Tolkien, whose Lord of the Rings trilogy would set the standard for genre fantasy, used the pseudomedieval secondary world to re-enchant an England disenchanted by industry and war. Unlike Morris, who contented himself with showing readers a portrait of heroism and virtue no longer possible in Victorian England, Tolkien went further, casting the forces of modernity and industry as a sublime evil. His descriptions of Mordor are evocative of both industrial wastelands and trench warfare:

> All was ominously quiet. The light was no more than that of dusk at a dark day's end. The vast vapours that arose in Mordor and went streaming westward passed low overhead, a great welter of cloud and smoke now lit again beneath a sullen glow of red [Tolkien, *The Fellowship of the Ring* 202].
>
> Mordor was a dying land, but it was not yet dead. And here things still grew, harsh, twisted, bitter, struggling for life. In the glens of the Morgai on the other side of the valley low scrubby trees lurked and clung, coarse grey grass-tussocks fought with the stones, and withered mosses crawled on them; and everywhere great writhing, tangled brambles sprawled. Some had long stabbing thorns, some hooked barbs that rent like knives. The sullen shriveled leaves of a past year hung on them, grating and rattling in the sad airs, but their maggot-ridden buds

were only just opening. Flies, dun or grey, or black, marked like orcs with a red eye-shaped blotch, buzzed and stung; and above the briar-thickets clouds of hungry midges danced and reeled [Tolkien, *The Return of the King* 233].

    Down on the stones behind the fences of the Black Land the air seemed almost dead, chill and yet stifling. Sam looked up out of the hollow. The land all about was dreary, flat and drab-hued.... South-eastward, far off like a dark standing shadow, loomed the Mountain. Smokes were pouring from it, and while those that rose into the upper air trailed away eastward, great rolling clouds floated down its sides and spread over the land [ibid. 248–249].

In the words of Meredith Veldman, who argues for a link between Tolkien's work and environmental and anti-nuclear movements in mid-twentieth-century Britain, "The lifeless, mechanical, tyrannical Mordor became for Tolkien a powerful symbol of what was wrong in twentieth-century England. Rooted in a worldview that reduces people to objects, Mordor glorifies technology and the power it confers as the unquestionable, ultimate good" (Veldman 187).

    Tolkien's critique was a timely one that pointed to real problems in his culture—problems that have not been entirely eradicated in our own. However, he drew on a long-standing dichotomy that carried with it its own perils. William Cronon outlines the problems with separating the world into the authentic, beautiful, unpeopled, positively valued wilderness and the artificial, ugly, crowded, negatively valued city in his 1995 essay "The Trouble With Wilderness; or, Getting Back to the Wrong Nature." Wilderness as we know it, Cronon points out, is a cultural construct. Prior to the eighteenth century, unpeopled regions were generally regarded as sites of danger and menace. For example, Fred Botting writes that mountains had been "considered as ugly blemishes, deformities disfiguring the proportions of a world that ideally should be uniform, flat and symmetrical" (Botting 38). The Romantics, however, embraced these landscapes, seeing them as places where the supernatural seethed beneath the surface of the world (Cronon 73) and arguing for their sacralization. This drive emerged at a time when America was crafting its own separate identity, and what Cronon calls the frontier myth is still woven into America's national fabric:

> Among the core elements of the frontier myth was the powerful sense among certain groups of Americans that wilderness was the last bastion of rugged individualism.... By fleeing to the outer margins of settled land and society—so the story ran—an individual could escape the confining strictures of civilized life.... This nostalgia for a passing frontier way of life inevitably implied ambivalence, if not downright hostility, toward modernity and all that it represented. If one saw the wild lands of the frontier as freer, truer, and more natural than other, more modern places, then one was also inclined to see the cities and factories of urban-industrial civilization as confining, false, and artificial [Cronon 77].

Cronon's critique of Western culture's construction of wilderness is twofold. First of all, in America, the land was in fact occupied by indigenous people; it took acts of genocide to create vast uninhabited tracts, which were then purchased by white males of the upper classes. In other words, wilderness as we know it has been constructed under false pretenses and through grave injustice, and relies on the structures of the society to which it has been set in opposition. Secondly, he writes, it denies the possibility of

> discovering what an ethical, sustainable, honorable human place in nature might actually look like.... Worse: to the extent that we live in an urban-industrial civilization but at the same time pretend that our real home is in the wilderness, to just that extent we give ourselves permission to evade responsibility for the lives we actually lead [Cronon 81].

Cities, in this scheme, are irredeemable by their very nature, and therefore not worth working to improve—a conclusion that can prove disastrous for the segment of the population not wealthy enough to leave.

Fantasy, the Country and the City

The fantasy genre as we know it arguably grew up around Tolkien's work on one hand, and sword-and-sorcery that partakes of the frontier myth, such as Robert E. Howard's stories of Kull the Conqueror or Conan the Barbarian, on the other. Mid-twentieth-century authors such as Susan Cooper, Alan Garner, and Ray Bradbury, while they set their fantasies in the modern world, almost always confined them to small towns and rural environments. For Cooper and Garner, these small communities are the heart of Great Britain; for Bradbury they are the heart of America. It could be argued that Cooper and Garner in particular are less interested in critique, however, than in drawing an unbroken line from the glorious past to the modern world. But it is Tolkien's contribution that has defined a generation of fantasy, to the point that the pseudomedieval setting is still considered a staple of the genre.

High fantasy has the potential to be innovative, challenging, and transformative. But as Brian Attebery points out, "Some writers seem to be so intimidated by the potential anarchy of the fantastic, so eager for a guaranteed response, that they retreat to the opposite extreme, which results in the predictability of formula" (Attebery 9). The formula is set up thus: "Take a vaguely medieval world. Add a problem, something more or less ecological, and a prophecy for solving it. Introduce one villain with no particular characteristics except a nearly all-powerful badness.... To the above mixture add one naive [sic] and ordinary hero who will prove to be the prophesied savior" (Attebery 10).

This formula—although its adherents may subvert it in their own work—is rooted in Tolkien's rejection of the urban in favor of pastoralism and depictions of sublime wilderness. That the vaguely medieval world depends on it is reasonably obvious. However, the ecological problem and the all-powerful badness of the villain are also (paradoxically, given the city's association with evil) easier to manage in rural environments, where great blocks of land can be set aside as the domain of evil, presided over by a dark lord; and where evil can poison the land itself in ways that are immediately measurable, even visible. Arguably, formula fantasy lends itself to rural environments not just because of its Tolkienian heritage, but because its essential components become difficult if not impossible to negotiate in urban settings. And so, the technological world with its scientific underpinnings is exchanged for a magical world with mystical, mythic underpinnings, in which life is simpler, nobler, and truer; and the possibility of high adventure makes ordinary people into potential heroes.

In short, both formula fantasy and the North American concept of wilderness are based on dualities in which our modern, urban world is judged to be the poorer, drabber, sadder, less authentic of two choices, the better of which we have no power to live in. In order to have a healthy relationship with nature, Cronon says, "we need to embrace the full continuum of a natural landscape that is also cultural, in which the city, the suburb, the pastoral, and the wild each has its proper place, which we permit ourselves to celebrate without needlessly denigrating the others" (Cronon 89). Likewise, Terry Gifford calls for "'[a] mature environmental aesthetics'" in order to "achieve a vision of an integrated natural world that includes the human" (Gifford 148). This prescription could be adapted to apply to a healthy relationship between our own psyches and the stories we tell ourselves: the reader of high fantasy knows that magic wardrobes and trains to Hogwarts are in short supply, so how does one live an authentic and fulfilling life in the world that we have?

These are the questions that Charles de Lint seeks to answer in his fantasies, using the fictional city of Newford to bridge the disconnects between magic and realism, urban space and wild space. Rather than seeing ugly, stifling modernity and vibrantly alive myth in terms of different geographical areas, he posits them as states of mind, writing,

> Myth ... provides a metaphorical blueprint which allows us, often subconsciously, to define our spiritual state in context to the rest of the world; it's what gives an underlying sense of vibrancy and meaning to the workaday world, to that sense of commonality which can often lead a man or woman to feel that his or her spirit is being stifled.... Sometimes all that can awaken one from such negativity is a mystical experience. It need not be of occult origin; it can be as

simple a thing as appreciating the flight of a crow across an afternoon sky [De Lint, "Considering Magical Realism in Canada" 117].

De Lint's Newford stories all work to reproduce the wonder and sense of connectedness that he characterizes as essential parts of the mystical experience. Part of this connectedness is "the simple verification of humanity's need to take care of one another and their planet" (De Lint, "Magical Realism"118).

I would like to stop for a moment and unpack what de Lint means when he talks about mythical thinking. In a time when science is being defunded and religious dogma influences policy,[1] it is not immediately clear that mythical thinking is a positive thing. Mythical thinking attempts to pull back and capture the world as a whole, what Wendy Doniger calls the telescopic view. If the view being promulgated is a world in which large numbers of people are evil, wrongheaded, or beneath notice, then mythical thinking can indeed be dangerous, but de Lint is arguing for something quite different.

It is a widespread practice among fantasy authors to make magic a moral force, or at least a force that serves, or acts according to, a certain moral scheme. This makes sense: to create a world, or to add a dimension to our own world, requires one to take a position on how the world works, and the systems one creates will reflect that. De Lint uses magic in his fiction to create connections, or arguably, to make explicit the connections that he sees already existent between human beings, events, and the natural world. A small act of kindness, such as Lizzie Mahone's burial of a deer carcass in *Widdershins*, is magnified so that Lizzie's friends find magical aid when they are in trouble, whereas an act of callousness or selfishness, such as Adrian Dumbrell's enlisting of the fairies to win an argument with a girl he wants to impress in *The Blue Girl*, creates mayhem and suffering. These are fairy-tale rules, by which a slight to the wrong person precipitates the tale and a boon to the right one resolves it. The difference is that in de Lint's world, there are no stock characters whose bad end can be safely and smugly predicted; nothing and no one is so securely outside of the web of reciprocity that one can afford to ignore his/her/its suffering. In other words, for De Lint, environmentalism and social justice are a natural outgrowth of this mythic worldview. There is no way of telling which fools are holy and which woods are enchanted, but they are all worth protecting.

In addition to this emphasis on connectedness, which makes binary opposites unwieldy to maintain and challenges the notion that any kind of space can be divorced from any other kind of space, de Lint takes several opportunities to blur the line between the city and the wild. He describes the country, with the "mossy scent in its air, deep with the smell of the forest's loam and fallen leaves and the sharp tang of cedars and pine" (de Lint, *Memory and Dream* 24) just as lovingly as the city and its "buzz in the air.... Part electric hum, part the press and proximity of so many other souls" (ibid. 138–139). Both *Memory and Dream* and *Spirits in the Wires* contain the motif of an apartment, furniture and all, set up in the middle of a clearing on a perpetually fair day. In "Romano Drom," the main character discovers that ley lines run through the city, creating continuity through time and across cultures. The short stories "The Conjure Man" and "The Forest is Crying" link the presence of green space and the well-being of trees to the well-being of humans, albeit through intangible means.

While characters encounter Otherworlds of desert and primeval forest—both of these populated—the quintessential wilderness in the Newford novels is the Tombs, an urban neighborhood razed by developers and then abandoned when the project fell through. One character describes the area as being "just like a wilderness ... a piece of the city gone feral" (de Lint, "Waifs and Strays" 2) Another casually places the Tombs outside of civilization (de Lint, "That Explains Poland" 109). Just like any other wilderness, the Tombs are populated, in this case by those on the margins of society. They even have a Sasquatch.

Creating links between urban space and wild space not only makes it difficult to argue that the two are polar opposites, but forces one to consider: if they must and do co-exist, then what is the best way to fit them together? The Tombs are one way, and although it is difficult to call them an optimal combination, they are a site for wonders. Places such as Fitzhenry Park or the Butler University campus, with their green space and sense of community, might be better examples of a functional relationship between nature and the city.

De Lint tackles problematic binaries from another angle as well, arguing that technology and magic can occupy the same space. In "Ten for the Devil," an electric guitar is just as capable of calling up the spirits as a fiddle. "Saskia," "Embracing the Mystery," and *Spirits in the Wires* all deal with the Wordwood, a website that has taken on a life, and a magic, of its own. The incorporation of technology into the Newford mythos leaves no question as to whether or not there is a role for magic in the modern world, and also works to redefine the role of myth. It is not a static thing fixed in the distant past or on another world, but a living tradition that responds to the needs of the people who create or modify it.

Another way in which De Lint brings the modern urban technological world back into the natural world is by stretching the boundaries of personhood. At this exercise's most basic level, he continually reminds the reader of the humanity of the homeless and the poor, for example—but not all of his characters are human, and yet they are no less worthy of consideration and respect. One of the many mythic motifs that de Lint takes up in his work is that of the more-than-human masquerading as the most humble among us: a flute player is the Oak King's daughter (de Lint, "Ghosts of Wind and Shadow" 212); a slightly mad cyclist is an elemental force from the beginning of time (de Lint, "The Conjure Man" 235); Professor Dapple's ill-tempered servant Goon moonlights as the goblin king (de Lint, "The Stone Drum" 57); Licorne, a homeless woman living in the Tombs, is really a unicorn. This is another fairy tale motif—a mythic motif, really. Zeus visited Lycaeon, Tantalus, and Baucis and Philemon as a traveler, finding only the latter two worthy; the central deity of Christianity was incarnated as an infant in a stable; Tara appeared to the sons of Eochaid as a hideous old woman asking for a kiss, and rewarded the kisser with the kingship of Ireland. De Lint's stories join many others counseling basic respect for the lowly and marginalized. However, one does not treat the lowly and marginalized well simply because they may be great. De Lint has a resource that the conveyers of these other examples did not: he can use the form of the novel to *demonstrate* the personhood of, say, Christiana Tree, who is actually Christy Riddell's Jungian shadow, or Pelly, Imogene Yeck's imaginary friend in *The Blue Girl*. The reader has access to their thoughts and feelings, including a concern for others that clearly marks them as part of a community. They do not need to be great, or to reward those who treat them well, for the reader to understand that they deserve a basic level of dignity, kindness, and respect.

Personhood is a major theme in *Memory and Dream*, in which the protagonist, Isabel Copley, learns to use her paintings to bring creatures from the Otherworld—the numena—into this one. Several of these are consumed by the desire to be fully human—to be "real." But Isabel's mentor, Vincent Rushkin, feeds off them, arguing that the numena are not and never will be real, and are nothing more than a resource. In the end, Isabel realizes that the fact that the numena are not human makes them no less real; they are just different. This conclusion is the foundational assumption for virtually all of De Lint's other depictions of ghosts, faeries, fictional characters, angels, and other assorted non-human creatures. Christine Mains, in her article "Old World, New World, Otherworld: Celtic and Native American influences in Charles de Lint's *Moonheart* and *Forests of the Heart*," writes that this perspective is rooted in Canadian urban multiculturalism.[2] It can also, however, be fruitfully applied to environmentalism. According to Cronon, "We need to honor the Other within and the Other next door as much as we do the exotic Other that lives far away—a lesson that applies as much to people as it does to (other) natural things" (Cronon 89). Cronin the environmentalist writes of the tree in the forest and the tree in the garden; the words could just as easily have come from a de Lint character.

De Lint also works to redeem modernity and urbanness by championing some of the things that make cities more livable. Adam Guzkowski has written on the role of community in De Lint's Newford novels. Volunteer work, of the sort that benefits the city's least fortunate, is a recurring theme. Characters visit seniors, spend Christmas working in soup kitchens, donate the fruits of their talents to charity auctions, and offer street kids shelter. De Lint reinforces the value of these acts by making his centerpiece character, Jilly Coppercorn, an ex-street kid who has benefited from the charitable efforts of others and become both a moderately successful artist and a role model for others. Jilly has ties to, as her friends joke, every fourth person in the city; she is connection embodied.

Art is also depicted as essential. It makes the city livable by transforming spaces and by building community. At the very least, it requires careful thought and attention to one's environs, and often it goes further, cultivating feelings of wonder and connectedness. Indeed, most of the recurring characters are visual artists, musicians, poets, or writers, and more often than not it is the practice of their respective crafts that bring them into contact with their fellow human beings, and with magic. *Memory and Dream* contains several lengthy discussions on the role of the artist, and culminates in the creation of a place where street kids can do art: after the basic necessities of life, the book posits that this is the most important thing that can be given to them.

Such impulses can be, and have been, read as reductive, sentimental, or naïve. However, de Lint is careful to emphasize, particularly in stories that deal directly with abuse and homelessness, that it is not a matter of painting pictures and telling stories in order to make everything all right again. Jilly's coming to terms with her abusive childhood is a process that takes decades, and magic, while it helps her cope, also imperils her when her own psyche gives substance to her memories of her abuser. In *Memory and Dream*, Katharine Mully kills herself to escape the memories of her childhood. Other characters commit suicide, die unjustly, or disappear forever, sometimes in spite of the magic that surrounds them and sometimes because of it. For others still, abuse is the catalyst that turns them into antagonists. Characters such as Adrian Dumbrell in *The Blue Girl,* Aaran Goldstein in *Spirits in the Wires,* Raylene Carter in *The Onion Girl,* and Rabedy Collins in *Widdershins* are sympathetic characters who behave destructively because their treatment at the hands of others has damaged their ability to interact with people in healthy ways. Because de Lint uses magic to intensify existing connections, abuse and mistreatment have immediate and far-reaching consequences that are impossible to ignore. This constitutes a call for people to treat each other well, to intervene when it looks like abuse is happening, and to react to destructive and self-destructive behavior with a view towards healing and restitution rather than punishment. Magic in de Lint's books can provide a coping strategy, and it can take injustice out of the shadows and make its effects external and manifest, but it cannot actually take the place of human responsibility and a just, ethical, and well-resourced social system.

That said, de Lint's representation of pain, grief, and hardship is not perfect. The planetwide malaise and urban decline he often speaks of are sometimes hard to glimpse amidst his portrayal of bustling gallery openings, hip coffee houses, and thriving bohemian neighborhoods with magic and wonder lurking around every corner. Although many of his recurring characters make just enough of a living to get by, his books lack representations of desperate urban poverty. It can be argued that not only might representations of desperate urban poverty undermine the effort to convince middle-class readers that the city can be made into a more livable space, but also that the terms of such poverty are deeply resistant to mythical thinking: that, for example, a single parent working two full-time jobs cannot afford the distraction of faeries and shapechangers, let alone green space and art, and is therefore not a good candidate to feature in de Lint's fiction. Under the terms of de Lint's ethics of reciprocity, a case can be made that the well-being of such people still matters, even if circumstances exclude them from this set of narratives. De Lint makes a gesture in the direction of no easy answers and no unequivocally happy endings, indeed no endings at all—at least, not without sacrificing the very complexity that his fiction tries to acknowledge.

De Lint is one of the pioneers of urban fantasy. In the 1980s and 1990s, he and other authors such as John Crowley, Mercedes Lackey, Peter S. Beagle, Will Shetterley, Emma Bull, and Ellen Datlow and Terri Windling (editors of the Borderlands series) made North American cities a legitimate setting for fantasy fiction. This effort overlapped with political initiatives in Canada and the United States to increase green space, fund public transit, and provide space and resources for the arts in urban areas, suggesting that urban fantasy both fuelled and reflected a broader cultural drive to reclaim the city in North America. The reclamation of cities is ongoing, but the drive to reinfuse the city with myth and magic has been largely successful, judging by the health of the urban fantasy genre. Of course, telling stories can never take the place of policies that make cities livable, but the livable city must be imagined first, and Charles de Lint has helped a generation of fantasy readers to imagine it, moving the sphere of meaningful action and weighty moral decisions from the secondary world and the idealized past to the here and now.

Notes

1. In his book *The Carbon Wars*, Greenpeace activist Jeremy Leggett tells how he stumbled upon this otherworldly agenda. During the Kyoto climate change negotiations, Leggett candidly asked Ford Motor Company executive John Schiller how opponents of the pact could believe there is no problem with "a world of a billion cars intent on burning all the oil and gas available on the planet?" The executive asserted first that scientists get it wrong when they say fossil fuels have been sequestered underground for eons. The Earth, he said, is just 10,000, not 4.5 billion years old, the age widely accepted by scientists. (Glen Scherer, *E Magazine*, qtd. in Clark, 2003/10/17)

2. I do, however, find Main's defence of de Lint's representation of First Nations People and his appropriation of indigenous voices problematic.

Works Cited

Attebery, Brian. *Strategies of Fantasy*. Bloomington: Indiana University Press, 1992. Print.
Botting, Fred. *Gothic*. London: Routledge, 1996. Print.
Clark, Fred. "*Left Behind* Is Evil." *Slacktivist* October 17, 2003. <http://www.patheos.com/blogs/slacktivist/2003/10/17/left-behind-is-evil/> Web. Accessed March 14, 2014.
Cronon, William, ed. "The Trouble with Wilderness. Or, Getting Back to the Wrong Nature." *Uncommon Ground: Rethinking the Human Place in Nature*. New York: Norton, 1996. 69–90. <http://www.uvm.edu/rsenr/rm240/cronin.pdf> Web.
De Lint, Charles. *The Blue Girl*. New York: Tor, 2004. Print.
———. "Considering Magical Realism in Canada." *Out of This World: Canadian Science Fiction & Fantasy Literature*. Ed. Allan Weiss and Hugh Spencer and comp. Andrea Paradis. Kingston: Quarry Press; Ottawa: National Library of Canada, 1995. 113–22. Print.
———. *Dreams Underfoot*. New York: Tor, 1994. Print.
———. *The Ivory and the Horn*. New York: Tor, 1996. Print.
———. *Memory and Dream*. New York: Tor, 1994. Print.
———. *The Onion Girl*. New York: Tor, 2001. Print.
———. *Spirits in the Wires*. New York: Tor, 2003. Print.
———. *Widdershins*. New York: Tor, 2006. Print.
Doniger, Wendy. *The Implied Spider: Politics and Theology in Myth*. New York: Columbia University Press, 1998. Print.
Gifford, Terry. *Pastoral*. London and New York: Routledge, 1999. Print.
Guzkowski, Adam. "Memory, Magic, and Meaning: Storytelling and the Creation of Community in Charles de Lint's Newford Collections." *Further Perspectives on the Canadian Fantastic: Proceedings of the 2003 Academic Conference on Canadian Science Fiction and Fantasy*. Ed. Allan Weiss. Toronto: ACCSFF, 2005. 113–17. Print.
Mains, Christine. "Old World, New World, Otherworld: Celtic and Native American Influences in Charles de Lint's Moonheart and Forests of the Heart." *Extrapolation* 46:3 (2008): 338–350. Print.
Morris, William. *The Well at the World's End*. Ed. Lin Carter and John Gregory Betancourt. Vol. 1. Berkeley Heights NJ: Wildside Press, 2000. Print.

Reenstjerna, Frederick. "Paradise or Purgatory: The City in French and British Children's Literature." *Cincinnati Romance Review* 9 (1990): 87–97. Print.
Tolkien, J.R.R. *The Fellowship of the Ring.* London: HarperCollins and Clio Press, 1990. Print.
———. *The Return of the King.* London: HarperCollins and Clio Press, 1990. Print.
———. *The Two Towers.* London: HarperCollins and Clio Press, 1990. Print.
Veldman, Meredith. *Fantasy, the Bomb, and the Greening of Britain: Romantic Protest, 1945–1980.* Cambridge UK: Cambridge University Press, 1994. Print.

The Word and the Flesh: Natural Law vs. Catholic Dogma in Rikki Ducornet's *The Stain*

Tammy Dasti

ACCSFF '09

Of all the world's numerous religions, none has so heavily influenced the arts as Christianity and of all the types of Christianity that have existed, none has been as powerful or as divisive as the Roman Catholic Church. Few other religious institutions have been such a powerful influence on western culture and history, and even fewer evoke such strong emotions within parishioners, both positive and negative. Those who remain within the folds of the church are eager to share stories about how their faith has helped to guide them throughout their lives, while those who have left are just as eager to point out how the church is out of touch, useless, and possibly even dangerous in modern times. There have been numerous writers who have dismissed the importance of organized religion, including Sigmund Freud and the Marquis de Sade, to name but two.

Canadian author Rikki Ducornet follows de Sade's example in dismissing the usefulness of the institution of the Church in her 1995 novel *The Stain*. Unlike de Sade, however, she replaces it with a more practical, useful religion based on the lessons learned from nature. The image of the Catholic Church in Ducornet's novel is that of a rampantly corrupt institution that is totally out of touch with the lives and the needs of its parishioners, while at the same time attempting to exact total control over the population through fear, misinformation, and intimidation. The image of God the Father is notable only by His complete absence from within the walls of the church. The God of Nature, by contrast, rules not by fear and intimidation, but through subtle signs and practical, life-affirming information. In *The Stain*, God is not absent entirely, as He is in de Sade; rather, He dwells in the details of Nature, not the church.

A student of the writings of the Marquis de Sade (whom she casts as a major character in her 1999 novel, *The Fan-Maker's Inquisition*), Ducornet has certainly been influenced by his opinions on religion and religious institutions. De Sade's writings are filled with characters who, while appearing to be pious in public, participate in countless sexual and immoral acts in private. In addition, de Sade uses his writings as a means of expounding his atheistic views of society, the world, and the universe. De Sade writes: "[above] all, beware of religion, nothing is more apt to lure you astray than religion's baneful institutions" (*Juliette* 19). For example, de Sade writes that the existence of God is a "fantasy" and that

> God has its origins in nothing but the mind's limitations. Knowing not to whom or what the universe about is to be attributed, helpless before the utter impossibility of explaining the inscrutable mysteries of Nature, above her we have gratuitously installed a Being invested with the power of producing all the effects of whose causes we are profoundly ignorant [*Juliette* 29].

For de Sade, God is simply not needed, since Nature and the natural law is independent from religious dogma. He goes on to write:

> God nor religion ... runs the universe.... [Since] the universe runs itself, and the eternal laws inherent in Nature suffice, without any first cause or prime mover, to produce all that is and all that we know; the perpetual movement of matter explains everything: why need we supply a motor to that which is ever in motion? ... We need not fret if we find nothing to substitute for chimeras, and above all let us never accept as cause for what we do not comprehend something else we comprehend even less [*Juliette* 43].

Like de Sade, Ducornet also holds the physical world as being of the highest importance, and she once said: "I love the sensual world, I love the body, and I love the physical, natural world" (Gregory and McCaffery) and that *The Stain* "is about the Christian idea of sin—the world and the body seen as satanic vessels" (Gregory and McCaffery), a facet of Catholic dogma which is in direct contrast to her personal views. The idea of the body as sinful, a thing to be tamed and controlled, however, is fundamental to "the Catholic tradition, you grow up being taught that the flesh is bad. The world, the flesh and the devil, those are your enemies" (Riley 148).

This concept of the flesh as evil is personified by Edma, who constantly represses not only her own body, but also the bodies and physical needs of those around her. Edma frequently links physical pain and suffering to religious devotion and expression, first seen when she forces Emile and Charlotte into daily prayer on their "knees upon the unforgiving linoleum of the kitchen floor—daily torture for Emile, a seasonal sufferer of gout" (14). Edma does not stint on her own pain either, as shown in the scene where she takes Charlotte to church prior to the meeting between the Mother Superior from St. Gemmes School, and the Exorcist. After settling Charlotte in a chair and telling her to pray for the recovery of her voice

> Edma fell to her knees and made her way from the chapel down into the transept's north arm, down the north aisle and across the nave into the south aisle, the transept's south arm, the ambulatory and the apse, and on into the axial chapels—[...] in a harrowing ritual that lasted well over two hours and left her panting for breath and her knees badly bruised [67].

For her pilgrimage to Lourdes, Edma goes even further, crawling around the entire compound, being

> satisfied only when her knees began to bleed ... she knew from her pain that she, at least, was worthy of salvation. "I'm bleeding for you, Lord," she needled....
>
> Each day Edma traced the same itinerary until the flesh of her knees was mashed to jelly. By the time she was ready to go home, she could only stand with the help of a cane she had bought from one of the numerous souvenir shops [94].

Edma also refuses to eat on her fourteen-hour train ride to Lourdes even though she "packed a voluminous luncheon-basket"; she is "unable to eat in public, before strangers, as if mastication was as much a sin as fornication" (92). Indeed, any type of bodily function is repugnant to Edma, who even poisons the domestic animals of the neighbors "which she despised for fornicating and defecating in public, in the street, without shame" (40). Edma's continual physical and verbal abuse of Charlotte, evident throughout the novel, is only suspended when Charlotte completely represses her own physical desires by refusing food and by frequent bouts of vomiting. Charlotte's tendency to vomit results in "unqualified sympathy from her Aunt Edma" who praises the child's illness and lack of appetite by exclaiming: "Imagine! The angel lives on water and air! The little nun" (52). This is, indeed, the only time in the entire novel when Edma praises Charlotte for anything. Even when Charlotte enters the Catholic school of St. Gemmes, Edma is more pleased with the fact that the child is "off [her] hands at last" (105) than with Charlotte's finally receiving a formal education.

While Edma's extreme repression of the flesh could be dismissed as religious fanaticism, her views on the connection between physical torture and divine grace are mirrored by Mother Superior from St. Gemmes school who sets out to meet Charlotte, not because the child is seen as especially devoted to Christ, but because Charlotte's "devastating ... act of violence upon [her] mortal husk" (65) catches her attention. The Mother Superior "believed that it was only the punished bodies which received visits from God" (60) and so is convinced that "this child, dramatically marked from birth—who had *eaten glass*—was a rare clay body destined for Purification in the Fiery kiln of Beatitude" (60). Mother Superior is thrilled by Charlotte's act of self-mutilation, as she is convinced that it is the act of a future martyr, and the Mother Superior is "interested in Martyrdom professionally" (60) and she encourages Charlotte to emulate the physical suffering of other, "contemporary" (65) martyrs, whose feats of physical torture and self-denial are recounted to the child as examples of perfect piety. Indeed, Charlotte is told that if she is not judged "to be worthy to shine with" these modern martyrs by God, then Charlotte will be "excluded" from heaven and "God's Divine Grace: Excluded forever" (65) since Mother Superior believes "that the price of Redemption [is] Disgrace" (61). Mother Superior is thrilled to have found Charlotte, and feels certain that attending St. Gemmes will cause the child's spirit to "shine forth, illuminating God's Glory, the Glory of St. Gemmes and, above all, the Glory of the Mother Superior. Hallelujah! she sang within herself.... What a prize! What a prize!" (65).

The repetition of the phrase "what a prize" creates the impression that Mother Superior sees Charlotte more as a prized calf at the county fair than a spiritual being in need of guidance. Indeed, Charlotte's spiritual needs and questions are completely ignored by both Edma and Mother Superior, both of whom are intent on using Charlotte for their own ends and whose treatment of the child is hardly virtuous. Indeed, de Sade pointed out that "the virtuous sentiment ... is a low, base impulse that stinks of commerce: *I give unto you in order that I may obtain from you in exchange ...*" (*Juliette* 144). Edma's only concern is to keep the child from embarrassing her in front of the neighbors, while at the same time exacting pity from them for raising her orphaned grand-niece, while the Mother Superior wants to turn Charlotte into a holy martyr in order to elevate her own standing within the church. Neither has any concern for Charlotte herself, as she is just an instrument of their desires, a means to an end, rather than a young soul in need of guidance. Clearly, if Charlotte wants any kind of spiritual guidance in this world, she must look beyond the walls of the Catholic Church.

The appearance of virtue and duty, the appearance of piety, the appearance of devotion to God are all that matter for many of the characters in *The Stain*. Edma for example, decides that she will save the thick scabs from her knees after she returns from Lourdes as proof that "she, at least, was worthy of salvation" (94), while Mother Superior is only interested in how Charlotte's eventual horrific death as a martyr will glorify the Mother Superior by making her look better in the eyes of the Church Fathers. Edma even dislikes her local parish priest since "God knows a man who is satisfied with ill-fitting dentures cannot be trusted as a spiritual leader" (20). Appearance, however, can be deceiving and while it is clear that neither Mother Superior nor Edma is as pious as they might appear to be, Ducornet underscores the deceptiveness of appearance in one critical scene. During the first meeting between the Exorcist and the Mother Superior, the Exorcist attempts to impress the nun by incorporating several Latin quotations into his conversation, for example, "*Ingentio formae damna repenndo meae*" (75) and "*In toto corde meo exquisiui te...*" (78). The Mother Superior cannot resist adding her own Latin quotation, and chimes in with "*Ignitum elquium tuum vehemnter*" (75). Since most readers are unfamiliar with Latin, and are likely to be more interested in the rather intense erotic game that the Exorcist is playing with the Mother Superior under the table anyway, these Latin quotations are most likely to be skimmed over by the vast majority. Even the narrator adds a quote at the end of the chapter, "*Dominus vobiscum. Ite, Missa, est!*" (80), a line that the reader would assume is a comment on the preceding chapter. However, once these seemingly learned quotes are translated into English, it becomes clear that none of them actually make any kind of sense at all. Rather, they are a literary hodgepodge of Latin words that are strung together in a way that appears to have meaning, but actually does not. For example, "*Ingentio formae damna rependo meae*" (75) actually translates into: "Cleverly form condemnation to ransom meae," while "*In toto corde meo exquisiui te...*" (78) translates to: "Upon all together corde meo sought after you." Indeed, some words, such as "meae" and "corde meo" are not Latin at all. The Mother Superior's quote: "*Ignitum elquium tuum vehemnter*" (75) is no better, and means "unknown eloquent your violently." Even the narrator's Latin quotation translates into so much nonsense: "Master you. Go, Holy Mass is!" The reader simply assumes that the characters and the narrator understand the meaning behind the Latin, not realizing that they are in fact, gibberish. In direct contrast to the important sounding, meaningless Latin is the passage from the opening of the novel, a quotation that appears before the novel begins. Ducornet credits the quotation as coming from "Jesus, the First Book of Jesu (from *Changing Concepts of the Bible* by Werner Wolff...)" (6); however, the quotation itself appears to be nothing but gibberish. It reads in part: "œaaa ooo zezophazaz-zaieozaza eee iii zaieozoakhoe..." (6). When an interviewer commented on the nonsensical quality of this quote, Ducornet corrected her, saying that this nonsense "is a Gnostic mantra. Its intention is to empower the navigating soul as it passes the planets—all guarded by demons—on its way back 'home'" (Gregory and McCaffery). If one thinks of reading a novel as taking a mental journey, then the phonetic spelling of a mantra to guide the reader on their journey through the world of the novel is certainly appropriate.

Clearly, Ducornet is playing with the reader's pre-conceived notions regarding not only religion, but the writer's craft itself. The lay reader (as most are, since so few people understand Latin) assumes that the characters are using quotes and a language which they are familiar with, and certainly the reader would assume that the writer would also have inserted Latin quotations into a novel in order to serve a purpose. Indeed, the Latin quotations do serve Ducornet's purpose, but not the one assumed by the reader. The Latin appears to have meaning which it actually lacks, while the quotation that appears to have no meaning, in fact, has a meaning. The same is true for the church itself, since the Mother Superior, Edma, and even the Exorcist's belief in the Devil lends the Church an appearance of credibility and purpose which it clearly does not actually have. None of these characters are interested in saving anyone's soul, not even Charlotte, and are only interested in using the authority of the church for their own purposes. Clearly, this is an atheistic view of the church, any church, regardless of denomination, as a decaying and corrupted institution which does not care at all about the people that it is supposed to serve, an institution that has long since outlived its usefulness.

Sigmund Freud, an avowed atheist like de Sade, referred to religion as "the universal obsessional neurosis of humanity" (*Future* 76) but he nevertheless also acknowledged that "religious ideas have exercised the very strongest influence upon mankind" (51). However, while de Sade encourages the complete rejection of religion as useless, Freud admits that "countless people find their one consolation in the doctrines of religion, and only with their help can they endure life" (*Future* 61). Ducornet must have been keenly aware of how many people do rely on God in order to get through life, since, despite her criticism of the Catholic church, the image of God is not absent from *The Stain*. Again flouting reader expectations, Ducornet takes great pains to include images of a God who does not dwell within the walls of the church, but instead can be found in the natural, physical world. God may not be in his stone house, but that does not mean that He does not exist entirely.

According to Sigmud Freud, the purpose of religions or culturally based moral systems is threefold: "they must exorcise the terrors of nature, they must reconcile one to the cruelty of fate, particularly as shown in death, and they must make amends for the sufferings and privations that the communal life of culture has imposed on man" (*Future* 30). Freud also adds "that the two main points in the modern educational programme are the retardation of sexual development and the early application of religious influence" (82). Throughout *The Stain*, Ducornet shows the Catholic church as failing Charlotte in each of these areas, save the last one, while the God of the physical and natural world fulfills these purposes. It is the God of nature who supports Charlotte and teaches her practical lessons that allow her to live and even thrive, while the church leaves her feeling frightened and alone.

As mentioned previously, both Edma and the Mother Superior repress the needs of the physical body as a means of becoming closer to God, since "it was only the punished bodies which received visits from God" (60) and the "world, the flesh and the devil" (Riley 148) are the ultimate enemies of mankind. Flesh and the natural desires of flesh hold a special terror for them, as shown by Edma's fury with her neighbors' animals for "fornicating and defecating in public ... without shame" (40) and Edma's praise of Charlotte's rejection of food (52). Rather than using religious teachings to exorcise the terrors of nature, Edma uses her own "unremitting hatred for the imperfect universe" (14) and the animals around them to inspire fear in the child and to frighten Charlotte into submission. The natural world is uncontrolled and dangerous, and even the garden is fraught with danger:

> Aunt Edma's yard, like a medieval forest, afforded little pleasure and much to fear. The charming, furry rabbits, munching comfortably in their greenwire hutches, were lascivious creatures given over entirely to the dubious delights of fornication. It was impressed upon Charlotte that the rabbits were diseased, that at any moment their ears would fall off, and that this malady was highly communicable. Charlotte ... must not go near the chickens either, for fear they fly into her face and peck out her eyes, mistaking them for grubs [34].

None of the animals around her are safe, and even Charlotte's stain is in the image of a dancing rabbit, one of the diseased, lascivious creatures that Charlotte must avoid at all costs. Indeed, the hare is seen as a symbol of the Devil (16) and is viewed by Edma as the mark of the sin of "licentiousness," a sin committed by Charlotte's mother which has been branded on the child.

The stain of the hare also becomes a social stigma which prevents Charlotte from attending school (35), and which Charlotte interprets as "a mark that God Himself had laid upon her to set her apart from the cruel, snot-nosed creatures who went to school" (36). While Edma is furious at the stain's existence, it is Charlotte's interpretation of its meaning that comes closest to Freud's concept of religion making "amends for the sufferings and privations that the communal life of culture has imposed on man" (*Future* 30). Rather, Charlotte's religious interpretation justifies her exclusion and rejection of communal society, rather than making up for being a part of it.

While Edma impresses fear of the natural world upon Charlotte, Mother

Superior impresses upon Charlotte fear of the afterlife by telling her that she will be "excluded forever" from God's Divine Grace (65) and therefore cast into Hell if Charlotte is not worthy of becoming a martyr. The acceptance of death is not merely a means to the end of becoming a martyr; rather it is portrayed as the ultimate state of perfection. In other words, Charlotte must be perfect in order to become a martyr, which causes the child to come to the conclusion that "to be as perfect as an egg, perfect people must be dead" (34). Rather than using religion to accept the inevitability of death, again as per Freud's suggestion, Mother Superior uses it to glorify and celebrate the possibility of a horrifically painful death to match Christ's sufferings. In the end, there is no aspect of the world which does not contain an element of fear. One really cannot win for losing, so it is unsurprising that, when Charlotte writes to the "Priories of the Convent of the Thorny Agony" (151) to ask to become a nun, she begins her letter: "Dear Mother Marked by evil since birth, I have lived in horror of life and dream only of Salvation" (152). It is only towards the end of the novel that Charlotte realizes "she had always been afraid, that it was above all fear, not faith, that was driving her on" (167).

The physical world of flesh and death, however one might try to repress it, will not be denied, and the result of religious rejection of that fleshy world climaxes in Charlotte's terrifying vision of God's pyramid temple constructed from "pieces of red meat, sewn together with thick, black thread, and that the whole thing stank of rotten chicken offal" (51). This nightmare edifice is the true "House of God" (51) a world of flesh, death, and decay that cannot be denied. While the God of Nature presents His dark face as a counteraction to the attempts to repress him, both Charlotte and the reader have already seen his kinder side. The God of Nature first appears as Charlotte uses Emile's seed catalogues and the Bible as reading textbooks; Charlotte chooses to pray to "the Lord God, the God of the Tulip and the Tomato, the God of the Strawberry and the Scarlet Gem" (40). Charlotte also uses nature to illustrate lessons from the Bible, by using pastel crayons to draw "faces on the smooth pebbles … of the garden path" (38); these "pebble-people" become Biblical figures in Charlotte's games. God-the-Father is one of Emile's pails, who nevertheless punishes the wicked with as much severity as the Old Testament God, as shown when "God-the-Father" punishes the pebble Joseph by "dropping Joseph down the well—a punishment so severe that Charlotte was riddled with guilt for days" (39). Charlotte moves this severe God-the-Pail back into the shed, and covers "Him with rags so that he could no longer be witness to what she was doing. Yet, even when blinded and banished to a sunless corner, He continued to exert a weird influence. Whenever she thought of Him, a monstrous wing would blot out the sky" (39). The influence of the Old Testament God is "weird" to Charlotte's natural pebble-people, He is a "monstrous" figure whose capricious wrath is something to be feared and avoided at all costs. Rather than alleviating the fears of Charlotte and her pebble-people, this Old Testament God adds to them, just as the figure of God as taught by Mother Superior and Edma adds to Charlotte's "horror" of life and the world around her. Charlotte's attempt to reconcile these two images of God clearly demonstrates how one image is incompatible with the other. The God of the Old Testament is a monster who blots out the sky, while the God of the Tulip and the Tomato quietly answers Charlotte's prayers and provides all that the garden plants require to survive and thrive. The decaying pyramid of meat, while an integral part of the God of Nature, is but one side of a much larger message.

Every religion needs a holy spokesperson from whom the parishioner can receive the divine word, and the same is true for the God of Nature, whose human spokesman on earth is Archange Poupine. Unlike Edma and the Mother Superior, Poupine not only accepts the natural world as it is, he revels in it by choosing to live in the woods rather than in the town. Poupine stands in direct contrast to Edma and the Mother Superior in that unlike either of them, he tells Charlotte "all he knew (and was there anything he did not know?) about life, love the seasons and dogs" (96). It is Poupine who tells Charlotte that her bleeding is not a kind of stigmata, as she believes, but means that she "can have babies" (170). This is the only instance where the Catholic Church fulfills one of Freud's principles, namely "the retardation of sexual development" (82). Indeed, despite her rigorous education by the nuns at St. Gemmes, no one has told any of the girls anything about their approaching puberty. Therefore, when Charlotte begins her first menstruation cycle, she is at first horrified and then decides that it must be a kind of stigmata. It is only the "sensible" Poupine who realizes that such information is "damn ... important" (173) and is willing to explain the reality of the situation to Charlotte. Even more specifically, he answers Charlotte's questions about her parents, while Edma "won't tell [her] anything" (98) about either of them.

Unlike the townsfolk, Poupine is unafraid of the gold colored she-wolf that has been seen around town. He tells Charlotte, "'Wolves aren't like men.... It's just famine that makes them cruel and that's the truth.... The roots of all things whisper together in the earth. The wolves know far more about the world (Oh, they know things!) than most people—living among the roots as they do'" (97). While the townsfolk, including Edma, see the wolf as a sign of evil, Poupine understands its ways and is unafraid of the animal. Even after the wolf attacks him, kills his dog, and rips off Poupine's ear, he wisely harbors the animal no ill will, saying that the loss "doesn't matter" because he can "still hear the dear singing" (172). After all, it is only men who are cruel without reason, while the wolf only becomes cruel when it is starving.

Poupine knows "all the names of the wild flowers in the woods, roadsides and meadows" (98) and which plants of the forest can help heal Charlotte's broken arm: "everything in these woods is a medicine or a mystery" (172), he tells her. The mysteries of the woods do not frighten Poupine, who recognizes the gold hare and the sulfur-colored she-wolf for what they are; images of the God of Nature, they act as His messengers, His agents for change. It is a gold-colored hare that Charlotte's father kills while his wife is in labor and it is this hare that stamps its image onto Charlotte's face (11); it is the sulfur-colored wolf who humbles Poupine by ripping off his ear, thereby causing him to give up liquor (172); it is the gold hare who causes Charlotte to leap from the train and escape into the woods (168); and it is the hide of a yellow wolf that the Exorcist uses to disguise himself, thereby attempting to masquerade as a messenger of the God of Nature in order to justify his own madness and murders (186). Unlike the gold of the church, the gold color of the hare and wolf are natural gifts given to them by the God of Nature that marks them as His messengers, but only to people like Poupine, who are not fooled by appearance and who have the eyes to see these agents of change for what they really are. It is Poupine's practical lessons that ultimately save Charlotte, and the townsfolk from the Exorcist's murderous rampage. Charlotte tells Poupine: "You gave me the eyes, Archange, to see ... to see how mad he was. Always" (189). It is the God of the Tulip and the Tomato who gives Charlotte the eyes to see what the Exorcist is, and the knowledge to survive without fear in the wilderness. Indeed, it is God of the Natural world as voiced by Poupine that allows Charlotte to at last become her own person, a creature free of fear and the physical suffering demanded by the Catholic church. It is only in the woods, away from the church, that Charlotte is able to find spiritual salvation.

While both de Sade and Freud completely reject the idea that there is a God of any sort, Durcornet clearly does not entirely agree with them. While her depiction of organized religion and Catholic dogma in *The Stain* is of a decaying institution more concerned with appearance and inspiring fear in the populace than with actual spiritual salvation, the idea of a Divine Being, however, is not totally absent; He is to be found in the natural world rather than within the walls of a church. The God of Nature is one who loves the physical world, who speaks to His followers through subtle signs and the wisdom of the body, a deeply personal God who is more powerful and wise than the Old Testament creation. For a writer who follows in the footsteps of an avowed atheist like de Sade, it is an usually spiritual message and one that is not expected within the context of a novel like *The Stain*; again Ducornet flouts our expectations and presuppositions about her work, which makes her such a powerful and interesting novelist.

Works Cited

De Sade, Marquis. *Juliette*. Trans. Austryn Wainhouse. New York: Grove, 1968.
Ducornet, Rikki. *The Stain*. London: Dalkey, 1995.
Freud, Sigmund. *The Future of an Illusion*. Trans. W.D. Robson-Scott. London: Hogarth, 1928.
Gregory, Sinda, and Larry McCaffery. "A Conversation with Rikki Ducornet." *Review of Contemporary Fiction* 18.3 (1998). Web. 15 May 2009.
Riley, Michael. *Conversations with Anne Rice*. New York: Ballantine, 1996.

Writing About Invented Places: Esther Rochon's Archipelago of Vrénalik

MAUDE DESCHÊNES PRADET

ACCSFF '13

> *Ainsi donc Phileas Fogg avait gagné son pari. Il avait accompli en quatre-vingts jours ce voyage autour du monde! Il avait employé pour ce faire tous les moyens de transport, paquebots, railways, voitures, yachts, bâtiments de commerce, traîneaux, éléphant.*
>
> [So Phileas Fogg won his bet. He had accomplished this trip around the world in eighty days. To achieve this he had employed all means of transportation, cruise ships, railways, cars, yachts, commercial ships, sleighs, elephant[1].]—Jules Verne, *Le tour du Monde* 217

Introduction

Now that earthly and cultural borders are more porous than ever, communication more complex and travel faster, it seems that we cannot apprehend the world but by fragments, as if it had become too wide. Easier access to the most foreign places, frequent uprooting, and moving transform our relationship to time and space. According to Fredric Jameson, postmodernity is characterized by a loss of historicity and a feeling of discontinuity (Jameson, *Le postmodernisme* 525). As individuals, as people, how do we understand space? How do we perceive distances, borders, and maps? How do we plan and organize the spaces we live in? Since the invention of the steam locomotive in the nineteenth century, our perception of distance and speed has been radically altered; suddenly, the possibility of readily travelling across huge territories in little time has become conceivable. Ever since the discovery of the steam locomotive, the means of transportation have been evolving at a high pace, and in turn, the world has become more accessible. In addition, obtaining information about far and foreign places has never been more convenient, as satellites and the Internet carry news from around the world at an incredible speed. Indeed, our relationship to time and space is being irreversibly reshaped.

Researchers have noticed such changes and have become more and more interested in spaces, a shift in perspective known as the *spatial turn*. Since Edward Soja's major work *Thirdspace*, place and space have continued to grow into a major center of inquiry in various fields of humanities, including literature. In the last few decades, among other place-related literary approaches, geocritical studies have grown in importance. According to Robert T. Tally, Jr., geocriticism is "a way of looking at the spaces of literature" (*Geocritical Explorations* 8). Some important contributions to geocriticism are Bertrand Westphal's *Géocritique*, which was the first comprehensive attempt to define geocritical studies; Christiane Lahaie's *Ces mondes brefs*, a geocritical study of Québec short stories; and Robert T. Tally, Jr.'s *Spatiality*, which ends with a philosophical plea in favor of the geocritical study of imaginary places. He writes: "Looking at what we might call *otherworldly* literature, I maintain we also gain a clearer sense of our own 'real' world" (147). In this case, *otherworldly* literature is to be understood as inclusive of all non-realistic genres. Let us recall the proposal put forth by Darko Suvin (*Poétique*), that if we were to divide fiction into two large groups, realistic and non-realistic, the latter includes the spectrum of fictional works whose world does not conform to reality as we know it.

In fact, the nineteenth century saw, almost simultaneously, the development of the steam locomotive and the birth of modern science fiction and fantasy. To our knowledge, modern science fiction is generally said to have begun, depending on which criteria we favor, with Mary Shelley's *Frankenstein* (1818), H. G. Wells's *Time Machine* (1895), or Jules Verne's *Voyage au centre de la Terre* (1864). Modern adult fantasy literature, for the most part, also originated in the nineteenth century, arising with George MacDonald's *Phantastes* (1858) and William Morris's *The Well at the World's End* (1896). Therefore, it appears that, interlaced with the transformation of our relationship to space, an interest has grown for imaginary worlds and non-realistic genres. In the academic world, there has been, since the 1970s, an increasing attention to the study of non-realistic genres. From such works as Darko

Suvin's *Poetics of Science Fiction* (1977), whose theoretical tools are still presently used in most studies, to Mark J. P. Wolf's *Building Imaginary Worlds* (2012), in which he looks at invented worlds through the scope of intermedial studies, the academic publications are numerous.

As Darko Suvin observed (*Poétique*), invented worlds, which he proposed to name "novums," act as "distorting mirrors" of our own reality, of us, that may be suggesting more about our perception of our world than we are aware of. Fredric Jameson, whose work has brought him to think both about postmodernism and space (*Le postmodernisme*), and science fiction and utopia (*Archéologies*), writes in the later work that we should examine the possibility that science fiction and fantasy describes more our relationship to space rather than our relationship to time (*Penser avec la sf* 162). In geocritical studies, there is agreement that non-realistic places can and should be looked at, although they have not yet been among the main targets of geocriticism. Thus, such an approach to imaginary places remains, mostly, a theoretical possibility. Those other places of the fantastic literatures may tell us much about our actual relationship to space. That intent may require that some critical tools from the science fiction, fantasy and geocritical field be adapted, or that some new tools be created, as invented spaces might present some distinct problems.

The focus of this analysis will be the invented archipelago of *Vrénalik*, in the fantasy novel *L'aigle des profondeurs* [*The eagle from the depths*] from Québec writer Esther Rochon. This novel is the second volume of a cycle, *Le cycle de Vrénalik*. In the non-realistic spectrum, this cycle is considered a fantasy novel, according to the criteria proposed by Fredric Jameson (2005), among which are the important presence of magic, the cyclic or mythical perception of time, and the relationship to literary myths. This paper is not a proper geocritical study, as it will focus on a single novel, but it has a geocritical perspective, or a place-oriented viewpoint. I chose this particular novel because it describes Vrénalik in detail, and illustrates the strength and importance of boundaries which tie the people to their land. When looking deeper into its places, throughout the process of writing this paper, I even came to think that the story is fundamentally all about places.

In this novel, Rochon creates an original fantasy land, a cursed archipelago cut off from the outside world, with a hostile environment and climate, a small population barely surviving, and very scarce visitors. However savage, Vrénalik is nevertheless a place where the ancient art of sorcery has survived, where legends are history and the land itself is alive, for those who can perceive it. What is Vrénalik? What means are used to describe it? How does this invented archipelago, with its history, legends, and geography, determine its plot? In fact, it appears that, when entering *Le cycle de Vrénalik*, one reads two stories at the same time: that of the characters, and that of the invented archipelago. Moreover, the invented archipelago works as a narrative entity, almost as if it were the main character.

About Invented Places

> I began reading science fiction in the 1950s and got from it a message that didn't exist anywhere else then in my world. Explicit sometimes in the detachable ideas; implicit in the gimmicks … most fully expressed in the strange, strange, wonderfully strange landscapes was the message: "things can be really different." —Suvin, *Defined by a Hollow* 10

Suvin, a major theoretician, and perhaps the first to ennoble science fiction as a legitimate field of study, expressed his epiphanic astonishment when he first discovered this literature. He discovered, mainly through those "wonderfully strange landscapes," that science fiction allows us to dream of infinite possibilities within our world.

What shall we call these strange landscapes? I prefer the term "invented places," referring to the concept of non-realistic or non-referential places. Suvin's "novum" concept includes all non-realistic or differentiated elements that form an invented world, and therefore is broader than "place." The concept of "imaginary places" may be somewhat more confusing, because one could consider all places in fiction, in a way, "imaginary," even if their name or description reminds one of referential places. For this reason, when mentioning places in a fiction that do not relate to existing places in our world, for example Middle-earth in Tolkien's invented world, I will refer to them as "invented places." How can a space- and place-oriented reading of a non-realistic novel, fantasy in this case, enlighten the multiple layers of its meaning? Among the tools that might prove pertinent to the reading of invented places, I will make reference to mainly two fields of research: cultural geography and semiotics.

Despite the fact that cultural geography's concepts have not been developed for invented places, they are of high relevance to this study because they concern the symbolic meaning of places. In fact, all places in fictional stories may have a substantial symbolic meaning, but this phenomenon is intensified in non-realistic literature, where places have to be thoroughly invented and described, since we cannot rely on any previous knowledge. In that sense, cultural geography meets a geocritical approach of invented places:

it is all about meaning, about how the experience of space is also an experience of otherness, thereby allowing us to better understand our way of being in the world. These spaces created by human beings which we find in fictional stories reveal, therefore, a way to question our relationship to our world. In the case of Vrénalik, my hypothesis is that the entire archipelago, and its parts, is a "sleeping *haut-lieu*" (Bédard 49–74), signifying a place with a potent symbolic meaning, yet whose potentiality is "asleep," or dormant, hence not fully active. In this particular case, the land is cursed, whereby most places are abandoned and deserted, although the sorcerers can still feel the particular energy and deep meaning of these sacred places, natural or man-made.

As for semiotics, they play a vital role in understanding the "making" and "writing" of invented places. I will mainly explore some writing strategies that may allow a writer to create invented places without impeding the pace of the story with overdrawn and lengthy descriptions, or losing the reader because of a lack of description. In this regard, my analysis fits into the theoretical lineage of Umberto Eco, Marc Angenot, and Richard Saint-Gelais. The different concepts I will rely on will be described later, but for now let us turn to Vrénalik.

Places in *L'aigle des profondeurs*

Esther Rochon's Vrénalik is an invented archipelago. That, already, is meaningful: what does an archipelago look like, if not an island broken into pieces? Therefore, this is a broken land, cut off from the rest of the world. It does not even belong to itself, as it is legally dependent on another country on the south continent. Four centuries ago, this land was rich and prosperous, but it is now ruins and decay. The people of Vrénalik, the Asven, are convinced that an ancient curse condemns them to remain isolated on their islands. They seem to have accepted this faith, as they no longer fight against the deadly children's diseases, poverty, and the inevitable extinction of their kind. The archipelago itself is described as a sleeping (if not dying) entity, organic and sensitive.

The narrator, Anar Vranengal, pupil of the sorcerer, learns about her country and herself by taking the pulse of the land. In fact, while following Anar Vranengal's whereabouts throughout this land, one reads two stories at the same time: that of the characters, and that of the invented archipelago. Moreover, the archipelago works as a narrative entity, as if it were virtually the main character. When we read this novel with a geocritical eye, the importance of places becomes obvious.

L'aigle des profondeurs begins with a description of the Citadel of Frulken, the main city in the archipelago. These very first sentences of the tale provide a good indication of Esther Rochon's rhythm of writing. From the very beginning, this first excerpt also illustrates the importance of places:

> La Citadelle de Frulken a sept étages de haut, sept étages de pierre, sept étages de roche, et quatre étages de cave sont creusés dans la falaise, quatre étages perdus, quatre étages déserts, quatre siècles de malheur tombés sur le pays.
>
> [The Citadel of Frulken is seven stories high, seven stories of stones, seven stories of rock, and four stories of caves dug into the cliff, four bygone stories, four abandoned stories, four centuries of malediction befallen on the land] [1].

And on that first description, the story begins. It is told by Anar Vranengal, one of the few living children of the archipelago, whose name, a powerful and meaningful one, was chosen after a place. Anar Vranengal was, in fact, the name of an ancient city that was swallowed up by the sea as a consequence of the curse that imprisoned the archipelago four centuries ago. A few hours per year, at solstice, part of the ruins emerge: this is where she was conceived. The sorcerer of Vrénalik, Ivendra, who chose her to succeed him, enlightens her on the significance of her name:

> Tu portes bien ton nom, Anar Vranengal. Une ville entière avec ses tours, ses palais, ses terrains vagues, émergée pour quelques heures, engloutie pendant de longs mois...."
>
> [Your name suits you well, Anar Vranengal. A whole city with its towers, palaces, wastelands—emerged for a few hours, submerged for long months...] [57].

Ivendra also teaches Anar Vranengal about the "directions" of people. According to him, a person has a direction, an orientation that defines them. He is from the North, from where sunlight does not come (70), and she is from underneath, from the depths, where the dead rest. He also teaches her how to stay still for hours in a certain place, meditating, with the purpose of connecting to the land. He advises her to become like the land:

> Deviens comme ici, Anar Vranengal. Un endroit ordinaire, pas plus propre que le terrain d'à-côté. Deviens telle quelle. Jusqu'à la fin de tes jours.
>
> [Become like here, Anar Vranengal. An ordinary place, no purer than the next land. Become as it is. Until the end of your days] [70].

By the end of the novel, Anar Vranengal winds up helping a stranger out from the caves of the Citadel, where he had chosen to live isolated from everything and everyone, for seventeen years. Due to an old tradition, his lengthy stay in the cave automatically gave him legal ownership of it. He then eventually returns to his homeland, where he begins publishing translations of Vrénalik's legends. Before leaving, he bequeaths the caves of the Citadel to Anar Vranengal. She then—from the depths, owner of the four stories of caves dug into the cliffs underneath the citadel, including one of the only two libraries in the whole country— becomes a famous citizen, someone of influence.

The caves of the Citadel are one of the most significant places in the novel. These depths reveal that *L'aigle des profondeurs* does not bring good and evil into a duality, but rather depicts a nuanced vision of elements such as death and decay. In fact, Vrénalik is a nuanced world, where ruins and deep and dark caves underneath the Citadel possess their own charm and value. Moreover, the quests of the characters and the history of the land itself are more ontological than Manichaean. Even if each character builds his or her own relationship to the world and the sacred, what is at stake, ultimately, is the existence and meaning of the land. We will see in the next paragraphs that the caves are, on the one hand, described as a dark and sordid place, and yet on the other hand a place of initiation, transformation, and contemplation.

The many descriptions of the caves of the Citadel are useful in building this nuanced vision of the world as well as illustrating the unique imagery of Rochon's invented land. It is no surprise that the caves are seeping, black, humid and slippery, and that they are a labyrinth where one could easily get lost and never return; that these abandoned caves have no staircase, no access leading to them—they are like an immense hole, an abyss filled with silence and solitude. They contain dungeons, oubliettes, detritus, and ghosts. Horrific events happened there in the past, like torture and even murders. All such characteristics can predictably be applied to many imaginary castle caves.

But, as we read further, the personal quest of Anar Vranengal leads her to help Jouskilliant Green escape the caves, and from that point on we get another dimension of the caves' depths. For Jouskilliant Green, longing for silence and solitude, it was a refuge. And, when he finally was ready to come back to the world, after seventeen years, he entrusted the caves to Anar Vranengal, which made her a person of power among her people, and, mostly, transformed her. She writes that when she followed Jouskilliant Green into the caves, she roused herself from childhood and was able to contemplate the world: "*Par le même mouvement, j'ai arraché mon enfance et j'ai contemplé le monde*" (2).

After her adventure, and once the caves had become her domain, Anar Vranengal goes there to commune with herself and the land. For her, this place becomes a peaceful refuge; it is now her home. And thus, the caves of the Citadel are not only dark, they also possess grandeur and a beauty of their own. Even the blind, giant white spiders that inhabit the area, first perceived as ugly by Anar Vranengal, manifest a certain magnificence. As she becomes familiar with the caves, Anar Vranengal realizes how important they are. Older than the Citadel itself, they are a place of savage splendor, something secret, hypnotizing, and unlimited. Parts of the caves even open up on the ocean. In these areas the sun gets in and a garden can be cultivated. One of the caves also shows a magnificent underground torrent. Finally, we can find in the caves the Library of the depths, one of the two libraries in the entire archipelago, full of wisdom and history. Indeed, when the people of Vrénalik long ago destroyed the staircases and blocked the trapdoors to the caves, it is as if they had cut themselves off from their own roots, their history and identity. Therefore, when Anar Vranengal goes looking for Jouskilliant Green, makes a ladder for him to get out, and then later dwells in the caves herself, she, in a way, initiates the symbolic reconnection of the Asven people to their roots.

At this point, I will introduce some concepts from cultural geography, and more precisely geosymbolism. Even though cultural geography is meant for "real" places, some tools may apply to invented places and reveal as much, if not more, about our existence in the world. In fact, in works of fiction, places are often, if not always, highly symbolic. Mario Bédard, a well-known cultural geographer and professor at *Université du Québec à Montréal*, thinks that places have no intrinsic meaning: "*Les lieux n'ont aucun sens en eux-mêmes. Ils n'ont que celui qu'on leur donne*" [places themselves have no meaning per se but the meaning we give them] (70). He asserts that it is of utmost importance to study intangible and symbolic aspects of places because they reveal how we, as humans, relate to "being" in the world, collectively and individually.

How, then, would cultural geography qualify the caves of the citadel of Vrénalik? Indeed, this is not an actual place, but a construction within the text, made mainly of partial elements of description and action creating the "illusion" of a proposed possible existence in which Vrénalik is real. Nonetheless, a reader accepts an implicit reading contract when he or she enters a fictional story: so what if Vrénalik existed (somewhere)?

Then the caves of the Citadel would be a "*haut-lieu*" (Nora), that is, a place filled with dense meaning and temporality, and even more precisely a "sleeping *haut-lieu*" (Bédard), because it was, before Jouskilliant Green and Anar Vranengal, abandoned, and even after Anar Vranengal inherits the caves. It is still a place of latent power and history, a place of loneliness and meditation, a powerful microcosm and mini–Vrénalik—that is, itself dormant since the curse hit the archipelago four hundred years ago and most of the land was deserted by humans. The archipelago could be compared, in this regard, to the castle of the princess in *Sleeping Beauty*, as people and nature, if not literally asleep, were cursed into inertia. In the following paragraphs, we will see many signs of this sleepiness of places in the novel, a sleepiness that is, paradoxically good and bad, beautiful and hard. It is as if this death of all places, of the Asven people and the land, was not a definite end, but a necessary phase of a natural cycle.

Perceptions of Space in Vrénalik: Contrasting but Not Contradictory

> *Jadis, ils avaient gagné la haute mer avec joie, rien ne les avait arrêtés, ils avaient fait le tour du monde. Maintenant les eaux profondes leur inspiraient la crainte, et s'ils savaient toujours bien manœuvrer leurs bateaux, ils ne les menaient jamais loin des côtes. L'océan les retenait prisonniers; ils attendaient que sa colère se calme.*
>
> [Once upon a time, they had sailed to the ocean with joy, they had traveled around the world. Now the deep waters instilled them with fear, and if they still knew how to manoeuver their boats, they never sailed them far from the coasts. The ocean kept them imprisoned; waiting for its anger to dissipate.]—Rochon 26

In addition to analyzing descriptive places in the novel, it is essential to look at the experience of the world that is transmitted through the characters' perceptions of space. We are then looking for clues to the individual or collective relationship to places. In this case, as in the example of the caves, we can find apparent contradictions, like two sides of a mirror, that nuance the image of the land. On a first or a very literal reading, one would mostly notice the feeling of imprisonment and degeneration. However, when we look closer, or read between the lines, everything is not black or white. On the one hand, Vrénalik is a lost country that two ships per year connect to the rest of the world (14), a country that does not even belong to itself (223), if the Asven people no longer navigate the wide ocean (26), and if even the stones want them to leave (23); on the other hand, there is no such thing as jails any more in Vrénalik.

One can observe, on such a land and among such people, many symptoms of degeneration: wild sexuality, ravages of madness, cynicism, inertia, and high child death rate; the abandoned towers of the Citadel now shelter eagles' nests, which Anar Vranengal sees as a sign of the place's nobility. In addition, everywhere on the archipelago, the forest is growing back amid ruins of abandoned cities and factories, proving that nature reasserts itself after all. Another interesting aspect of Asven society is gender equality: in the rich and developed societies of the outside world, women are considered inferior, whereas in the poor land of Vrénalik, they are equals. It is suggested in the novel that gender equality came about with the curse and thereby the consequences of the curse, hence implying that survival necessities overshadowed notions of rank, cast, or gender discrimination.

Despite such bleak times, there are places in Vrénalik that are untouched by madness and degeneration—places protected by an aura of their own, like the Bay of Svail. There, Anar Vranengal experiences a feeling of utter freedom, because the temple at the bay of Svail, traditionally the domain of the sorcerers, has a different atmosphere from the rest of the land. In this place, Anar Vranengal feels that the land is free of the curse and of appearances, as if it were out of time. She says:

> *Ici, le vent n'était pas comme ailleurs; je pouvais si facilement lui parler. La roche n'était pas ordinaire; c'était évidemment mon amie. Tout s'animait, résonnait, était un rappel, que je pouvais aisément comprendre, de notre tradition.*
>
> [Here, the wind was not as elsewhere; I could easily talk to it. The rock was not ordinary; it was naturally my friend. Everything was alive, vibrant, and was a reminder, easy for me to understand, of our tradition.] [91]

Although the temple of Svail itself is mostly abandoned and demolished, except for a few rooms where the sorcerers live, the young woman perceives the countryside as free: "*Quoi de plus libre que ce paysage?*" [What's freer than this countryside?] (90). The temple of the bay of Svail also illustrates an essential characteristic of places in Vrénalik: they are invested with a sense of history. Intrinsically, everything on the archipelago is memory. The whole land therefore possesses a dignity—a pride that the reader can feel between the lines.

When one examines the perception of space in this novel, one gets the impression of an inner debate about the positive and negative aspects of the curse which isolate yet protect Vrénalik, thereby condemning the Asven people to misery and extinction, but at the same time a sense of freedom from outside influences and greed is observed, not to mention a privileged relationship to nature. As a critic stated quite accurately in *Lettres québécoises*, Rochon's writing shows a democracy of thought that makes her books an homage to difference and transformation (Rochon, back cover).

If we were to go further regarding which specific tools might apply to a geocritical study of invented places, it would be interesting to verify the following hypothesis: fantasy is more likely to be rich with "places of the heart" ("*lieux du coeur*"), that is places with a strong personal affective meaning for the characters, and "sleeping places," because of its relationship to myth. Science fiction, on the other hand, is more likely to show an abundance of non-places, in-between places, and exemplary places, because of its links with utopias and dystopias (or, as Margaret Atwood prefers to call them, eustopias—reminding us that one never really goes without the other). But, then again, there are many hybrid forms that would be harder to separate—which nuances our conclusions.

On Writing Strategies …

Another major input to a place-oriented approach of non-realistic fiction would be semiotics—the study of signs and signs systems, especially when it comes to the "absent paradigm" theory (Angenot) and the "model reader" theory from Umberto Eco, and some adaptations proposed by Richard Saint-Gelais. We will see that some concepts can bring some transparency to the writing strategies specific to invented places.

With otherworldly literature, we read two interlaced stories: that of the world, and that of the characters. Places participate in the coherence of the imaginary world, but, because they have no direct referent in reality, the novel must provide sufficient clues to the reader so that he/she can build an inner imaginary atlas, or, one may say, a xeno-atlas, that is more or less realistic. Even if invented places are never quite wholly detached from the world as we know it, we can postulate that there are specific writing (and reading) strategies related to fantastic worlds.

In "The Absent Paradigm," Angenot shows that one particularity of science fiction (and perhaps fantastic literature in general) might be the kind of reading it demands: a large part of the information given cannot be verified in the real world—it does not exist outside of the book—thus the reader has to cope with an "absent paradigm" that can only be informed by the text itself. Richard Saint-Gelais, along the same lines, proposes that the reader of such non-realistic fiction has to accomplish a double-reading task: reading the story that is being told, and, at the same time, building an inner representation or a mental database about the fantastic universe, a xeno-encyclopaedia—which contains enough information to understand and appreciate the story (Saint-Gelais 108). This xeno-encyclopaedia is built throughout the reading by adjusting one's reader's encyclopaedia[2] to the novum.

Since this specific reading has to be informed by the text, the non-realistic fiction writer must pay particular attention to how to provide enough details about the novum to make it coherent. My hypothesis is that writing strategies are of major importance when it comes to creating invented places that are part of a "xeno-atlas"—my proposal to designate the part of the xeno-encyclopaedia that concerns geography and places. Such writing strategies may or may not be specific to fantastic literature, although some are possibly used more frequently than others in these genres. What is probable, though, is that the omnipresence of such mechanisms is a constant characteristic of fantastic literature.

The challenge with invented places is to find the right balance between telling enough so that the reader does not feel lost, but not telling too much, which would slow the pace down constantly. According to Richard Saint-Gelais, this difficulty is specific to otherworldly literature. Parts of the tools developed are outside the text: fantasy novels, for instance, often contain maps. Other tools are encoded within the text.

Concerning Rochon's invented archipelago, we can observe three main writing strategies in *L'aigle des profondeurs* that are used to inform the reader's xeno-atlas. The first one could be described, according to Saint-Gelais, as pseudo-realistic. This is very close to what Murphy calls a fake manuscript: the novel is not presented as fiction, but rather as a *témoignage* written by a girl named Anar Vranengal. This is the difference between "Once upon a time" and "I will tell you something that happened to me." It creates an effective illusion of reality. In *L'aigle des profondeurs*, Anar Vranengal, the narrator, writes what she remembers of Jouskilliant Green, because she thinks that someday someone might come to read it, and because she needs to process the events for herself. That "someone" is us, readers, or so we imagine.

The second strategy concerns the identification of places with memory. In *L'aigle des profondeurs*, since the archipelago is dying, every place is a ruin, an artifact, a trace of a glorious past. This partakes in the illusion of realism: the land has so much history it appears complex, layered, just like a "real" land. In the novel, Anar Vranengal travels with her teacher, the sorcerer Ivendra, as a major part of her education. With her, the reader travels and discovers important and sacred places of the country. On one island, the forest has grown back over the ruins of ancient industrial cities—but the ruins are still visible everywhere, reminding us of those times. Deep in the forest, in a hidden place, Ivendra shows the young girl an ancient sacred place, a "door" to other worlds that is now unusable—but that is vibrant with past history and other dimensions. In other places, like in the temple of the bay of Svail, or in the capital city, Frulken, people live in the decaying buildings, which are still inhabitable, as in a phantom city, and share those falling walls with the animals: rats in the basements, eagles on the towers of the Citadel, giant white spiders in the caves, etc. They do not dare to repair the walls, fortress, or houses, because they think they deserve to live like that and remind themselves of the curse at all time. It is as if every place is thick with history—places speak of the people, and therefore seem complex and "real."

The third main strategy is metonymic. It consists of using the places to show something about the characters and the plot. There is a strong symbolic relationship between places and characters, starting with Anar Vranengal, who was named after a place herself, who is, in some way, a place herself. Because of her powerful name, she bears her whole world within. Ivendra wants his pupil, during their errands, to immerse herself into the archipelago, to understand intuitively its rhythm and its pulses, and to "become the land" herself. That allows for some useful shortcuts: when the narrator tells something about a place, the plot—Anar Vranengal's initiation—continues to progress through the description, and we learn more about the invented world. It allows for an easier interlacing of the story, the world and that of the characters, instead of stopping the plot every time a description is to be made. For example, at one point in Anar Vranengal and Ivendra's initial trip, they explore the island of Strind, geographically and symbolically the deserted earth of the archipelago.

> *Que d'édifices étranges, suspendus au-dessus des eaux; que de poutres rousses, émergeant d'en-dessous! Les rives nous enserraient. Parfois, aux lieux les plus étroits se dressaient des ponts immenses, à demi écroulés. Nous passions sous des arches plus hautes que des maisons ... nous voguions au-dessus de caravelles submergées et de cargaisons englouties; le soir, d'une voix feutrée, nous parlions du passé de Vrénalik et de sa mort à venir.*
>
> [What strange buildings, hanging above the waters; what rusted beams emerging from beneath! The river banks were encircling us. Sometimes, in the narrowest places, the most immense bridges rose, half collapsed. We passed under arches higher than houses ... we were sailing over flooded caravels and engulfed shipments; at night, with a whispering voice, we talked about Vrénalik's past and its imminent death] [62].

The above scene plays, regarding the plot, three narrative roles at the same time. Since it is so strongly metonymic, what appears to be a simple description becomes much more. It describes an invented place, the island of Strind, informing the reader about the setting of the novel; it continues to tell the story of an initiatory trip taken by the sorcerer and his apprentice, what they see and what they talk about. It also tells the history of the country and its inhabitants, of their lost industrial activities and monuments, and of their past prosperity and grandeur.

The reader knows, of course, that Vrénalik does not exist, and that he/she is reading a work of fiction. However, such strategies build an illusion of coherence and realism which facilitates, for the reader, the sliding into the implied reading contract: "let's suppose for a moment that there was a place called Vrénalik…"

Conclusion

Is it so different, we might ask, so meaningful, to look into invented places rather than realistic places? Here is Carl Freedman's thought about science fiction, that applies to fantasy as well: "The science fiction world is not only one different in time and place from our own, but one whose chief interest is precisely the difference that such difference makes" (Freedman xvi).

This reading of Esther Rochon's *L'aigle des profondeurs*, based on the places in the novel, shows how fertile the possibilities of a geocritical reading of invented places may prove to be to enlighten the meanings of fantastic fiction. We have examined, through this analysis, some elements of this approach: conceptual tools from cultural geography such as different types of "*haut-lieux*" might be pushed further, like the semiotic concept of xeno-atlas and the writing strategies necessary to build it in the text. More elements are to come in further research, but looking deeper into invented places in fictional works might raise wonderfully rich questions about the ways we inhabit this very world.

Notes

1. All translations from French in this text are my own.
2. The reader's encyclopaedia is a concept elaborated by Umberto Eco in *Lector in Fabula* (1979). Saint-Gelais has adapted the concept to fantastic literature, but the basic principle remains the same: Eco's theory is that the text feeds an implied reader, a "model reader," with sufficient information for him to decode it. The amount of details that the text contains is based on an estimation of how much the model reader already knows (his reader's encyclopaedia).

Works Cited

Angenot, Marc. "The Absent Paradigm. An Introduction to the Semiotics of Science Fiction." *Science Fiction Studies* 6.1 (March 1979). Web. 28 Feb. 2014.

———. "Le paradigme absent: un peu de sémiotique." in Lehman, Serge et Benoît Laureau ed., "Futur et fiction: Quel langage?" *La Quinzaine littéraire* (août 2012). Web. 28 Feb. 2014. <marcangenot.com/wp-content/uploads/2013/02/Paradigme-absent-version-QL.pdf>

Atwood, Margaret. *In Other Worlds: SF and the Human Imagination*. Toronto: McClelland and Stewart, 2011. Print.

Augé, Marc. *Non-Lieux: Introduction à une anthropologie de la surmodernité*. Paris: Le Seuil, 1992. Print.

Bédard, Mario. "Une typologie du Haut-Lieu ou La quadrature d'un géosymbole." *Cahiers de géographie du Québec* 46.127 (2002): 49–74.

Eco, Umberto. *Lector in fabula: Le rôle du lecteur ou la coopération interprétative dans les textes narratifs*. Trans. Myriam Bouzaher. Paris: Grasset, 1979. Print.

Foucault, Michel. "Des espaces autres." *Architecture, Mouvement, Continuité* 5 (1984): 46–49. Print.

Freedman, Carl. *Critical Theory and Science Fiction*. Hanover: Wesleyan University Press and University Press of New England, 2000. Print.

Jameson, Fredric. *Archéologies du futur: Le désir nommé utopie*. Trans Nicolas Vieillecaze et Fabien Ollier. Paris: Max Milo, 2007. Print.

———. *Penser avec la science fiction*. Trans. Nicolas Vieillecaze et Fabien Ollier. Paris: Max Milo, 2008. Print.

———. *Le Postmodernisme ou la logique culturelle du capitalisme tardif*. Trans. Florence Nevoltry. Paris: Beaux-arts de Paris, 2011. Print.

Lahaie, Christiane. *Ces mondes brefs: Pour une géocritique de la nouvelle québécoise contemporaine*. Québec: L'instant même, 2009. Print.

Murphy, Patrick D. "Reducing the Dystopian Distance: Pseudo-Documentary Framing in Near Future Fiction." *Science Fiction Studies* 17.1 (1990): 25–37. Print.

Nora, Pierre, ed. *Les lieux de mémoire III*. Paris: QuartoGallimard, 1997. Print.

Rochon, Esther. *L'aigle des profondeurs*. Lévis: Alire, 2002. Print.

Saint-Gelais, Richard. *L'empire du pseudo: Modernités de la science-fiction*. Québec: Nota Bene, 1999. Print.

Shelley, Mary. *Frankenstein*. New-York: Dover Thrift, 1994. Print.

Soja, Edward W. *Thirdspace: Journeys to Los Angeles and Other Real and Imagined Places*. Cambridge, MA: Blackwell, 1996. Print.

Suvin, Darko. *Defined by a Hollow: Essays on Utopia, Science Fiction and Political Epistemology*. New York: Peter Lang, 2010. Print.

———. *Metamorphoses of Science Fiction: On the Poetics and History of a Literary Genre*. New Haven: Yale University Press, 1979. Print.

———. *Pour une Poétique de la science-fiction: Études en théorie et en histoire d'un genre littéraire*. Trans. Gilles Hénault. Montréal: Presses de l'Université du Québec, 1977. Print.

Tally, Robert T., Jr. *Spatiality*, London: Routledge, 2013. Print.

———, ed. *Geocritical Explorations: Space, Place, and Mapping in the Literary and Cultural Studies*. New York: Palgrave, 2011. Print.

Tolkien, J.R.R. *Le Silmarillion*. Trans. Christian Bourgeois. Paris: Pocket, 2013. Print.

Turgeon, Laurier. *Les entre-lieux de la culture*. Québec: Presses de l'Université Laval, 1998. Print.

Verne, Jules. *Le tour du monde en 80 jours*. Paris: Le livre de poche, 2007. Print.

———.*Voyage au centre de la terre*. Paris: Le livre de poche, 2012. Print.

Wells, H.G. *La machine à explorer le temps*. Trans. Le Mercure de France. Paris: Gallimard, 1997. Print.

Westphal, Bertrand. *La géocritique: Réel, fiction, espace*. Paris: Minuit, 2007. Print.

———. *Le monde plausible*. Paris: Minuit, 2011. Print.

———, ed. *La géocritique: Mode d'emploi*. Limoges: PULIM, 2000. Print.

Wolf, Mark J.P. *Building Imaginary Worlds: The Theory and History of Subcreation*. New York: Routledge, 2012. Print.

Speculating Diversity: Nalo Hopkinson's *Brown Girl in the Ring* and the Use of Speculative Fiction to Disrupt Singular Interpretations of Place

Derek Newman-Stille

ACCSFF '13

Nalo Hopkinson does not create easy notions of race, ethnicity, and diaspora in *Brown Girl in the Ring* (1998), but, rather, embraces the complexity of a diasporic identity and the multiple draws on the diasporic person. Her characters show a complex and conflicted engagement with the notion of *home*, pulled toward multiple forms of "home" and displaying the multifaceted nature of diasporic identity. Smaro Kambourelli notes that diasporic identity is hybridized, constantly under revision, and does not lend itself to easy subjectivity (21–23). Place is inscribed with multiple levels of meaning for diasporic populations, being read through lenses of the present and past simultaneously (Kambourelli 20).

Situated in a Toronto of the not-so-distant future, which has been cut off from the rest of Canada and ghettoized due to its economic and perceived social issues, Hopkinson's Toronto is made into a conflicted space, unsure of its own identity and place of belonging. It has been designated an unsafe space and becomes a place where radicalized and economically disadvantaged people are trapped. It is a place where riots have occurred between people with various claims to space and is called a "war zone" (11). It is disconnected, searching to establish an identity for itself in exile. Like people in diaspora, it represents a simultaneity of past and present, a doubling or multiplication of identities. It is the ideal setting for a woman in diaspora to search for her own identity, notions of belonging, and sense of place, and to challenge singular notions of place and home.

Ti-Jeanne is a woman of Caribbean descent, comfortable with aspects of her Caribbean identity (food, clothing, and other forms of identity expression that Canadian Multiculturalism views as "safe") but she is uncomfortable with religious notions from her familial homeland and the religious traditions of her grandmother, Gros-Jeanne.

> Ti-Jeanne herself wasn't so sure. There was the drumming that went on in the crematorium chapel, late into the night. The wails and screams that came from the worshippers. The clotted blood on the crematorium floor in the mornings, mixed with cornmeal. Obviously, other people than Mami still believed in "that duppy business." Ti-Jeanne didn't understand why Mami insisted on trying to teach her that old-time nonsense [36–37].

Yet, these traditions are a part of her, expressing themselves against her wishes through dreams, visions, visitations from Vodoun gods, or Loa, and her magical abilities. She fears these moments when her Vodoun heritage interacts with her body, imposing what she considers to be uncomfortable, unwanted, and foreign presences on her body. Her grandmother stresses to her the importance of expressing and understanding this part of herself in order to ensure that her magical abilities do not override her. Anthropologist Erika Bourguignon echoes this sentiment when she suggests that

> We cannot act without memory, nor can we understand ourselves unless we understand our own pasts.... Our capacity both to remember and to share our memories with others is distinctly human, since it involves the use of language and of other complex symbolic representations.... The tension between our contradictory desires to remember and to forget, that too is distinctly human [64–65].

Ti-Jeanne cuts herself off from her cultural memory when she resists the expression of her magical abilities, and yet the symbolic system surrounding those repressed memories resurface in the form of her confrontation with the Loa. The identity schism she has created means that the unexpressed parts of her are warring for expression, desiring manifestation, and the Vodoun gods are tired of being ignored. It is significant that Bourguignon states that "silence is looking away, unwillingness to confront reality. Ignoring, denying the past, we risk madness, yet the call to action of mythic history may have grave consequences" (84) since Ti-Jeanne, told stories about how her mother resisted her Vodoun gifts and became mad, fears that her own power will lead to her madness and loss of sanity. Her power and selfhood are divided between the traditions that still encompass her life and her desire for a perceived "normal" Canadian life, free of what she sees as complications of her past. She is diasporic and split between two homes, each laying claim on her and influencing her identity and each expressing themselves through her diasporic body.

She, like her Toronto, is in a conflicted place about identity, uncertain, and on shaky ground. Her body is a place of duality, simultaneously representing her cultural past and cultural present and complicating easy notions of "home." At times, she experiences a double vision, a doubling of her sight of the places around her, seeing both a modern Toronto roti shop, for example, and an overlay of a green tropical meadow with Caribbean plants in it and the figure of the Jab-Jab, a creature from Caribbean myth:

> She dragged the door open and ran into the roti shop. The warm, fragrant air on her face was a shock. How come she was outside, and why was it warm? ... She appeared to be in a green tropical meadow. A narrow dirt path ran through it, disappearing in the distance as the road curved gently downward. The scent of frangipani blossoms wafted by on the gentle breeze.... A figure came over the rise, leaping and dancing up the path. *Man-like, man-tall on long, wobbly legs look as if they hitch on backward. Red, red all over: Red eyes, red hair, nasty pointy red tail jooking up into the air. Face like a grinning African mask. Only is not a mask; the lips-them moving and it have real teeth behind them lips, attached to real gums....* The Jab-Jab turned its appalling grin of living wood in their direction [17–18, italics in original].

She enters an in-between space, complicating the Toronto landscape with her dual vision of two different homes. Toronto is a changing space, and Hopkinson uses this doubling of Toronto and changes in the Toronto landscape to resist singular notions of space or easy allocations of identity. Places cannot be read through a single lens or with a single idea of meaning, but, rather, are shifting places, acquiring new identities and shifting meaning as new people interact with their features. Toronto in *Brown Girl in The Ring* is a place in flux, shifting, changing, and representing different things for different people, reflecting the reality of "home" for people in diaspora. Her dual vision inscribes the place both with different physical features and also a different mythical reading, inserting elements from Caribbean socio-religious beliefs into the Canadian space.

As a Caribbean-Canadian author, Hopkinson is keenly aware of the ability of places to take on different meanings and of the complexity of being a person who has moved from one nationality to another. When she first arrived in Canada, she noted that she began reading Canadian speculative fiction as a means to understand her new place ("Final Thoughts" 380), and therefore she knows the potentiality that speculative fiction holds to give voice to notions of place and to capture the complexities of locality. She recognizes that landscapes are texts, texts that are read in certain ways that are shaped by the narratives told about them, and she uses the text of *Brown Girl in the Ring* to suggest an alternative reading of the Toronto environment, injecting it with aspects of Caribbean myth to illustrate the Canadian myths of single nationhood that are imprinted on the city.

In order to assert a form of belonging in a space that traditionally denies racialized and ethnic others, Hopkinson rewrites the Toronto landscape of the future. Denied a past in Canada because of the erasure of blackness from the Canadian landscape, she instead writes diversity into the Canadian future. Bourgouignon notes that "in spite of (often selective) memory work, we also have efforts at silencing, forgetting, repressing, and denial" and this is precisely the erasures that Hopkinson resists, focusing on re-asserting a Caribbean presence onto a Canadian landscape that often ignores it or relegates it to a space of Otherness. Rinaldo Walcott notes that blackness has been systemically erased from Canadian history, branded as a recent thing, which denies the long history of blackness in Canada (*Black Like Who*). Blackness has been systemically denied a place in Canada and cast as new, and unsettled—as something foreign. Images of nationality have cast Canada as a white space, a place with two founding peoples (French and English) and a European cultural context. Himani Bannerji suggests that constructions of nation in Canada "constantly [signify] the White population as 'Canadians' and immigrants of colour as 'others'" and that "the state and media jointly portray immigrants from non–White, poor countries as 'the problem'" (295). Casting non–White populations as "Other" has created a White Canadian exclusivity in the notion of national construction. Non-White Canadians are configured as threats, dangers to the Canadian imaginary and as virtual presences on the landscape that are *in* Canada, but not *of* Canada. Frances Henry refers to this process as "differential incorporation," whereby certain groups are "more incorporated or integrated into mainstream society than others" and have different access to economic, social, and cultural capital in a given society (11). She notes that this is the case for Caribbean people in Canadian society who have been differently incorporated than other groups whose ethnicity or race was configured as being more desirable in Canadian constructions of national belonging (ibid. 11–12).

Hopkinson uses the speculative fiction medium to take an iconic image of the Canadian cityscape, the CN Tower, and transform it through a Caribbean-inspired Vodoun ritual into the world tree and pillar of the

Vodoun temple. Toronto becomes temporarily a space where the Loa (Vodoun gods) walk the landscape. Ti-Jeanne climbs the CN Tower and calls upon the Vodoun gods, inviting them down through the pillar that the tower can be seen to represent (rather than hegemonic masculinist notions of progress) in order for them to transform Toronto into a ritual space, a space of Caribbean identity that is not limited to regular multicultural portrayals of "hyphenated" Canadians through their foods, clothing, and other consumables. This transformed Toronto becomes a mythic space, a ritual space, and a space that defies its image as an urban location of commerce and commercialism:

> She remembered her grandmother's words: *The centre pole is the bridge between the worlds*. Why had those words come to her right then? Ti-Jeanne thought of the centre pole of the palais, reaching up into the air and down toward the ground. She thought of the building she was in. The CN Tower. And she understood what it was: 1,815 feet of the tallest centre pole in the world. Her duppy body almost laughed a silent *kya-kya*, a jokey Jab-Jab laugh. For like the spirit tree that the centre pole symbolized, the CN Tower dug roots deep into the ground where the dead lived and pushed high into the heavens where the oldest ancestors lived. The tower was their ladder into this world. A Jap-Jab type of joke, oui [221, italics in original].

It is significant here that Ti-Jeanne's memory focuses on the nature of the center pole as a bridge between the worlds because it becomes a bridge not just between the urban and supernatural worlds, but also between the different mythic constructions of Canada, allowing for multiple readings. Hopkinson plays a "Jab-Jab type of joke" on the notion of urban space, illustrating that it is multifaceted, complex, and not easily limited to one interpretive framework. This mythical play destabilizes the notion of a singular interpretive framework, teasing out the inconsistencies. Walcott indicates that in his perspective

> The project for black Canadian artists and critics is to articulate a grammar of black that is located within Canada's various regions, both urban and rural. The invention of a grammar for black in Canada that is aware of historical narrative and plays with that narrative is crucial in the struggle against erasure. A grammar for black needs to occupy a number of different positions, social and cultural identities, and political utterances [149].

This is something that is characteristic of Hopkinson's work—her desire to play with notions of stability, to question narratives and insert presences that resist erasure.

The CN Tower becomes a point of intersection within the text allowing the dead to rise up from the ground and the Loa to descend from above. It becomes a place that has memory summoned into it, imbued into its structure, preventing the erasure of the past by inserting it into the structures of the present. It becomes a literal shaky ground where multiple readings intersect: "The chandelier was swaying. In fact, the whole structure of the CN Tower was shaking. An 1,800-foot needle, trembling" (222). Memory and the dead, the erased, and disempowered, become present and act on their landscape, resisting erasure or removal from the cultural and economic politics of their place. Characters who had been killed or had their willpower taken away now become actors in the world, arising from the grave, illustrating Hopkinson's assertion that memory and myth have power and can act in our world to facilitate change.

She transforms the Canadian landscape by disrupting notions of the set role that artifacts and architecture are constructed to represent and by suggesting another dialogic possibility. She reconfigures aspects of the traditional Canadian landscape into a traditional Caribbean landscape, marking the space as multivalent and subject to multiple interpretive frameworks. She illustrates that meanings are not static, but constantly shifting, being reinterpreted and reconfigured by new people with new ideologies and new systems of meaning. The CN Tower in Hopkinson's proposed future Toronto is not a static thing, but, rather, is transformative, changing with the populations that change in Canada. The landscape and its meanings are constantly altered as our social and political landscapes shift and things that are traditionally Canadian, like the CN Tower, are able to be reinterpreted as Canada's traditions and ideologies move to include a more diverse group of Canadians with more diverse readings of the features of heritage.

Hopkinson calls attention to the way that the future (where *Brown Girl in the Ring* is set) interacts with the present and past, and all are interwoven in a complex way. Walcott suggests that "the gaze or look is a return of sorts to the past and at the same time a gesture to the future-present" (148). The past has implications for the lens with which we view our world and our vision of the future shapes our present reality. By bringing attention to temporality and implications for national narratives around ethnicity, Hopkinson illustrates the complex way in which the past continues to arise and influence our present and the development of our future.

By calling up the dead in her ritual, Ti-Jeanne is ritually enacting the intersection of past and present. David Lowenthal notes that people of the Caribbean embrace their long-dead ancestors along with the present, and that remembered places often converge in our memory, collapsing disparate images into a few dominant ones (28). When people emulate (or in this case, literally invoke) the past, they make the past anew, creating entirely new ideological frameworks (33).

As Bannerji suggests, Caribbean identity in Toronto is mediated through racist notions of stereotypes that Canadian multiculturalism applies to communities viewed as "ethnic." Communities are commoditized according to current "fashion and current market tastes" (295). Multicultural identities are mediated through festivals like Toronto's Caribana, which essentialize cultures and cast them exclusively through performative elements like clothing, dance, music, and food (ibid: 296). They become consumable cultures to be feasted upon by a presumed White majority spectator.

> As long as "multiculturalism" only skims the surface of society, expressing itself as traditional ethics, such as arranged marriages, and ethnic food, clothes, songs, and dances (thus facilitating tourism), it is tolerated by the state and "Canadians" as non-threatening. But if the demands go a little deeper than that (e.g., teaching "other" religions or languages), they produce violent reaction, indicating a deep resentment toward funding "others" arts and cultures [ibid.].

By focusing on a structure associated with commercial tourism in Toronto, the CN Tower, Hopkinson brings attention to the way that commercialism has an overpowering influence over relationships and our understandings. When she destabilizes the commercial focus of the Tower and asserts a Caribbean religious presence, Hopkinson centers the notion of depth to understanding and the sense that understanding can be disrupted and changed with new ideological growth and the introduction of different perspectives.

By asserting a religious presence on the Canadian landscape through the imposed duality of Toronto as both an urban Canadian locale and as a Vodoun temple, Hopkinson brings out these uncertainties within the Canadian multicultural program. Even Ti-Jeanne herself, who evokes the Vodoun gods, fears the dual presence in her own body of her Torontonian identity and the simultaneous treatment of her by the Vodoun gods as a vessel, a figure that can be possessed and treated as a priestess. She is initially threatened by her own religio-cultural difference and views it with fear and suspicion despite the fact that she is willing to readily cook and eat the food of her grandmother and use creolized language. She rejects the religious heritage her grandmother represents because it threatens her ideas of normalcy, ideas that are hegemonically imposed through the "taming" of cultural difference in Canadian multicultural policies. Yet, Frances Henry, in her ethnographic study of the Caribbean diaspora in Toronto, notes that religion is an extremely important institution for diasporic Caribbean societies (148). She also suggests that the migration of Caribbean people to Canada changes their religious life, and religious activity declines in the second generation (ibid. 151). Henry's informant 'Margaret" described her experience with religion in

Canada: "Here you get lost in the milieu because nobody cares" (ibid. 152). Ti-Jeanne, as a third generation Caribbean Canadian, has experienced a life shaped by distance from her Vodoun religious roots.

When she encounters the presence of Vodoun spirits interacting with her, "Ti-Jeanne felt the gears slipping between the two worlds" (19). She feels a heightening of her instability of place and identity. This duality is figured in Ti-Jeanne's mind as a form of madness since she hears voices in her head and sees visions from her second sight. She seeks to ignore these visions, fearing them since she views them as something that drove her mother mad and could potentially drive her mad as well (ibid. 20).

Frances Henry's study revealed that Caribbean women tend to be more attracted to religion than Caribbean men and see it as a source of "solace and support. For many women whose lives are extraordinarily difficult, religion and reliance on God is their main source of emotional and spiritual support" (150), which may be why Ti-Jeanne's grandmother encourages her to engage more strongly in Vodoun. Indeed, Henry suggests, "The deep-seated religiosity of Caribbean women, especially working class women, means that religiosity is transmitted to their children" (ibid.). Vodoun religion becomes a means for Ti-Jeanne to not just connect with home, but also with her family lineage.

The doubling of place is not only religious, it is also cultural and extends to the vegetative level. Ti-Jeanne's grandmother tries to teach her healing remedies that combine Caribbean knowledge with a Canadian landscape:

"What you does put on a cut to heal it?"
Damn. One of Mami's spot tests. "Ah, aloe?"
"And if we can't get aloe no more? Tell me a Canadian plant."
Shit. It was the one with the name like a tropical plant, but it was something different. What, what? Oh, yes: "Plantain leaf" [36].

Her herbalism is doubled, representing both Caribbean landscapes and traditions and a simultaneous re-reading of the Canadian landscape to represent a resource for Caribbean notions of healing. The land can be re-purposed for new uses. Furthermore, knowledge about that land can be re-purposed as "Mami freely mixed her nursing training with her knowledge of herbal cures" (12), combining knowledge she acquired in Canadian schools with that discovered through her investigations in Caribbean herbalism. Knowledge itself is capable of transcending cultural barriers and mixing and combining into new forms that adapt to diverse situations. The fact that this combination of traditions is used to treat the body and bring it to health illustrates Hopkinson's interest in the implications of combining traditions both for the landscape as well as the bodies of individual participants—there are literal bodily implications for the combination of traditions and bodily health and understanding is culturally constituted and constructed.

Walcott suggests that black works of art and fiction "are not merely national products ... they occupy the space of the in-between, vacillating between national borders and diasporic desires, ambitions and disappointments. These works suggest the possibilities of the 'new,' but in many cases can not leave various kinds of 'old' behind" (xii). Hopkinson blends the "new" and "old" and blurs notions of national boundaries through her insertion of Vodoun and Caribbean mythology onto a Canadian landscape, a cultural landscape that is often uncomfortable with ideas of Vodoun and any non–Judeo-Christian-normative religious structure. She makes Canada a space *of* Vodoun and where Vodoun can occur and suggests that this combined space and combined use of space has implications for the healthy bodies of those contained within national boundaries.

It is significant that Vodoun serves as the scaffolding for constructing a dualistic vision of Canada and Canadian landscapes. As Bourguignon suggests, "In Haiti mythic history is told mostly through ritual practice and the explanations associated with it" (79). Vodoun itself is a blend of traditions, made from a combination of African rituals within a Catholic colonial structure. Vodoun is particularly apt for exploring dual visions and the intersections of multiplicities of place because it represents an intersection of African-derived beliefs and Roman Catholicism. It is a religious system that is already configured in the African diaspora. As Frances Henry notes, "The so-called 'voodoo' of Haiti is the best known of these, but African-derived syncretic religions are to be found in almost every country in which Roman Catholicism was the colonizing European religion" (148–9). It is a religion of re-inscriptions, using icons from the Catholic religion of the previous slave owners in Haiti to express figures of a religion that incorporated aspects of a previous African religious structure, including elements of spirit possession, direct appeals to multiple gods, and requests to gods or Loa through the offering of rum. Vodoun participants often use images of Catholic saints as representations of their own gods, substituting Erzule, the goddess of love, for Mary, using images of St. Patrick to represent Damballah, the snake god, etc. It is a religion that itself represents the reinterpretation and re-ascription of meaning onto symbols of oppression or exclusion. Vodoun in Haiti was also used as a means of resistance, attached to movements like the Maroons, who sought to create a free Haiti by resisting colonial rule and empowering slaves to escape. Vodoun represents a combination of narratives, an incorporation of different visions of the past within the present, and the power to re-inscribe symbols for an empowering objective.

Spirit possession, in which the Vodoun Loa are invited into the body of a practitioner, is a common aspect of Vodoun (Henry 149), highlighting the multiplicity of the individual's experience.[1] By being possessed involuntarily, Ti- Jeanne is literally being possessed by a past home, overcome by memory, and her body is subsumed by her spiritual roots. This possession of Ti-Jeanne's body mirrors that of the city itself when the Loa descend down the CN Tower and thereby create a bridge between Ti-Jeanne's two homes—Toronto and the Caribbean.

Vodoun can serve as a method for re-inscribing history and re-asserting a historical presence of blackness. This is particularly significant in Canada, where, as Walcott (*Black Like Who*) notes, blackness is systemically erased and the black historical presence is denied. Canadians, seeking to construct the Canadian nation as a just society, ignore the Canadian history of slavery (for example, when portraying Canada as the open end of the underground railroad rather than accurately portraying the railroad as going both ways and the act of border-crossing as being the feature causing freedom) as well as ignoring the historical oppression of black people in Canada. Hopkinson seems to be using Vodoun to assert a historical presence of blackness in Canada and assert a longevity of black experience, as well as using it as a symbol for the ability of people to re-inscribe and reinterpret symbols. It serves as a discourse for discussing a multiplicity of historic narratives. Vodoun becomes a space where place is inscribed and where a claim to the landscape is made.

Walcott identifies reinterpretation, reinscription, reimaginings, and Creolisation or hybridization of cultures representative of many diasporic black texts in Canada, as part of the "grammar of blackness in Canada" (*Black Like Who*). He argues that "black diasporic cultures are most engaging and critically affirmative when the practices of (re)invention are highlighted and displayed in complex fashion" (xii). There is no easy cultural borrowing or consistent reinscription of meaning, but rather a complicated structure of asserting new meanings and shifting meanings while combining diverse symbolisms. It is a process that can be simultaneously nostalgic and critical of the past and present. Hopkinson displays this diasporic critical analysis through the medium of science fiction, complicating the present by introducing a different, though still similar and possible future in which Toronto has become a ghetto. Canadian science fiction itself is a genre of complexity that questions literary media and invites the audience to not simply read the text, but question it, engage with it, and often end up with further questions than when the text began. It is not a text of easy answers, but rather of edgy spaces that allow for multiple readings and multiple engagements. Hopkinson further complicates the genre by using the "apocalyptic future" trope of science fiction while mixing it with the magical realist trope of fantasy. She combines folklore, which is often inscribed as being something of and from the past, with an urban landscape of the future and Toronto's landscape becomes an interstitial space between the modernity of science fiction and the fantastic mythical power of a formative mythology. Hopkinson questions the notion of reality, adding complexities to the way we view the world, investing her characters with visions, the ability to become invisible, and the capacity to interact with spirits through Vodoun magic and rituals. She uses the genre of the fantastic to acknowledge the fiction of her text, but simultaneously reacts against a Canadian political text written onto the black Canadian body that is equally fictitious—portraying black Canadians as new, as threats, and as not belonging. By setting her text in an urban landscape and using realistic settings and realistic possibilities which blur the boundaries between Canadian reality and the fictional world, she calls on her readers to question the messages that they receive daily from pop culture and the media which portray blackness as threatening.

Walcott suggests that "In a Canadian context, writing blackness is a scary scenario: we are an absented presence always under erasure" (xiii). The black Canadian presence in Hopkinson's novel is literally cut off from the rest of Canadian society when barriers are erected around the city of Toronto and it is declared an unsafe, threatening space (modeling the image of blackness as dangerous), and this segregation and ghettoization of blackness absents blackness from the Canadian society of the future created by Hopkinson, but simultaneously makes it hypervisible by, in fact, noting the area as a ghetto and creating visible walls that would hide it but simultaneously make it conspicuous as an area that *is* walled. Like Walcott's description of black Canadians as simultaneously invisible and hypervisible, systemically erased and ignored while their bodies become fixed in the gaze of spectatorship (*Black Like Who*), Hopkinson's Toronto is a racialized space that is cut off but simultaneously noticeable.

Hopkinson plays with ideas of invisibility of difference by having her characters literally become invisible through Caribbean magic. Ti-Jeanne and her partner try to escape from Toronto, hiding their presence in order to get past border security by using a technique and practice from their Caribbean homeland. She seems to be suggesting in her narrative that the only place that Canadian racial geographies can be transformed is in a science-fictional reality.

The strongest assertion of Caribbean identity on a Canadian landscape occurs when Ti-Jeanne uses Vodoun magic to call down the Loa, the gods of Vodoun, through the CN Tower, a fixture and figure of Canadian modernity in order to assert the idea that places can have multiple meanings. She calls the Loa through the tower as a Vodoun priestess would call the Loa through the pillar of the Vodoun temple, turning the CN Tower into this pillar symbolically, and, by extension, all of Toronto into a larger Vodoun temple, a place where magic can happen and Vodoun spirits can roam and influence and change the world around them. She asserts a Caribbean identity on Toronto, inscribing it with diversity and the notion that place can be read through the experiences of all members who call it home, rather than through an exclusive lens that privileges one group's vision and ideology. She breaks down hegemonic visions of place by looking at places as hybridized, dualistic, multiplistic, and conflicted. Places are not easily interpreted by one paradigm, but under constant shifts and fluxes, changing in meaning as various people see and experience them.

There is no ease of identity, no simple ascriptions of ethnicity as Canadian multiculturalism would like to pretend. People are complex and places are complex and understood through multiple, diverse, intersecting lenses.

Literature has the ability to create diverse spaces even when it seems as though it is impossible to transform the physical landscape. Speculative fiction can propose an alternative reading to the landscape and allow a space for diversity. For New Canadians, literature and the arts can become a space where the Canadian landscape can be transformed into an inclusive space that challenges dominant narratives of belonging and suggests an alternative reading of the world and its spaces. The meaning of objects can shift in the consciousness of diasporic people as they assert their own identities and prevent their erasure from the Canadian landscape. Hopkinson uses literature as a space for the assertion of the idea of *home* for people in diaspora.

Notes

1. I want to thank Siobhan Carroll for a great discussion at the *International Conference of the Fantastic in the Arts* following her paper "Transforming Urban Space and Female Bodies in Nalo Hopkinson's *The Chaos*" about the role of the body in Nalo Hopkinson's work, which drew my attention to the way the body interacted with space in *Brown Girl in the Ring*.

Works Cited

Bannerji, Himani. "Geography Lessons: On Being an Insider/Outsider to the Canadian Nation." *Unhomely States: Theorizing English-Canadian Postcolonialism.* Ed. Cynthia Sugars. Peterborough: Broadview, 2004. Print.

Bourguignon, Erika. "Memory in an Amnesiac World: Holocaust, Exile, and the Return of the Suppressed." *Anthropological Quarterly* 78.1 (2005): 63–88. Web.

Henry, Frances. *The Caribbean Diaspora in Toronto: Learning to Live With Racism.* Toronto: University of Toronto Press, 1994. Print.

Hopkinson, Nalo. "Final Thoughts" *Tesseracts Nine: New Canadian Speculative Fiction*. Ed. Hopkinson and Geoff Ryman. Calgary: Edge, 2005. 379–81. Print.

———. *Brown Girl in the Ring*. New York: Grand Central, 1998. Print.

Kamboureli, Smaro. *Scandalous Bodies: Diasporic Literature in English Canada*. Waterloo: Wilfred Laurier University Press, 2009. Print.

Lowenthal, David. "Past Time, Present Place: Landscape and Memory" *Geographic Review* 65.1 (1975): 1–36. Web.

Walcott, Rinaldo. *Black Like Who? Writing Black Canada*. Toronto: Insomniac, 1997. Print.

"God's Country," Evil's Playground: Susie Moloney, Michael Rowe, Brian Horeck and the Northern Ontario Gothic

Cat Ashton

ACCSFF '13

Despite the amount of research that has been done on the Canadian Gothic, and even the Ontario Gothic, relatively little critical attention has been paid to the Gothic possibilities of Northern Ontario. This paper will explore the Northern Ontario Gothic through four novels: Susie Moloney's *Bastion Falls*, Brian Horeck's *Minnow Trap* and *Frozen Beneath*, and Michael Rowe's *Enter, Night*. I will show that central to Northern Ontario Gothic is the idea of who belongs to the north and what that means, and that each author is saying something very different when they call the north "God's country."

The Gothic

Louis Gross defines Gothic fiction as "literature where fear is the motivating and sustaining emotion" (Gross 1), while Kim Michasiw calls it "a mode of fantasy that facilitates the molding of anxiety" (Michasiw 237). Fred Botting identifies excess and transgression as two of the markers of the Gothic

(Botting 89), and Joseph Crawford writes about the Victorian Gothic, "Gothic was a network of tropes which, collectively, served to either literally or metaphorically demonise its subject matter, whether that subject was a person, a house, a social group, or an entire civilisation, by describing it as though it was an object of numinous dread" (Crawford vii). Cynthia Sugars and Gerry Turcotte add:

> The Gothic, as a mode, is preoccupied with the fringes, the unspoken, the peripheral, and the cast aside. It is populated with monsters and outcasts, villains and victims, specters and the living dead. The Gothic is often located in a realm of unknown dangers and negotiates both internal and external disquiet. It is a literature of excess and imagination, but one that is used as well to reassure and compartmentalize unreason. It is therefore a literature that both enacts and thematizes ambivalence [Sugars and Turcotte xv].

It is challenging to arrive at a satisfactory definition for a genre term that has been applied to works as disparate as Ridley Scott's science fiction film *Alien* (1979) and the realistic novels of Alice Munro, but generally, Gothic fiction deals with anxiety about identity, about the fragility of stability, and about the present's uneasy relationship with the past. The disruption of stability, identity, and the past have the potential to make the Gothic into the uncanny shadow of the national narrative, and Gothic fiction very easily becomes a regional phenomenon.

The Gothic translated very easily to North American soil, with its sublime landscapes and its suppressed foundation of genocide. According to Cynthia Sugars, Gerry Turcotte, and Justin Edwards, among many others, the Canadian version of the Gothic derives from the land's colonial past. Sugars and Turcotte write:

> Historically, Canadian writers have used gothic tropes to articulate their sense of the contingency of their presence in Canada. Initially, it is fair to say, the Gothic emerged as a way of responding to the unfamiliar by demonizing and even fetishizing the "unknown"—be it human or landscape. Often this monstrous presence was figured as an Indigenous one—a danger lying just beyond the garrison but not sufficiently removed. Over time, Canadian writers began to appropriate this force, to bend it to a national purpose, and to map the parameters of an identity that might embrace what was resonantly local so that the Gothic became a way to insist on, rather than deny, a colonial history. In effect, the gothic mode was used to articulate a suitably "haunted" version of Canadian identity, one that lent the Canadian locale a "feel" of authenticity because it had been rendered "(un)homely" (that is, both familiar and unfamiliar at the same time) [Sugars and Turcotte xvii].

Edwards adds, in *Gothic Canada: Reading the Spectre of a National Literature*:

> The imagined sense of self—as white, European and a product of the "two founding nations"—must be held responsible for, among other things, the genocide of Natives in the wake of European settlement, the residential schools for the children of First Nations and the horrors of Japanese internment during World War II. The effects of marginalization, segregation, ostracization and oppression haunt Canada's history with violent acts that refuse to be hidden. The nation's unjust acts force us to view the country as a fragile entity that is pieced together out of the ideological abominations of a disturbing past.... But just as a reading of history exposes a monstrous side to Canada, the nation itself has tried to construe its others as threatening, and to imbue those who challenge the imagined stability of the nation, the dominance of Euro-Canadianness, with gothic discourses.... Within this process, disparity can be socially constructed as "abnormal" or "unnatural" and lines drawn to separate the "natural" from the "grotesque." Power, we must remember, is always about the ability to include and exclude, to determine who inhabits the centre and who is forced to live on the periphery [Edwards 110–111].

This tension between center and periphery, southerner and local, is one of the central tensions in Northern Ontario Gothic, and two of the three authors featured here wrestle with the connection between membership in the center and the crimes of colonialism.

With 87 percent of Ontario's land mass, but only 6 percent of Ontario's population, Northern Ontario has higher unemployment rates than the south, lower life expectancy, and higher substance abuse rates (OLHIN Strategic Plan 13). Its population is 85.6 percent white, and 12.8 percent Aboriginal. It is a marginalized, economically depressed area whose citizens often resent the more southerly, better serviced, wealthier center. Its residents, like those of the American South, are often stereotyped as being uneducated, uncultured, and ill-spoken drunks. However, where American Southern Gothic is an established literary tradition, Northern Ontario Gothic is relatively new.

Bastion Falls

Susie Moloney's *Bastion Falls* was published in 1995. In it, during a freakish September blizzard, the Northern Ontario town of Bastion Falls is attacked by vague dark shapes that lure victims by posing as deceased loved ones, and then suck out their lives. Why they have chosen this moment to attack is never revealed, but their presence is centered on the old garrison for which the town is named, which "served as a remote outpost, supposedly as a guard station, but was really the place to send those bad seeds that broke the laws of the settlement while serving the country. Murderers, thieves, rapists and drunkards served in Bastion, a punishment fitting most any military crime" (Moloney 4). Many of these men have descendants living in Bastion Falls, evoking the Gothic motif of tainted families. The horrors are banished when young Shandy Johnson sneaks out at night to burn the fort down.

The book opens with a description of the town, small and remote—613 residents (2), and northerly enough to enjoy a ten-month winter. Moloney says, "It is beautiful country, and although all over the world places with their own share of beauty claim the title, the people around Bastion are quite sure that it is God's country" (1–2). But this is what Moloney says about the God of Bastion Falls:

> Everyone stays in bed on Sundays. Babies are baptized at home, if at all. There is, however, a spirituality in the town. A deep belief in and fear of God. God makes gardens grow, brings rain for five days in a row, picks a good fishing spot and gives all your babies measles at once when you have a cold. God also makes you sorry when you slap your wife or shake your child; God is going to punish you for doing that bad thing. Once in awhile, when you shoot your neighbor, or rape a town girl, God, you protest in the traveling court, sent you voices. God is omnipresent in Bastion, as much part of the town as Natty Spencer, the town's most obvious drunk. God might be scorned, hated, feared, worshipped, carried like a luck charm or dead, but he is a force, and his principles, if ignored, are still present, just like Natty [4].

This God is remote and ambivalent, just as capable of stirring residents to crime as to penance, and as much a part of the fabric of the town as its criminal history. The people feel very strongly about at least paying lip service.

Although its white citizens are inheritors of the crimes of their ancestors at the garrison, in the service of European culture, Bastion Falls is clearly on the periphery of Canadian society:

> The thing was, Bastion was way up, the station was way down, and Joe suspected they didn't pay too much attention to Bastion even though he called them whenever something interesting happened. Joe suspected that they took most of their news from Springhill, up where the ski hill was. A bigger market. Everything was market these days, even the CBC [61].

However, while the revenants from the garrison threaten all white citizens equally, in terms of narration there is a clear divide between those who were born to the town and those who come from outside. Shandy Wilson, the psychic teenager, and her mother Lydia; store manager Don Clanstar and his unfaithful wife Emma; Allen "Hickory" Tinsdale, the gay and lonely phys. ed. coach; and school principal Candace Bergen have all sought out Bastion Falls as a haven from the outside world, and their points of view are narrated sympathetically. Characters *originally* from Bastion Falls, however, such as Natty Spencer, Chester Hawkins, Hardly Knowles, Lawrence Ross, and Mrs. Thurston—whose conviction that Candace is just a city slicker unused to the snow actually delays emergency procedures (73–74)—are written from a distance, and often given a degree of comic grotesqueness. For example, this is Natty Spencer:

> Oh, those zombies used to scare Natty. If she'd been a better-educated woman, like a university-educated Ms. Bergen, then she might have made the connection between the zombies who lived for only one thing maybe and the alcoholic monkey on her own back, but thankfully she wasn't. She could live in a healthy, connection-less world where things were exactly as they seemed. But when that last guy, Natty didn't know his name but had seen him around, came tumbling in the front door, he'd looked to Natty exactly like one of those zombies from the Park Theatre [140–141].

The locals are caricatures, and Moloney's tone, when dealing with them, is wry and detached. The exception is Marilyn Barefoot, a First Nations woman who also receives sympathetic narration. (Mall manager and Marilyn's brother Joe Nashkawa, and Johnny Nahgauwah, the mayor, are other First Nations people who are treated more sympathetically than the other townspeople, but both are minor characters.) Marilyn is one of the first caught outside in the freak storm, yet somehow survives the attack of the black shapes once, and returns outside later to help Shandy burn down the fort (250). One way to read this is that Marilyn, as an Indigenous person, cannot be culpable for the atrocities committed at the fort, does not benefit from the colonial system of which the fort was a part, and therefore is not punished. She is a Northerner, but she is the only major character in the novel for whom the north is not a space haunted by ancestral crimes.

Moloney's portrait of the white citizens of Bastion Falls carries with it more than a hint of elitism, but she partakes of the longstanding Gothic tradition of making the inhabitants of a haunted locale themselves grotesque. Who, after all, would call a haunted place home but the faintly monstrous, the deliberately obtuse, or those fleeing a tragic past? But as a northerner herself—if not a born Northern Ontarian—Moloney is a part of the demographic that she mocks. In this case, the demonization of which Crawford speaks is at least partly playful, fond, and self-deprecating. Moreover, the failure of existing government structures to serve Bastion Falls properly is depicted not as a proper and just result of the town's grotesqueness, but rather a cause of it, a shirking of responsibility that results in tragedy.

Minnow Trap and Frozen Beneath

Brian Horeck is another author who identifies as part of the north, but his two self-published novels, *Minnow Trap* (2005) and *Frozen Beneath*

(2008) show a different picture of who is in the center, who is on the periphery, and who is grotesque, monstrous, or laughable. Both books are set in or around Blind River, where Horeck is based.

Minnow Trap tells the story of a group of well-to-do white couples who live in lakefront homes—Steve and Mary, their daughter Sarah and her boyfriend Tom, Bob and Carol, Mike and Janis, and the widowed Brenda. Steve's minnow trap captures a strange, aggressive, unidentifiable crustacean, the first wave of a water-based alien invasion. The couples, together with Russian soldier Nick, use a combination of military firepower and leisure-oriented gadgetry to repel the threat. The book is set in the area around Birch Lake, a real lake north of the towns of Webbwood and Massey. Horeck tells the reader, "The area has a high summer population of cottagers who travel from as far away as Chicago and Detroit to, as they say, get a taste of God's country" (Horeck, *Minnow Trap* 10). Later, Nick, faced with a "beautiful peaceful lake" (143), tells Mary, "'Now I can see why they call this God's country'" (ibid.). The book's few descriptive passages are devoted to extolling the virtues of the landscape.

Frozen Beneath is set closer to Blind River, on Lake Matinenda, and this too is "God's country" (74). Lake Matinenda is the landing site of an alien spacecraft, which has become frozen beneath the ice. Its distress calls are disruptive and dangerous (131, 136). Sharklike creatures emerge from beneath the ice, damaging gear and killing a young man (276–79). Two military men, John and Kevin, use their vacation time to investigate, and find themselves siding with the locals against NORAD and Homeland Security, who are about to drop a nuclear device on the spaceship (389). The men and their civilian friends hatch a plan to use explosives, a snowmobile, and a fish-finding camera to lure the spacecraft to open water (383–84), where it is able to escape before the nuclear weapon is dropped.

In *Minnow Trap* and *Frozen Beneath*, legitimate northerners are straight, white, upper middle-class, Anglo-Saxon Christian men and their wives (note: *not* men and women). Their northernness is both the reward of correct life choices, and itself a virtue, as *Minnow Trap* demonstrates with this exchange between Tom and Sarah:

> "You have super parents, Sarah. And your dad is really cool. Lots of middle-aged men would love to have his lifestyle—living on a lake in a remote cottage like this. And such privacy with no neighbors on either side. This sure makes for great skinny-dipping! And it sure beats living in the city with all that noise, hustle, and bustle."
>
> "It took them years of planning and work to set this stage. I guess it all boils down to choices and sacrifices we have to make in life. Like you and I going to university" [Horeck, *Minnow Trap* 75].

This idea of northernness as the condition of hard-working white males and their wives is reinforced through casual racism, sexism, and the mocking of characters who fall outside of the norm. Brenda, a Canadian-born woman of Ukrainian descent, is referred to as "our perogie princess" (144). In *Frozen Beneath*, JP, a French-Canadian, is depicted as a buffoon, with his accent played for comedy. His friend Greg Kawalsky is made fun of for being of Polish descent. In *Minnow Trap* even Nick, the Russian soldier who is effusively praised for his courage, knowledge, and good looks, makes a good first impression only "despite the accent" (132).

If foreignness, then, is a quality that is penalized, it is also instructive to look at what qualities are valued. Among the most prized are the ability to take a joke at one's own expense (so that those who fall outside of the white Anglo-Saxon male paradigm are admitted to the center as long as they are willing to endure merciless teasing), and the ability to enjoy the finer things in life. Characters spend pages praising each other for their fine food and drink, their cottages and boats and snowmobiles, and particularly their technological gadgets. The plot of *Frozen Beneath* hinges on a character's fishfinder, while *Minnow Trap* depends similarly on a telescope with a digital recorder and night vision, and a four-wheeler with GPS. Technology—particularly technology adapted to traditionally male leisure activities—occupies a central role in Horeck's work, and it is possible to read both of his novels as both a celebration of, and justification for, consumption, with the caveat that it is only permissible when certain kinds of humans do it.

Both books express admiration for the military—not as a function of nationalism, but as an institution itself, as Canadian, Russian, and American military men are celebrated equally. Characters in Horeck's books are very secure in their mastery of power structures. Even when they bend rules or break laws, they clearly have right on their side. Characters use recreational vehicles while drunk and drop copious hints about hunting and fishing illegally. In *Frozen Beneath*, Kevin assaults a fellow bar-goer for sexually harassing a waitress (124–27). When the victim turns up dead (sliced in half by the alien spacecraft), the Lodge owner tells Kevin that the police will not investigate him because the man had assaulted two of their number (211). Kevin is not a local, but he is the right kind of person, so in the eyes of the police he can get away with murder. Enforcers of the rules—such as John, the conservation officer in *Minnow Trap* who tickets Nick for fishing without a license (242–44)—are stuffy, self-important bureaucrats. The book takes considerable joy in seeing him put in his place with a single phone call to the powerful (245).

This illuminates some of what Horeck means when he uses the phrase

"God's country" to describe the setting of his novels. Horeck means it quite literally. His straight, white, upper-middle-class characters enjoy what they insist is an Earthly paradise. For all their swearing, lasciviousness, and perpetual drunkenness, the protagonists of *Minnow Trap* say an explicitly Christian grace before meals, and share a group prayer before defeating the aliens. They have nothing to fear from authority, because they are so closely aligned with the terrestrial and celestial forces of good.

Where in Moloney's work—as in Rowe's, as we will see—the source of horror lies in the community's past, in Horeck's work, where the community is celebrated and its power structures secure and just, the Gothic threat is displaced onto the radically external, with aliens from outer space invading the idyllic north. However, there are indications that the horror is preinscribed on the landscape. In *Minnow Trap*, one of the characters claims to have never liked the pond where the alien creatures have only recently been planted, while in *Frozen Beneath*, the Graveyard Narrows is a patch of ice that claims the lives of snowmobilers long before any alien threat appears.

Colonial guilt bubbles up in other places. Characters in *Minnow Trap* initially mistake the alien landing site for a First Nations ceremonial ground "from hundreds of years ago" (35). This prompts them to cover it up as quickly as possible. There are in fact several Ojibway communities in the area, but Horeck dismisses First Nations people as long-disappeared relics of a distant past, even as his characters admit that they have a right to the land:

> "So why didn't you guys want anyone to see what you thought at the time to be Indian drawings in the rock, anyway?" asked Brenda.
> "Because if it was discovered by some archaeologist, we would have our hunting area closed off in a heartbeat," said Steve. "The First Nations might claim it as a place of worship, or something like that. Not that I would blame them, after all, they were here first." [215]

If the problem of colonialism is addressed here, however imperfectly, with a grudging admission of wrongdoing, it is treated more obliquely elsewhere. There is friction between Nick, the Russian soldier, and Brenda, who is of Ukrainian descent, over past Soviet expansion, although Horeck is very clear about where his sympathies lie in the following exchange, after Brenda has said that she is not from Ukraine, and Nick corrects her to "Russian Federation":

> [Nick] felt some kind of resentment from [Brenda]. And refused to tip toe around her, including any prejudices she may have against Russians. "I am sorry I had to pick Russia for my place of birth, if that helps any." His point got through to Brenda, as she sat on what he had said for a few seconds and realized how much of a poor sport she must seem to be in his eyes.

"I'm so sorry. Forgive me Nick. You, like me, weren't there during those hard times. I guess if I wanted to hold grudges from histories past, then I shouldn't have bought this Honda outboard motor for my boat because the Japanese were once our enemy." [171–172]

Brenda hasn't objected to Nick's place of birth; she has objected to his verbal erasure of the Ukraine, especially to correct her understanding of her own heritage, and yet she is the one at fault. If the invasion is over, in other words, it is better to let bygones be bygones; airing any sort of grievance after the fact, even in response to objectionable statements, is being "a poor sport." Of course, the characters are themselves battling alien colonists keen on exploiting the area for its water resources.

Cynthia Sugars and Gerry Turcotte write, of Canadian Gothic fiction:

> Instances of [the uncanny] include scenes where the distinction between past and present, real and spectral, civilized and primitive, is tenuous and disjunctive. When the uncanny is combined with the Gothic, elements of the supernatural, the monstrous, or the paranormal are foregrounded. When these are conjoined with the postcolonial, it takes a variety of possible tacks: fears of territorial illegitimacy, anxiety about forgotten or occluded histories, resentment towards flawed or complicit ancestors, assertions of Aboriginal priority, explorations of hybrid cultural forms, and interrogations of national belonging and citizenship" [Sugars and Turcotte ix].

Horeck's work can hardly be called postcolonial, but even his books wrestle with many of the above issues, however clumsily. As part of both a privileged class and a marginalized minority, Horeck moves back and forth on the question of who belongs to the land and how, although he demonstrates no awareness that he is doing so.

Additionally, Horeck's work serves as a combined manifesto and snapshot of a certain kind of Northern Ontarian life, and arguably a faithful representation of how many affluent, white Northern Ontarians see themselves: as underestimated and dismissed by urban centers in the south, and beset by foreign threats. Horeck's protagonists enjoy the best of Northern Ontario, and their wealth protects them from the worst; if they are indeed at the margins, it is because they choose to remain apart from the fast-paced, morally bankrupt south, but in their own communities they are squarely at the center, rather than the periphery.

Enter, Night

Michael Rowe's *Enter, Night* is the most recent entry, published in 2011. Rowe is the only author here who does not identify as being from or living in the North; he was born in Ottawa and lives in Toronto now, having also lived in Beirut, Havana, Geneva, and Paris.

Enter, Night takes place in the mining town of Parr's Landing, somewhere in the vicinity of Thunder Bay, in the early 1970s. A vampire who came to the area in the early seventeenth century, posing as a Jesuit priest, is entombed in a nearby cave system recently disturbed by archaeologists. The book begins with the return of five people to the town: Richard Weal, the erstwhile archaeology student who frees the vampire; Dr. Billy Lightning, residential school survivor and the son of the head archaeologist, who attempts to warn the townspeople; and Jeremy Parr, his sister-in-law Christina, and her daughter Morgan, who return to the Parr family mansion and Jeremy's villainous mother after the death of Christina's husband. Billy, Jeremy, Christina, Morgan, and Morgan's friend Finn must fight off a town suddenly full of vampires. Although the original vampire has been buried under the ground for centuries, the impression he gives his not so much one of being repressed as of being planted, to eventually sprout monstrous fruit. Parr's Landing does not need the supernatural to be unremittingly bleak. Even before the vampire surfaces, Jeremy Parr asks his sister-in-law Christina, "Have you noticed that love doesn't flourish in this town?" (Rowe 111) Elsewhere, he passes a street described in language that is the quintessence of Northern Ontario Gothic:

> He found he'd forgotten that even towns like Parr's Landing had streets like this one—rows of narrow, rectangular prewar shotgun houses with peeling paint and small chain-link fenced front yards where nothing beautiful ever grew, with fenced back yards that housed dogs who were never allowed to experience the warmth of the indoors. Houses that were smaller and meaner than even the other small, mean houses in a town full of them....
>
> To Jeremy, even the light seemed dirtier on Martina Street. It was as though the generations of men and women who'd offered their youth, their hopes, their dreams—indeed, the entirety of their lives—to the Parr family gold mines as a sort of terrible, ultimate rent had only their own despair left to plant in the patchy, ugly side gardens between the houses. If that was the case, it was a crop that thrived both in the heyday of his family's violent use of the land and its people and later, when the mines closed, throwing a town full of miners on the mercy of government welfare, and their own hardscrabble ability to survive. His own family's fortune had been long ago secure, of course, which had allowed his mother to continue to live like royalty, albeit lonely royalty, in her house on the hill on the other side of Bradley Lake [243–244].

The ugliness of the town notwithstanding, the landscape is beautiful:

> On either side of the car, the highway rose and fell, bracketed here and there by soaring granite cliffs of rose and grey stone. Forests of maple and birch planed off from the highway into the distant badlands like great wings of red and gold.

> Christina saw the edges of algae-encrusted swamps laced with dead logs and slippery rock, and deep pine everywhere. As they approached the town of Wawa, the maple and birch gave way to a mélange of birch and various other deciduous trees, as well as conifers, adding the blessed rigour of dark green to a palette from which Christina felt nearly drunk with colour [48].

Rowe juxtaposes the traditional ingredients of the sublime, cliffs and forests, with death, decay, and viscosity. Likewise, the phrase that Horeck uses earnestly and Moloney uses with wry detachment is laden with irony and menace when Rowe has Jeremy Parr use it, saying, "If I were home I'd be dancing with handsome men at the Parkside or the St. Charles right now, with my shirt off and a bottle of poppers in my nose. Ah, memories. They're all we'll have to sustain us out here in God's country" (59).

For those who exist on the margins in Rowe's north, God's country combines sublime beauty with undertones of corruption. Parr's Landing is controlled by Jeremy's mother Adeline, a Canadian industrial variation on the evil aristocrat. She is aloof from the community, so her behavior is not motivated by community pressure, but rather by a warped sense of *noblesse oblige*, the need to be better than everyone else in town. When she becomes a vampire, she remains virtually unchanged. Underneath the industrial exploitation is a deeper irony: the Jesuit missionaries who settled the area to well and truly make it God's country brought with them plague, genocide, residential schools, and a stowaway vampire.

That said, Christian religious symbols work against this vampire, and Jeremy, a gay man, is saved once by his St. Christopher medal. This invokes the trope, present in Gothic fiction but held over from the medieval romance, of higher powers protecting characters who are persecuted and despised by earthly hierarchies, implicitly criticizing those hierarchies. The North might be God's country, but Jeremy, Christine, and Billy occupy the moral high ground.

In the previous books, it has been instructive to examine the dynamic between locals and outsiders. *Enter, Night* does not involve outsiders—only characters who have left the north and come back. Even then, while Jeremy, Christine, Morgan, and Billy are sympathetic characters, they are not morally distinct from the other townspeople. Parr's Landing is, for the most part, populated by nice, normal, largely benevolent people, like Morgan's friend Finn and his parents, who are products of the attitudes of the time. Simply being from, or living in, Parr's Landing is no crime. However, characters who participate in the power structures of the town tend to become monstrous: Jeremy's old lover Elliott McKittrick first becomes a bigoted bully as a police officer (91–92) and then is one of the first to become a vampire; Adeline Parr is repeatedly referred to as an ogress (46, 57) before she is turned; and of course, the Jesuit missionaries had both their colonial mission and their murderous stowaway. To be an ordinary citizen of Parr's Landing is not to be living the good life, or comically grotesque; it is to be a victim. Exploitation is so deeply woven into the fabric of the town that the hockey team is called the Parr's Landing Predators (91).

Rowe draws explicit links between colonialism, the Parr family's exploitation of the land and people, and the vampire. Before he is aware of the vampire, Jeremy says to himself

> This is my inheritance.... This is my legacy. This land and the people my family has been feeding on for over a hundred years. Whatever seed was planted in those hills and under that earth, it's been held for me in trust all these years. It's been waiting for me to claim it. Or for its chance to claim me [244].

Elsewhere, he thinks

> I come from a family of ghouls. We've been feeding on the town for more than a century, in the same way the people who came from the old world to claim this corner of the new world fed on the people who lived here before us. My mother has fed on her own children. The "eternal return" in Parr's Landing isn't renewal, it's damnation [256].

Rowe uses Gothic tropes—the evil town, the tainted family, the resurgence of a dark past to claim the innocent—to critique the economic structure that defines many Northern Ontario communities. Practically speaking, this structure has its roots in Southern Ontario, but the Parr family is a handy personification, as well as a placeholder while the vampire sleeps.

Christina, Jeremy, and Billy have been so wounded by Parr's Landing that they have fled, and their ambivalence about coming back to Parr's Landing is characteristic of the Gothic blurring of boundaries and concern about horrific origins, but also very true to life. Poverty, child abuse, alcoholism, racism, homophobia, the exploitation of workers, and the systematic oppression of First Nations People are more than just atmosphere; they are real problems that face the north. In defiance of the Freudian uncanny, Rowe's book demonstrates that what or who gets pushed to the periphery does not always return in monstrous form; Jeremy, Christina, and Billy return to Parr's landing strengthened against the very forces that tried to identify them as monsters. Where the dominant culture itself is defined by predation and xenophobia, the return of the repressed can be liberating.

Conclusions

All four books negotiate what it means to be a member of the community, and by extension the north. Although "God's country" refers in every case to the extreme beauty of the land, the undertones change from book to book, and what it means to belong to God's country is likewise different in each case. This is closely linked to how each author regards the power structures in place in each community. For Horeck, whose straight, white, affluent male characters never doubt the virtue of their actions, the appropriateness of their humor, and the correctness of their life choices, "God's country" is so unambiguously wonderful that the only real threat can come from another star system. For Moloney, who writes with wry fondness of a small town tainted by dark beginnings and suffering decades of neglect by those in power, "God's country" is ambivalent, the God in question as remote and capricious as the CBC. And for Rowe, who writes from the point of view of characters marginalized by sexism, classism, racism, and homophobia, "God's country" has been rendered monstrous and corrupt by the very forces that have worked to turn it into God's country.

While the specter of colonialism seethes below the surface of *Minnow Trap* and *Frozen Beneath*, *Bastion Falls* and *Enter, Night* engage openly with the link between the Freudian uncanny and the colonial history of the region, with antagonists that have their roots in the settlement of their respective communities. In the latter two books, the ordinary problems of a Northern Ontario town—unemployment, poverty, alcoholism, and the hardship of remoteness itself—shade into the Gothic menace, which came with European settlers, and predates the community it threatens. In fact, there is a suggestion that the communities have always been contaminated by their presence.

All four novels, although they make Northern Ontario the site (and in two cases, the source) of horror, come with messages for Southern Ontario, and the world at large. For Brian Horeck, this message takes the form of demanding respect for the North, and declaring that its (affluent, white, male) citizens are as fit to wield power and make strategic decisions about the fate of the world as any others, and are in fact morally superior for choosing to remain in the North. Susie Moloney, too, is troubled by the disenfranchisement of the North at the hands of the South: it exacerbates an already bad situation, leaving Bastion Falls to fall to its hungry ghosts. And although Toronto is the center of light and life for Michael Rowe's characters, Rowe denounces the industrial exploitation that has economically depressed the North. In short, all four examples of Northern Ontario Gothic constitute protests against marginalization, and Moloney and Rowe make this marginalization itself the source of horror.

Works Cited

"Biography." <www.susiemoloney.com/#!bio>. September 19, 2013. Web.
Botting, Fred. *Gothic*. London: Routledge, 1996. Print.
Crawford, Joseph. *Gothic Fiction and the Invention of Terrorism: The Politics and Aesthetics of Fear in the Age of the Reign of Terror*. London: Bloomsbury, 2013. Print.
Edwards, Justin D. *Gothic Canada: Reading the Spectre of a National Literature*. Edmonton: University of Alberta Press, 2005. Print.
Gross, Louis. *Redefining the American Gothic: From* Wieland *to* Day of the Dead. Ann Arbor and London: UMI Research P, 1989. Print.
Horeck, Brian. *Frozen Beneath*. Willowdale, ON: wemakebooks.ca, 2008. Print.
_____. *Minnow Trap*. Altona, MB: Friesens, 2005. Print.
Michasiw, Kim. "Some Stations of the Suburban Gothic." *American Gothic: New Interventions in a National Narrative*. Ed. Robert K. Martin and Eric Savoy. Iowa City: University of Iowa Press, 1998. 237-57. Print.
Moloney, Susie. *Bastion Falls*. Toronto: Key Porter, 1995. Print.
"Northern Ontario." Wikipedia. <en.wikipedia.org/wiki/Northern_Ontario>. December 30, 2013. Web.
Ontario Local Health Information Network. *Leading Health System Transformation in Our Communities: 2010-2013 North West LHN Strategic Directions*. June 2010. <www.northwestlhn.on.ca/uploadedFiles/Home_Page/Report_and_Publications/Strategic%20Directions%20-%20Public%20Report%20v5TF.pdf>. December 30, 2013. Web.
Rowe, Michael. *Enter, Night*. Toronto: ChiZine, 2011. Print.
Sugars, Cynthia, and Turcotte, Gerry. "Canadian Literature and the Postcolonial Gothic." *Unsettled Remains: Canadian Literature and the Postcolonial Gothic*. Introduction. Eds. Sugars and Turcotte. Waterloo, ON: Wilfrid Laurier University Press, 2009. vii-xx. Print.

Can the Witch Speak? The Supernatural Subaltern in Kelley Armstrong's Otherworld

Adam Guzkowski

ACCSFF '09

While there has been much debate about the extent to which the persecution of witches can be read as a history solely predicated upon the violent subjugation of women by dominant patriarchal social structures,[1] the symbol of the witch continues to serve as a powerful cultural trope which persists as both a popular figure and a manifestation of historically specific discourses about feminism and female power. In the contemporary fantastic, the figure of the witch is a complex and oftentimes contradictory figure; witness for instance the significant differences in the portrayal of witches in texts such as Alice Hoffman's *Practical Magic* (1995), John Updike's *Witches of Eastwick* (1984), and Kim Harrison's Rachel Caine series (2004–2014), as well as in television shows and films such as *Bewitched* (1964–1972), *Charmed* (1998–2006), *Sabrina, the Teenage Witch* (1996–2003), *The Craft* (1996), and *The Good Witch* (2008).

On the one hand, seemingly liberatory narratives offer critical perspectives on sexism and patriarchy, while on the other hand, traditionalist and essentialist threads are woven through these narratives, offering constructions and reconstructions of women and women's power as biologically determined, lesser than men and men's power, or simply "Other." The figure of the witch in contemporary fantasy provides a subject that is at once marginalized and empowered, one that serves as a site for the exploration of notions of personal and political empowerment, gender, and representations of the

Other. My motivating assumption in this investigation is the belief that in studying contemporary fantasy literature, it is possible to gather new insights on the state of contemporary culture which reveal, and perhaps even generate, the potential for transformative personal and social change. As feminist literary scholar Anne Cranny-Francis notes:

> The maintenance of a particular social formation is largely dependent on the interpellation of the individual subject by the discourses (of class, gender, race, etc.) which constitute and describe that formation. If fantasy literature can reposition readers to evaluate critically and oppose hegemonic discourses, so modifying their own subject position, then a modification of the social formation is inevitable [106].

By focusing a feminist analysis on the figure of the witch and on the functions and potentialities of power and voice, it becomes possible to use texts of popular fiction to critically engage with "culturally entrenched narrative templates and representational conventions" (Meyers 5). The analysis herein will attempt to do so by addressing the construction of witches in Kelley Armstrong's Women of the Otherworld series, focusing on the second, third and fourth novels in the series: the 2002 *Stolen*, which first introduces witches into her imaginative landscape, though from the narrative perspective of a non-witch, and *Dime Store Magic* and *Industrial Magic*, respectively published in early 2004 and late 2004, both narrated by a witch protagonist who first appears in the novel *Stolen*.

At this point it is worth recognizing one of the limitations of this paper. Though certainly implicated in the descriptor "contemporary," an exploration of the manner in which the texts studied here serve as both products of, and critical reflections on, their particular historical moments is beyond the scope of this paper. This is a necessary choice, made in order to do justice to a conceptual mapping of a theoretical framework that might serve to enable a critical exploration of the figure of the witch in contemporary fantasy. Nevertheless, I engage in this exploration with an awareness that literature is, as Alan Sinfield notes in *Cultural Politics— Queer Reading*, deeply "involved in the processes through which our cultures elaborate themselves," and that while "literature is only one of innumerable places where this production of culture occurs," it is always already shaped by the ideological pressures of its particular social, cultural, and historical context (3; 4). At the very same time, literature shapes those contexts through the reproduction, contestation and/or reification of those ideological frameworks. In order to disentangle such complexities, it becomes important to examine the particularity of specific texts, while simultaneously developing a theoretical lens with which to reflect upon those broader contexts and ideological frameworks.

Having said that, let us look more closely at the Women of the Otherworld series, which began with the publication of the 2001 *Bitten*, narrated by the werewolf Elena Michaels. The series, featuring werewolves, witches, necromancers, half-demons and vampires, continued with *Stolen* (2002), again narrated by Elena, followed by two novels, *Dime Store Magic* (2004) and *Industrial Magic* (2004), both narrated by the witch Paige Winterbourne. The Otherworld series contains a total of thirteen novels. This includes two more novels narrated by the werewolf Elena (*Broken* [2006], *Frostbitten* [2009]), one narrated by a (dead) half-demon witch named Eve Levine (*Haunted* [2005]), one narrated by a necromancer named Jaime Vegas (*No Humans Involved* [2007]), one narrated by a half-demon named Hope Adams and a sorcerer named Lucas Cortez (*Personal Demon* [2008]), and one narrated in the third-person featuring multiple protagonists (*Living with the Dead* [2008]). The final three novels in the series are narrated by Savannah Levine, a young witch who first appears in *Stolen*, and eventually becomes the foster daughter of Paige Winterbourne (*Waking the Witch* [2010], *Spellbound* [2011], *Thirteen* [2012]).

It is noteworthy that while books three and four are narrated by the witch Paige, my analysis begins with the second book, where the possibilities for witches are to some extent delineated, though admittedly the seemingly fixed boundaries defined therein become blurred as the Otherworld series develops. Initially, most of what we learn about witches, their historical and contemporary relationship to both supernatural and mundane social and political contexts, is learned through characters talking about witches, rather than witches speaking for themselves. Unlike Elena, who begins as the speaking subject, defining the understanding of her world through her own narrative, however reliable that may be, Paige begins as the spoken subject, with the understanding of her world defined primarily through the narratives of others. She will continue on to narrate two books of her own, but will engage in that subjective position as the rhetor having always already been determined to some extent by the rhetoric of others.

In *Stolen*, Paige is depicted as a young woman striving to assume a leadership role while chafing under authority figures, and frustrated with antiquated models for decision-making and approaches to spellcasting that foster impressions of witches as weak and reactive (35, 55, 58, 61, 154). The hierarchical structuring of the Coven vs. non–Coven witches, and the monitoring and moral regulation that occurs within the Coven and is imposed on non–Coven witches by the Coven, come to be seen by Paige as systems that perpetuate injustice, and leave her determined to enact proactive change, initially from within the ranks of the Coven (*Stolen* 7, 25, 154; *Dime Store Magic* 7,

156). Paige articulates her vision of what the Coven could and should be in the latter part of *Dime Store Magic*:

> I could reform the Coven, make it into a place witches came to, not escaped from. Once the Coven had regained its strength and vitality, we could reach out to other witches, offer training and fellowship.... I'd make the Coven more flexible, more adaptable, more attractive, better suited to fulfilling the needs of all witches [288].

Even as she works to achieve broader political aims in her quest to reform the community of witches, Paige is also involved in the immediate application of her notions of liberatory pedagogy and social support systems for witches, once she becomes involved with mentoring the young witch Savannah.

One of the key elements in the figure of the witch in Armstrong's Otherworld is the coming of age ceremony associated with a witch's ability to access her full magical potential, which correlates with her first menstruation. At the time she is kidnapped in *Stolen*, Savannah is rapidly approaching that phase of her physical and supernatural development (122–23). Ruth Winterbourne, Paige's mother, is also kidnapped, and first encounters Savannah in the cell block where they are being kept awaiting testing and experimentation by a (human) billionaire who covets the powers and abilities of the supernatural races. Ruth decides to accelerate Savannah's development of her powers, recognizing that "the best [she] can do is give the child the tools she'll need to survive" (154); that theme of equipping young witches for future survival is one that is repeated throughout all three texts being examined here. Though Ruth dies before she can be rescued, her actions clearly enable Savannah to survive to be rescued, and to be adopted by Paige, who acts as both guardian and teacher for Savannah in *Dime Store Magic* and *Industrial Magic*. In her role as mentor to the young witch, Paige is responsible for performing the coming of age ceremony that supposedly opens a witch up to her full potential for magical power.

As the events unfold in *Dime Store Magic*, that ceremony proves to be more complex than Paige initially expects, as she and Savannah soon discover that the Coven's so-called traditional practices around the coming of age ceremony are in fact mere shadows of the powerful practices once handed down from one generation of witches to the next. The revised "traditional" version is in fact a variation designed by the Elders to help witches escape excessive attention from sorcerers' Cabals by limiting witches' powers (92, 196–97). This discovery brings to mind the words of Haudenosaunee scholar Dawn Martin-Hill, who in reflecting on the ways in which (internalized) colonization has affected her own community asks "How can we ensure that what we claim to be traditional is a tool for liberation and not a tool of oppression?"

(109). Indeed, the decisions being made by the Coven Elders, and enacted under the guise of "traditional" practices, seems to be heavily invested in shaping each young witch under the Coven's care into an iteration of the model Martin-Hill describes as "She No Speaks ... the woman who never questions male authority.... She is quiet ... she obeys ... she never questions or challenges domination—she is subservient" (108).

Having recognized the disempowering decisions that have been made by the Coven Elders, Paige and Savannah actively engage in the reclamation of traditional knowledge and practices, which Dawn Martin-Hill describes as part of the "project of decolonization" (111). They research the absences and silences they have noted in both spellcasting lore and the rituals for the coming of age ceremony, and succeed in finding and recovering the "lost" grimoires from where the Coven Elders had hidden them away (*Dime Store Magic* 202, 216–17, 232–36), and in doing so enact the political force of much postcolonial literature, which "comes from a concern with recuperating a lost history" (Söderlind 6). This process of recuperating the lost history of witches enables Paige and Savannah to start shaping a future that moves past the world created by the limiting beliefs of the Coven Elders, which Savannah summarizes as "a world where witches were stupid and useless" (*Dime Store Magic* 301). This process also enables them to visualize a future beyond the supposed freedoms and rewards touted by a Cabal witch paid richly for her subservient role; while trying to tempt Savannah to join the Cabal, the Cabal witch nevertheless describes a perspective anathema to Savannah's burgeoning feminist consciousness: "Sorcerer magic is the magic of power. With all respect to women and equal rights, witch magic just doesn't measure up" (*Dime Store Magic* 304).

Moving beyond the unsavory options offered by Coven and Cabal, Paige and Savannah continue to plan for performing the reclaimed coming of age ceremony for Savannah, two particular elements of which bear closer examination: an invocation "to grant the witch the power to wreak vengeance on her enemies and to free her from all restrictions on her powers," and the need for grave dirt for the ritual (*Dime Store Magic* 239, 245). Having discovered that the variations used by both Coven and Cabal for witches under their auspices contain limitations on the power that is enabled by the coming of age ceremony, Paige nevertheless struggles with the implications of a teenage spellcaster under her care having access to "full powers, without restriction" (*Dime Store Magic* 240). Yet in the end Paige chooses to perform Savannah's ceremony with the reclaimed invocation, driven by the desire to ensure that Savannah, and indeed all witches, have the power to choose their own paths without being limited by the oppressive moral regulation of the Coven Elders, or the surveillance and control of the Cabals (*Dime Store Magic* 243).

The need for dirt from the grave of someone who was murdered for the reclaimed ceremony also causes Paige some unease, yet in the end the choice of whose grave the dirt comes from serves to illustrate themes of both feminist empowerment and the reclamation of voice. The grave chosen is that of a woman "shot to death by her common-law husband during an argument because he ... wanted to shut her (obscenity deleted) mouth for good" (*Dime Store Magic* 246). This choice, combined with the invocation that calls for the power to wreak vengeance, carries a powerful feminist message that suggests that Savannah's future as a witch will be one deeply engaged with feminist concerns. When the ceremony is completed, there is sense of complete peace and utter certainty experienced by both Paige and Savannah, also suggesting that the reclaimed ceremony has opened new possibilities for the emancipation of a new generation of witches (*Dime Store Magic* 353–55).

Given the close connection between issues of voice and the project of decolonization, I will now turn to Gayatri Chakravorty Spivak to enable further critical engagement with the figure of the witch. One of the key insights offered by Spivak's classic essay "Can the Subaltern Speak?" (1988) is the notion that even the most seemingly innocuous or "straight-forward" acts of representation contain within them an overabundance of theoretical baggage—complex layers and nodalities of cultural, political, and ideological discursive legacies. Furthermore, according to the work of Spivak, and other postcolonial and feminist scholars, it is necessary to examine how the construction and representation of the subject "given voice" (or not)—speaking and spoken for—always already performs, produces and reproduces colonial relations of power, which are determined, or more accurately over-determined, by gendered, racialized and classed discourses. Voice, speech and the power of representation are absolutely vital tools in the work of what Spivak refers to as radical practice. Admittedly, focusing only on these facets of Spivak's argument is somewhat reductive, given that "Spivak's purpose in 'Can the Subaltern Speak?' is to trace the historical, economic and geopolitical conditions that prevent the agency and voice of the gendered subaltern subject on the other side of the international division of labor from being represented" (Morton 110). Nevertheless, Spivak's analysis of the historical and symbolic nature of voice and representation within that context provides a useful interrogative perspective from which to approach the discursive constructions of the witch in Armstrong's Otherworld.

Certainly this invitation to situate analysis within an acknowledgment of, and engagement with, the complexities and contradictions of power and discourse impels a reflexive look at the use of postcolonial theory here. Postcolonial theory is highly useful for the ways in which it facilitates the examination of constantly reinscribed subject positions of simultaneous agency and subjugation. Yet I am using this theoretical framework, which is deeply invested in critical examination of racialized colonial discourses, to discuss fictional characters that to the casual reader would appear to be white, middle-class, American citizens with the ability to "pass" when necessary, unmarked by difference, at least visibly, beyond that position of difference labeled "woman." At the same time, a close reading of the texts suggests that witches in Armstrong's Otherworld can be understood as racialized subjects engaged in decolonization and the reclamation of traditional knowledge. Recognizing these contrasting readings, the judicious application of postcolonial theory allows an analysis of the figure of the witch as both an empowered feminist and/or postcolonial magical rhetor, *and* as a subject bounded and silenced by discourses of domination and discipline.

Such discourses are both supported and further enacted by symbolic constructions of witches as fitting the characterizations of them as "sorceresses, murderesses and destroyers of male potency" (Biedermann 386). This history is certainly mobilized by Armstrong in the novel *Stolen*. At one point Paige, frustrated with the overbearing conduct of a male character named Adam, turns to another woman, and in front of Adam, relates the following:

> "Elena, did you know that one of the major accusations against witches during the Inquisition was that they caused impotence? ... Not just psychological impotence either.... Men accused witches of literally removing their penises. They thought we collected them in little boxes where they wriggled around and ate oats and corn..." [Elena] laughed. "Men," Paige said. "They'll accuse women of anything." She paused and slanted a look at Adam. "Of course, it's such an outlandish charge, one can't help but wonder if there isn't a grain of truth in it" [346–47].

Here we see humor used as a device by Armstrong to articulate for the reader the history of men's fear of the emasculating power of witches, and how that fear functioned in the context of witch hunts, a period of history which feminist scholar Marianne Hester refers to as one of the most violent, most disturbing, and most explicit manifestations of patriarchy, which revealed both the power and the insecurity and irrationality of patriarchal discourse.

Yet in Armstrong's Otherworld, history is also rewritten to include the roles played by sorcerers and witches, such as the following discussion of the Inquisition, and the reverberations of that history up to the narrative present:

> Sorcerers were among the first targeted by the Inquisition in Europe. How did they react? They turned on [witches]. The Inquisitors wanted heretics? The sorcerers gave them witches.... While witches burned, sorcerers ... became rich and

powerful. Today, sorcerers rule as some of the most important men in the world ... and witches? Ordinary women leading ordinary lives, most of them so afraid of persecution they've never dared learn a spell that will kill anything larger than an aphid [*Dime Store Magic* 20].

That fear continues to be a factor in the conduct of witches in the narrative present of Armstrong's fiction, as evidenced by one of the Coven Elders trading information to a sorcerer's Cabal that leads to the capture of Paige and Savannah, in exchange for protection and a guarantee of immunity from the Cabal's current activities (*Dime Store Magic* 310–11). Earlier in *Dime Store Magic*, this same Elder tells Paige that "the Coven doesn't exist to help those who bring trouble on themselves" (155), and throughout the text extols the virtues of "proper behaviour" and being unnoticed and virtually invisible (6–7, 154–56, 286–88). Such statements and actions illustrate the fact that "to internalize oppression is to incorporate inferiorizing material into the structure of the self—to see oneself as objectified, to value and desire what befits a subordinated individual, and to feel confident and empowered by skills that reinforce one's subordination" (Meyers 8). Despite strong pressure to conform to the standards accepted by the Elders of the Coven, Paige refuses to accept the confining strictures of the Coven's status quo; she believes that "the Coven exists to help all witches" (*Dime Store Magic* 155), and is determined to create a new kind of community for witches, even in the face of rejection from witches who readily accept the status quo (*Industrial Magic* 10–12).

Early in the novel *Stolen*, Paige demonstrates an interest in the coalition politics of the Council, a semi-regular "meeting of the supernatural races" that functions like an informal supernatural United Nations (48, 50–63). As *Dime Store Magic* progresses, Paige continues to learn more about other supernatural races (109–11, 160–61, 168), and sees herself as being involved in the work of the Council in the future. As she interacts with other supernaturals early in *Industrial Magic*, Paige is delighted to be introduced as follows: "'Paige used to be in the Coven, helping witches there, but now she works outside the Coven, so she can help all witches'" (131). By the latter half of *Industrial Magic*, Paige has repeatedly demonstrated her abilities as witch, investigator, and leader, earning the respect of other supernaturals; she soon begins to ponder how forming a new Coven for a new generation of witches can be combined with strengthening and revitalizing the Council (*Industrial Magic* 376, 526–28). Paige's musings on where to begin are answered by the end of *Industrial Magic*, as a Cabal employee turns to her with a request that she serve as the mentor for a young witch. The new Coven begins with Paige promising to teach the young witch, thus symbolically being entrusted with the future of the sisterhood/race of witches (528).

In their own way, each of the witch protagonists in Armstrong's world (Ruth, Paige, and Savannah) struggle to change the internalized oppressions and entrenched institutions shaped by gendered and racialized social norms; they work to confront the histories of power and control that have served to confine and subjugate witches for generations. In doing so, they also provide inspiration for doing similar political work in the communities and contexts of "the real world," demonstrating the fact that "generic fiction may be a site for the allegorical description of social injustices displaced in time and/or place from the reader's own society, but still clearly recognizable as a critique of that society" (Cranny-Francis 9). Armstrong's novels can also be understood in the context of other Canadian texts that can be read as postcolonial by virtue of their dependence on a "contestatory position vis-a-vis a centre defined in political/referential terms"; a text such as this "carries on a struggle from a cultural/linguistic margin which it vindicates and valorizes" (Söderlind 230). While that marginal position may be the supernatural subalternity of the witch, the fact remains that Armstrong's novels show one of the hallmarks of "the postcolonial situation," namely "the struggle for identity in a situation where self-representation is always tainted with alterity" (Söderlind 4). Söderlind, in *Margin/Alias: Language and Colonization in Canadian and Québécois Fiction*, argues that "any statement of identity is an assertion of difference, and that the postmodern interest in the ontology of difference is central to the postcolonial situation" (5). How difference comes to be, as well as how it comes to be known and understood, is an important facet in the positioning of the witch in Armstrong's work. The witches in the Otherworld are always already gendered and racialized subjects, and immediately recognize and are recognized by their patriarchal/colonial oppressor, as demonstrated when Paige encounters a sorcerer near the beginning of *Dime Store Magic*:

> Gabriel Sandford was a sorcerer. I knew this the moment I looked into his eyes, a gut-level recognition that registered before I could have told you what color those eyes were. This is a peculiarity specific to our races. We need only look one another in the eye and witch recognizes sorcerer, sorcerer recognizes witch [19].

Even if a witch or sorcerer has chosen to forego deliberate development of their powers, this recognition is always active. Complementing this visual acuity is a genetic guarantee of the ability to perpetuate the race of witches. In Armstrong's novels, being a witch is biologically inherited from the mother, and witches only bear daughters, never sons (*Dime Store Magic* 23). This creates a matrilineal transference of power that is, at the same time, coded as gendered, racialized, essentialist and biologically deterministic.

Yet witch power is not simply biologically determined, for as Caroline

Ruddell states, "in postfeminist texts that centre on the supernatural, female power is not only associated with the body, it is also aligned with speech, text and language" (35). Thus while the potential for the acquisition and use of magical power is biologically determined, the actual acquisition and use of magical power is reliant upon rhetorical agency. The witch, as Susan Latta articulates, is "an important icon because she represents the ability to use language to transform reality" (24). In the context of contemporary fantasy, the figure of the witch provides "an alternative mythology of women empowered by words, women who can, quite literally, change the world through both the power of their actions and the power of their words" (Latta 20). However, unlike the witches of Alice Hoffman's *Practical Magic* (1995), or of the television show *Charmed* (1998–2006), the witches of Armstrong's Otherworld series do not demonstrate the ability to create new discursive patterns. While witches in the aforementioned texts have the ability to create new spells and rituals as exigencies demand, Armstrong's witches are limited to re-discovering the spells of their foremothers. Thus while the witch protagonists in the Otherworld series are more explicitly positioned as liberatory figures in so far as they engage in the social and political spheres of their supernatural and mundane contexts, this is not necessarily so in terms of their acquisition and use of magical power. However, the character of Savannah, Paige's foster daughter, seems to offer the possibility of transgressing or altogether transcending those limitations in the future, being the first witch in at least a generation to complete a coming of age ceremony that invoked "power without bounds" (*Dime Store Magic* 355).

Feminist philosopher and cultural theorist Diana Tietjens Meyers, in her book *Gender in the Mirror: Cultural Imagery & Women's Agency*, describes the autonomous individual as "an evolving subject … a subject who fashions her self-portrait and shapes her self-narrative through a process of skillful self-discovery, self-definition, and self-direction" (22). By the conclusion of *Industrial Magic*, Paige Winterbourne has shaped a self-narrative that includes being a powerful witch, the founder of a new kind of Coven, and mentor to the next generation of emancipated witches, including her foster daughter Savannah. Savannah embodies the hope for full rhetorical emancipation in terms of magical power, and in doing so signifies the potentialities gestured to by Maria Lauret when she stated that "Feminist endings are open endings" (187). After all, a "methodology attentive to the subversive potential of postcolonial literatures must by necessity subscribe to a view of language which allows for resistance" (Söderlind 4); therefore, it remains absolutely vital to recognize in Savannah the potential for agency and resistance as expressed through magical means. At the same time, it is Paige who has already successfully illustrated Diana Tietjens Meyers' description of developing an emancipated voice:

> the emancipated voice would be the one that has unmasked oppression-perpetuating falsifications by joining with others to challenge social structures, by analyzing how these structures maintain the status quo and who is benefiting from this set-up, and by envisioning a society free of repression and exploitation [18].

Throughout the course of *Stolen*, *Dime Store Magic*, and *Industrial Magic*, Paige works for the betterment of witches as well as other supernatural races, and builds a community of both fellow witches and non-witch allies. She identifies and confronts those perpetuating and profiting from histories of oppression, and works to create new forms of political engagement and liberatory pedagogy for the next generation, combining reclaimed traditional knowledge with innovative ways of using both magic and telecommunications to further enable capacity building and community development for witches. In Paige Winterbourne, Kelley Armstrong has created a protagonist that exemplifies the complexities of negotiating gendered and racialized subjectivities, and illustrates the power and future possibilities of (re)claiming voice and agency.

As Bryan Palmer writes in *Cultures of Darkness: Night Travels in the History of Transgression*, "to be called a witch still remains a gendered insult of weight, harking back to the essentializing caricatures of centuries past" (50). Upon initial examination, some of the constructions of the figure of the witch in the work of Kelley Armstrong might appear sexist, essentialist, or biologically deterministic. And many of them are indeed all of those things, to some extent. Yet these texts also offer strong female (witch) protagonists who, as they mature over the course of the Women of the Otherworld series, achieve greater levels of rhetorical agency and power, and have greater spheres of impact and influence. While the figure of the witch in the contemporary fantasy literature of Kelley Armstrong is complex and oftentimes contradictory, it nevertheless offers a powerful and compelling allegory for feminist empowerment. By situating protagonists within a discourse in which they are always already coded not only as women, but as marginalized yet simultaneously threatening "Others," contemporary fantasy featuring witches may be a rich and interesting narrative mode within which to examine feminist agency realized within systems and structures of knowledge and power inimical to such agency.

Notes

1. For some examples of the debates on and depictions of witches as both historical and symbolic figures, see Baroja, Bartel, Faith, Hester, Moseley, Palmer, Purkiss, and Sanders.

Works Cited

Armstrong, Kelley. *Bitten*. Toronto: Random House, 2001. Print.
———. *Broken*. Toronto: Seal, 2006. Print.
———. *Dime Store Magic*. Toronto: Random House, 2004. Print.
———. *Frostbitten*. Toronto: Random House, 2009. Print.
———. *Haunted*. Toronto: Seal, 2005. Print.
———. *Industrial Magic*. Toronto: Random House, 2004. Print.
———. *Living with the Dead*. Toronto: Random House, 2008. Print.
———. *No Humans Involved*. Toronto: Random House, 2007. Print.
———. *Personal Demon*. Toronto: Random House, 2008. Print.
———. *Spellbound*. Toronto: Random House, 2011. Print.
———. *Stolen*. Toronto: Random House, 2002. Print.
———. *Thirteen*. Toronto: Random House, 2012. Print.
———. *Waking the Witch*. Toronto: Random House, 2010. Print.
Baroja, Julio Caro. *The World of the Witches*. Trans. Nigel Glendinning. London: Phoenix, 2001. Print.
Bartel, Pauline C. *Spellcasters: Witches and Witchcraft in History, Folklore, and Popular Culture*. Dallas: Taylor, 2000. Print.
Bewitched. Creator Sol Saks. American Broadcasting Company, 1964–1972. Television.
Biedermann, Hans. *Dictionary of Symbolism: Cultural Icons and the Meanings Behind Them*. New York: Facts on File, 1992. Print.
Charmed. Creator Constance M. Burge. WB Television Network, 1998–2006. Television.
The Craft. Dir. Andrew Fleming. Perf. Fairuza Bulk, Neve Campbell, Rachel True, and Robin Tunney. Columbia Pictures, 1996. Film.
Cranny-Francis, Anne. *Feminist Fiction: Feminist Uses of Generic Fiction*. New York: St. Martin's, 1990. Print.
Faith, Karlene. *Unruly Women: The Politics of Confinement and Resistance*. Vancouver: Press Gang, 1993. Print.
The Good Witch. Dir. Craig Pryce. Perf. Catherine Bell and Chris Potter. Whizbang Films, 2008. Film.
Harrison, Kim. *Black Magic Sanction*. New York: HarperCollins, 2010. Print.
———. *Dead Witch Walking*. New York: HarperCollins, 2004. Print.
———. *Ever After*. New York: HarperCollins, 2013. Print.
———. *Every Which Way But Dead*. New York: HarperCollins, 2005. Print.
———. *For a Few Demons More*. New York: HarperCollins, 2007. Print.
———. *A Fistful of Charms*. New York: HarperCollins, 2006. Print.
———. *The Good, the Bad and the Undead*. New York: HarperCollins, 2005. Print.
———. *The Outlaw Demons Wails*. New York: HarperCollins, 2008. Print.
———. *Pale Demon*. New York: HarperCollins, 2011. Print.
———. *A Perfect Blood*. New York: HarperCollins, 2012. Print.
———. *The Undead Pool*. New York: HarperCollins, 2014. Print.
———. *White Witch, Black Curse*. New York: HarperCollins, 2009. Print.
Hester, Marianne. *Lewd Women and Wicked Witches: A Study of the Dynamics of Male Domination*. New York: Routledge, 1992. Print.
Hoffman, Alice. *Practical Magic*. New York: Putnam, 1995. Print.
Latta, Susan. "Reclaiming Women's Language for Power and Agency: The Charmed Ones as Magical Rhetors." *Investigating Charmed: The Magic Power of TV*. Ed. Karin Beeler and Stan Beeler. New York: I. B. Tauris, 2007. 19–28. Print.
Lauret, Maria. *Liberating Literature: Feminist Fiction in America*. New York: Routledge, 1994. Print.

Martin-Hill, Dawn. "She No Speaks and Other Colonial Constructs of 'The Traditional Woman'" *Strong Women Stories: Native Vision and Community Survival*. Ed. Kim Anderson and Bonita Lawrence. Toronto: Sumach, 2003. 106–20. Print.

Meyers, Diana Tietjens. *Gender in the Mirror: Cultural Imagery & Women's Agency*. New York: Oxford University Press, 2002. Print.

Morton, Stephen. *Gayatri Spivak: Ethics, Subalternity and the Critique of Postcolonial Reason*. Malden: Polity, 2007. Print.

Moseley, Rachel. "Glamorous Witchcraft: Gender and Magic in Teen Film and Television." *Screen* 43.4 (2002): 403–22. Print.

Palmer, Bryan D. *Cultures of Darkness: Night Travels in the Histories of Transgression*. New York: Monthly Review, 2000. Print.

Purkiss, Diane. *The Witch in History: Early Modern and Twentieth-Century Representations*. New York: Routledge, 1996. Print.

Ruddell, Caroline. "The Power of Three: Strength in Numbers and 'Wordy' Witchcraft." *Investigating Charmed: The Magic Power of TV*. Ed. Karin Beeler and Stan Beeler. New York: I.B.Tauris, 2007. 29–41. Print.

Sabrina, the Teenage Witch. Creator Nell Scovell. American Broadcasting Company (1996–2000) and WB Television Network (2000–2003), 1996–2003. Television.

Sanders, Andrew. *A Deed without a Name: The Witch in Society and History*. Washington: Berg, 2000. Print.

Sinfield, Alan. *Cultural Politics—Queer Reading*. Philadelphia: University of Pennsylvania Press, 1994. Print.

Söderlind, Sylvia. *Margin/Alias: Language and Colonization in Canadian and Québécois Fiction*. Toronto: U of Toronto P, 1991. Print.

Spivak, Gayatri Chakravorty. "Can the Subaltern Speak?" *Marxism and the Interpretation of Culture*. Ed. Cary Nelson and Lawrence Grossberg. London: Macmillan, 1988. 271–313. Print.

Updike, John. *The Witches of Eastwick*. New York: Knopf, 1984. Print.

Navigating the Darkness: Blindness and Vampirism in Tanya Huff's Blood Books

Derek Newman-Stille

ACCSFF '11

Darkness: a symbol of fear and negativity for most people, a time when human beings are without our most prominent sense—our vision. We project our fears onto the darkness. Night, for us, has become a liminal period; a threatening time between one day and the next; a "temporal monstrosity" (Youngs and Harris 135). In her Blood Books series, Tanya Huff uses darkness to represent an intersection of multiple fears and threats. In particular, she allies the fear of darkness with one of the other most prominent fears of human society, fear of bodily invasion and corporeal damage.

Huff interweaves two figures with intimate connections to ideas of darkness and corporeal threat: Detective Vicki Nelson, who is losing her vision due to retinitis pigmentosa, a degenerative eye disease that causes the loss of peripheral and night vision; and Henry Fitzroy, the vampire bastard son of Henry VIII, who is only conscious during the nighttime hours and is badly burned by the sunlight when exposed. These figures *should* be confined to separate worlds due to difference in ability (literally confined to different temporal realms), but instead serve to accommodate one another's bodily difference or disability. Henry becomes Vicki's "seeing eye vampire" during the night due to his accelerated night vision, and Vicki becomes Henry's daytime assistant, helping him to get back to safety during the daylight hours, and accommodating his needs during the unconscious periods of the day.

Because we are deprived of a sense that we construct as the most vital, the darkness represents, for us, a symbol of ignorance or lack of awareness. In the dark, the sighted see themselves as deprived of their most vital mechanism for interpreting and understanding the world around them (Youngs and Harris 135). Blindness is also often situated in our society as a symbol or a method of discourse about ignorance. People are "blind to the injustices of society" or "can't see what is right in front of their faces." Rod Michalko, a scholar of disability who is blind, notes that blindness has been constructed in our society as denoting a lack of knowledge or experience, yet, "experiencing blindness, however, is not in any way synonymous with knowledge" (*Mystery of the Eye* 3). Our society's over-reliance on sight has constructed it as the primary means of discourse and way of understanding the world, so blindness is constructed as its foil, socially constructed as a "lack" of access to knowledge.

Huff plays with this image, but makes her central character a Teiresian[1] figure, embracing the ancient Greek notion that "only the blind man [or woman] truly sees." Her point of difference—her "constricted vision"—actually allows Vicki an expanded vision of reality, the ability to *see* outside the confines of her worldview and experience more about the differences in the world around her than others would. She is able to *see* Henry as a vampire even though he is passing as human in a world that does not believe in vampires, and she is able to notice signs of monstrosity around the city that others, *able-bodied, human* others, do not notice because of their natural propensity for ignoring the abnormal, the fringe, the different. Vicki is naturally different, an outsider because of her bodily difference, and therefore she can see this world around her. Her blinded eyes allow her to see difference, to accept and embrace the fringe of bodily difference and thus to allow her "narrow vision" to actually become an expanded vision of the world and the possible around her. Disability is exclusionary, it causes a distance from normalized society, but it is only through this distance from the normal that Vicki is able to see the abnormal. Vicki's glasses become a lens through which she can see the world as it is, ironically letting her see the "things that go bump in the night" while not letting her physically *see* them and thus ensuring that she, as a blind woman, is literally going bump in the night.

> More things in heaven and earth.... She didn't know if she believed in vampires, but she definitely believed in her own senses, even if one of them had become less than reliable of late. Something strange had been down in that tunnel, and nothing human could have struck that blow ... [Huff, *Blood Price* 31].

Vicki sees the truths of her world because of her altered vision, or, more accurately, because of her altered social situation that therefore focuses her attention on the fringe.

Disability in our world, like monstrosity in the world Huff constructs, is something hidden, something discursively veiled and removed from social attention. Dossa notes that people with disabilities have been rendered socially invisible:

> disability is our other self as it brings home the point that the boundary between them and the Other is not sharp. Rather than encountering our other self, we keep it hidden—an effort bolstered by a consumer society that lives us the message that we can remain young and able-bodied if we take responsibility for our own health and well-being [2528—note: "lives us the message" is in the original text, denoting a lived experience].

Society has a lot at stake in creating firm barriers between ability and disability and in rendering disability invisible, which is why the disabled are often institutionalized, removed from public roles, and ignored. Tanya Titchkosky suggests that "the very ways that disability is included in everyday life are, also, part of that which structures the continued manifestation of disabled people as a non-viable type" (*Reading and Writing* 5). This marginalization provides an ontological perspective of alterity, a difference in the way that the world is conceived of. Vicki is able to experience the fringes of society because her disability already distances her from the meaning-making system that depends on the erasure of social and bodily Others. Since she is one of those Others, the social masks placed on our world that hide the fringes and marginal are weaker for her, more susceptible to probing and questioning. She is able to experience things that other police officers immediately dismiss as impossible.

Dossa refers to this sense of a collective story embodied by those in marginal social positions when she states: "when marginalized people speak, they tell a collective story. This is because their individual stories are embedded in the larger social, political, and economic contexts" (2529). There is a larger narrative, a hegemonic structure that relies on the social construction of certain others as ontologically invisible, hidden. Yet, by being in marginal positions, the relations of ruling are more visible, more transparent (ibid.).

Vicki's retinitis pigmentosa means that she is literally probing the shadows for answers, trying to see into the shadows where her eyes are unable to discern details: "she twisted until she could see into the darkness beyond the end of the train…. What did the shadows hide, she wondered…. She'd never considered herself an overly imaginative woman … but *something* lingered in that tunnel" (*Blood Price* 11). Huff makes literal the ability of disability to render the socially transparent "visible," noticeable because of the shared alterity and marginality from hegemonic systems of power that rely on rendering social Others invisible.

The alternation between day and night becomes a point of intersection between these two figures (night-blind woman and vampire) and the symbol of darkness and blindness become central ones for the exploration of difference. Vicki mourns her loss of vision, while Henry mourns his loss of the day and sunlight. Centralizing a figure who is losing her vision, Huff makes disability a key issue in her narrative and situates the disabled body against the monstrous body as points of bodily difference from a normalized, ableist society.

The monster is a powerful symbol for explorations of social alterity. As Asa Mittman suggests, "monsters do a great deal of cultural work, but they do not do it *nicely*. They not only challenge and question: they trouble, they worry, they haunt. They break and tear and rend cultures, all the while constructing them and propping them up" (1). Monsters become a conglomeration of the fears, anxieties, issues, and questions of those in positions of hegemonic power in a society (Cohen, "Monster Culture" 4). They are the ultimate foils for conventions that those in hegemonic power have created as unquestioned "norms" that render other possibilities, the fringes that norms create, invisible while simultaneously hypervisible because they are foreign to that which is accepted.

Huff, like many authors of vampire fiction, constructs the vampire as a figure that represents bodily difference magnified. These are figures that, like the disabled body, are simultaneously marginal and central. As Nina Auerbach suggests, "They may look marginal, feeding on human history from some limbo of their own, but for me, they have always been central: what vampires are in any given generation is part of what I am and what my times have become" (1). Vampires, although expressing the Other, Auerbach suggests, are fundamentally about ourselves and bring attention to what we believe, do, and how we construct our understanding of the world around us. As figures who embody a society's fears and desires, the vampire and other monsters come to constitute a dark mirror in which we can see ourselves distorted, the hidden, suppressed things about us that we deny. In her work *Our Vampires, Ourselves*, Auerbach explores the notion that the vampire has evolved along with us, changing throughout history to match and reflect our insecurities, the salient issues of the day, and the perspectives of the members of a given society. Although imagined Others, they fundamentally come to speak fluently about our Selves (Auerbach). They are "personifications of their age" (Auerbach 3).

Huff, like other authors of Canadian urban fantasy, uses the figure of the monstrous protagonist to explore areas that are traditionally the realm of disability subject matter.[2] These vampires, werewolves, zombies, and

Frankensteinian monsters come to represent and magnify bodily difference, but they also in some ways serve as a presumed "safe space" for exploring disability issues without direct reference to disability. These monstrous figures undergo many aspects of the disabled experience such as difference from the normalized body, the imposition of a medicalized system for interpreting their bodies, encountering physical barriers, difficulties accommodating to an ableist world, differences in appearance (and in some cases "disfigurement"), and the challenge and experience of "passing" as "normal." However, the monster is also given characteristics in modern urban "dark" fantasy that allow it to be less of a threat to able-bodied society than the disabled body. The fears of bodily change and harm by the monster also come with the added bonus attached to them that mitigates many of the fears people have about becoming disabled. Becoming monstrous means bodily difference, but, unlike disability, it does not mean becoming "deprived" of senses, nor is it perceived as becoming weak (as disability is often portrayed in the ableist world). Instead, the monstrous body, although forced to change, often gains sensory abundance (the ability to smell, hear, or see better). Their bodies are also not weak (like the disabled body is perceived to be), but rather represent an abundance of strength. Their bodies are threatened and threatening bodies, but mitigated by an abundance of health (and often longevity), that thing which is often directly situated in opposition to disability (perceived as an absence of health) in modern disability narratives by able-bodied authors.

Tanya Titchkosky suggests that disability is constructed fundamentally as "loss." "What is wrong is seen to belong to disabled people in a more intimate or personal way than it does to others.... The inability to do things is one of society's primary definitions of disability" (*Disability, Self, and Society* 14). She suggests that "these people are referred to as "weak," or simply as the "vulnerable." Disability is made viable as a metaphor to express only that which is unwanted and that which is devastatingly inept" (*Reading and Writing* 4–5). Michalko speaks directly of blindness when he notes that blindness is spoken of as "lack," as "something missing" (*Mystery of the Eye* 6). The monster, similarly, can be associated with either lack or excess (Mittman 7), and in the case of the monstrous protagonist, the focus is often on abundance—senses keener than that of an "ordinary" human, exceeding humanity, beyond "normal" ability. Huff's vampire Henry is stronger than a "regular" human being, heals more rapidly, and has a sensory range greater than the human "norm" that extends to all of his senses—sight, smell, taste, touch, hearing. Yet, these sensory abundances can also be disabilities in a sense. For example, frequent mention is made of Henry's light-sensitive eyes, and the pain he experiences when seeing in bright environments. Like people with disabilities, Henry has found methods of adapting to his sensory excesses: "long years of practice kept him from recoiling, but he turned his back to give his sensitive eyes a chance to recover" (Huff, Blood *Price* 23–24).

Huff goes beyond simple allegory when she directly situates disability and monstrosity in a combined narrative in her Blood Books series. Vicki and Henry are both trying to pass as "normal," hiding their difference from a normalized world. Both figures have to find jobs that accommodate their bodily "limits": Vicki as a private detective instead of a police officer, and Henry as a romance author who has the ability to hide from daylight in his house to write and has an excuse for his "eccentricities" through his claim to an artist identity. Both need to change to adapt to their bodily difference: their perceived limits.

Huff uses the symbol of the monstrous as the extremified symbol of the outsider, of "difference made flesh" (Cohen, "Monster Culture" 7) and she allies this symbol of extreme, fictional alterity with an existing figure of difference, the disabled body. Huff illustrates a strong parallel between these two figures, making a connection that I hope to explore in my research about the interconnections between the fields of monstrosity theory and disability studies.

> Simi Linton introduces disability studies as a discourse that takes for its subject matter not simply the variations that exist in human behavior, appearance, functioning, sensory acuity, and cognitive processing, but, more crucially, the meaning we make of those variations. The field explores the critical divisions our society makes in creating the normal versus the pathological, the insider versus the outsider ... [2].

Jeffrey Jerome Cohen, when introducing monstrosity theory, suggests that

> the manifold boundaries (temporal, geographic, bodily, technological) that constitute culture become imbricated in the construction of the monster—a category that is itself a kind of limit case, an extreme version of marginalization, an abjecting epistemological device basic to the mechanics of deviance construction and identity formation.... The monster is a problem for cultural studies, a code or a patter or a presence or an absence that unsettles what has been constructed to be received as natural, as human.... The monster is that uncertain cultural body in which is condensed an intriguing simultaneity or doubleness ... binding one irrevocably to the other ["Preface" ix].

Both fields of research concern themselves with the social outsider, differences in interaction, biological difference, the sensorium, and fundamentally what it means to be human and "normal." Both look at what is considered "abnormal," either from a human perspective in the case of monstrosity studies, or from an able-bodied-centric perspective in the case of disability studies. The Linton passage defining disability theory could similarly be applied to monstrosity research. Disability theory looks at the variations *in* human behavior, while monstrosity theory takes as its focus differences *from* human behavior, taking that difference into excess since monstrosity is often used in narratives to exaggerate difference into the absurd. Linton's assessment of disability theory as a field that looks at appearance could also be applied to monstrosity theory, which takes as an essential part of its research the human vision of the monster and its visible difference.

The monster is a fiction, a construction of text and myth, and yet so is the disabled body. Titchkosky brings critical attention to the notion that the disabled body is a fiction, a textual construction (*Reading and Writing*). "Disability appears in the everyday life of text in a host of seemingly contradictory ways.... The very ways that disability is included in everyday life are, also, part of that which structures the continued manifestation of disabled people as a non-viable type" (*Reading and Writing* 5). Disability has been constructed as a metaphor for lack, ineptitude, and a "big problem" (*Reading and Writing* 4–5). This metaphorical construction of disability, the use of terms about disability in aspects of our social media to refer to an absence, points to the construction of disability as something that is both conceptually real and also mythical. Like the monster, disability has taken on a mythical quality in the way we narrate our experience of the world. Similarly, although monsters are not believed in, although they are textually constructed figures as well, "their importance, their significance, extends well beyond the base question of their reality" (Mittman 6). Monsters have social and cultural force. They act upon our world by drawing cultural interest and by coming to embody the fears and desires of our society as expressed through our popular culture.

The monstrous body traditionally displays difference in exaggerated ways, rather than subtle differences in interaction and appearance that exist in many cases of disability. However, there are also hidden monstrosities which are often paralleled with the idea of "passing" as normal. This is certainly true of Huff's vampires who need to hide themselves in society as a matter of survival and have hidden so well that they have become fiction. The appearance of the vampire matches our own so much that it can pass effectively. Huff regularly notes in her Blood Books that Henry has to restrain himself to keep his social mask in place, to hide behind it. Others temporarily note Henry's difference when he allows his social mask to slip, when he is unable to pass, evoking fear from the humans who witness his alterity unveiled:

> Slowly, making no sudden movements, Greg slid his chair back, putting as much distance as possible between himself and the man on the other side of the desk. He wasn't sure why, but in sixty-three years and two wars he'd never seen an

expression like the one Henry Fitzroy now wore. And he hoped he'd never see it again, for the anger was more than human anger and the terror it invoked more than human spirit could stand.... The fear in Greg's voice penetrated through the rage. There was danger in fear. Henry found the carefully constructed civilized veneer that he wore over the predator and forced it back on [Huff, *Blood Price* 26].

Henry recognizes, like many people with disabilities do, that the appearance of difference, the reminder of bodily alterity, can evoke fear and that fear can cause other negative responses. Huff brings attention to the effort that Henry extends in creating his human social mask and maintaining it. He has constructed an image of normalcy to allow him to pass unnoticed in the human sphere.

Similarly, Vicki spends a great deal of her time appearing as able-bodied as possible. She consistently tries to navigate dark environments (often to the detriment of her safety) in order to appear "normal." She takes any use of assistive devices as markers of "weakness" and tries to keep the progression of her disability a secret from friends and potential clients. Whereas Henry fears that the slippage of his mask of normalcy will lead to people configuring him as "threat" Vicki's social mask is erected to prevent people from configuring her as "vulnerable." As a former police officer, her identity is constructed around ideas of bravado and independence and she fears that the use of assistive devices will suggest a fundamental dependence that has been inscribed on her identity by her disability. Particularly when pursuing criminals or when in the presence of her former colleagues in the police department, Vicki feels a compulsion to take greater risks, to use her assistive devices less. It is significant that she tends to feel a greater impulse to pass as her pre-retinitis-pigmentosa-self when engaging in activities that related to her former identity as a police officer, a job that she felt she could no longer engage in as a woman who was losing her sight.

Goffman notes that, traditionally, the idea of visibility is a significant one for any issue of stigma (48). The more the able-bodied person has to change patterns of interaction with the disabled person, the more apparent to him or her the disability becomes and the more likely he or she is to socially situate it as an "issue"; this can lead to discrimination (Goffman 49–51). The issue of visibility is often dealt with in literary narratives about disability and monstrosity and in both the stigmatized person will often try to hide bodily difference in order to "fit in" to normalized society: the "passing" phenomena.

Disabled people often feel social pressure to change their own behavior so they can "fit in" with normalized society and "pass" as "normal." Rod Michalko, a disability scholar who has a visual disability, describes his own experiences with "passing" as sighted: "I could see hardly anything, but I belonged to the world that could see everything. What should I do and how should I live in this world? Simple, act as if I belong, act as if I can see" (*Difference That Disability Makes* 23). In order to avoid stigma and stereotypes, disabled people often try to keep their disability as hidden and unnoticeable as possible. Michalko notes that "passing, then, is an act of repression because the presence of disability in everyday life reminds us of the fragile character of social interaction and threatens its existence" (*Difference That Disability Makes* 10). He was passing as sighted because of his personal awareness that differences in social interaction with the able-bodied can lead to the end or increasing awkwardness of those social interactions and therefore felt a social pressure to conform and keep his disability hidden.

Disabled people develop "accommodation" strategies to adapt to an ableist world and ensure that their disability does not create too much of a difference from the able-bodied "normal" methods of interaction so as to mitigate discrimination. Michalko felt that

> passing as fully sighted became my strongest desire and I went about it with devastating single-mindedness.... I employed every interactional strategy possible to pass myself off as someone who was totally sighted. I could see, even if it was just a little, and I was sighted. That was my self, my identity, and even though blindness was creeping its way into me, I held it in abeyance on what I quickly came to experience as the interactional battlefield of passing [*Difference That Disability Makes* 9].

Not only are the social interactions of the disabled person at risk by not "passing" as able-bodied, in some cases, their entire situated identity can be at risk. Michalko, as someone who was originally sighted, invested personal identity in that normalized role and came to view his own progressive change to blindness as a threat to his own identity and therefore felt an internal pressure to accommodate, to make his disability unapparent to others and himself.

For Vicki, the knowledge of her disability led to her dismissal from the police force and to a continual struggle with the assumptions of people around her that she was "weak" or incomplete in some way. She perpetually felt the need to take on more dangerous tasks to prove her competence and strength. Her identity as a police officer and then as an investigator were invested in her ideas of strength and competence, which she tied to her identity as a sighted individual and made it difficult for her to rely on the use of assistive devices or other people for support. For Henry, the opposite was true. He had to struggle to downplay his strength—to appear passive and reduce the natural inclination of people around him to instinctively read his body as "predator" and thus "threat." Huff's series shows monstrous figures dealing with the social push to domesticate, humanize, and accommodate to human standards much in the same way that disabled people feel a push to accommodate to able-bodied standards—to find new ways of navigating able-bodied space and make their disability "not a problem" for able-bodied people to interact with them. Both the fictional and non-fictional stigmatized group feel the push to try to fit in and make their difference inconspicuous.

In the impulse to pass, disability is rendered invisible just as the vampire in Huff's constructed world of the Blood Books has been rendered mythical by the efforts of vampires over time to conceal their differences, to pass as human. Both Vicki and Henry are embedded in a system that requires that they render themselves socially invisible, that they hide difference and reinforce the notion of a normative body structure that leaves no room for diversity or bodily alterity.

Linton notes that differences in the functions of various characteristics are a key feature in disability studies research (2), and this is also true of monstrosity research that similarly looks at differences in ability: different strengths and different weaknesses that demarcate the monstrous as a separate category from the human. The sensorium is important to both fields and both look at the sensory organs as an important feature. In Huff's narrative, a particular attention is placed on the vampiric eye. The vampire possesses incredible visual range as well as night vision, and Huff physically marks that difference. The vampire's eye shines in an unnatural way, almost glows, particularly when he or she is relying on their vampiric abilities or is agitated and his or her human mask of control slips.

Disability studies tends to focus on the social belief about the absence or deficit of senses as a discourse, where monstrosity can look at both deficit and abundance. Huff shows significant interaction with the idea of the disabled eye, reminding the reader that Vicki has to turn her head to see her periphery and putting her in low-light situations where she loses her ability to see. Her difference is physically marked by her glasses, which are noted repeatedly when the character is prominent in the narrative by repeated need to adjust her glasses (sometimes multiple times per page). Similarly, attention is brought to assistive devices that enable her to navigate dark environments such as the flashlight she carries with her. Indeed characters are able to identify Vicki through looking into her purse and seeing her assistive devices. There is another interesting intersection here between the monstrous gaze and the disabled one: Huff notes the silver quality of the vampiric vision, evoking the idea of the glasses, the reflective, mirrored surface and the general role of the monstrous and disabled characters in Huff's narrative to serve as a mirror of social vision but one that includes difference where normalized vision often ignores difference and treats alterity as too problematic to engage with.

Sight and vision become almost a personified character in these novels: the personification of loss, alterity, ignorance, and darkness. Sight also becomes a symbol of acceptance: "blind" acceptance of difference and the ability to "see" beyond physical appearance. Henry pines for the loss of daylight, Vicki for the loss of the night.

These two parallel narratives intersect directly at the end of Huff's fourth book in the series, *Blood Pact* (1993), when Vicki faces a notion that many disabled people experience: the option of either dying or facing the possibility of a permanently transitioned and "different" or foreign body. Vicki chooses to allow Henry to transform her damaged body into a vampiric body, and has to deal with the consequences of this action and the resultant further change in her experience of the world in addition to developing new accommodation techniques. She collapses the small, tenuous difference she has constructed between disability and monstrosity by having the disabled character become the monster and embody Henry's difference as her own.

The intersection of narratives and transition of difference is made clear when Vicki's able-bodied lover, Mike Celluci, first encounters her after her change into a vampire. Huff describes Vicki as having become "thinner, paler, and her hair was different" (*Blood Pact* 330). Mike's first impression of Vicki's change shows the prevalence of sighted discourse: "It took a moment for the *most obvious* change to sink in. 'Your glasses?'" he asks. Vicki replies with "I don't need them any more … good thing too … can you imagine a vampire with no night sight? Biting by braille—God what a mess that would be" (*Blood Pact* 330). In these words, Huff defines Vicki by her disability and situates it as her most defining feature (thus, "the most *obvious* change"). Like many disabled people, she has been socially situated as an extension of her disability as though the disability defines her and any other aspect of her identity is inseparable from her existence as a disabled person.

In some senses, Huff fulfills the typical able-bodied wish fulfillment for disability narratives and Vicki gets cured of her disability by being transformed into a vampire,[3] but this *does* represent a further transformation for the character, a need to accommodate to a newly differentiated, and further changed body and a need to further learn accommodation and adaptation skills. Vicki has to rely on Henry as a mentor to help her accommodate to the world in her new body. She needs a full year to learn how to adapt to a world that she been altered to no longer naturally fit into: how to hunt, how to sense, how to move, and how to pass as "normal." This plays on the idea of disability mentorship that is common in the experience of many disabled individuals, the need to learn from someone with similar body conditions how to best navigate a "normalized" world with a body that is judged to be abnormal and rely on their longer experience of difference to learn how to best accommodate. Vicki's body is still disabled, but it is disabled in a different way, situated as abnormal by nature of being uncanny. Near her description of Vicki's transition into a vampire in *Blood Pact,* Huff illustrates the transition of disabilities—instead of having to squint to see in the dark, Vicki "tried not to flinch from the sudden spill of light" (329). She has to adapt to her abundance of strength, her abundance of senses, instead of her perceived deficits in those areas as a disabled individual, but the need for adaptation to bodily difference is the same.

Linton notes that the most crucial characteristic of disability studies is the "meaning we make of those variations" (2), and, similarly, monstrosity studies—dealing with fictional subjects—dwells entirely in the metaphorical and, having no physical, "real" parallels, tends to symbolize social anxieties. Monstrosity, as a subject, is about looking at the meaning behind differences: what do they represent? What do they tell us about "humanity" and "normalcy?" Huff uses her monstrous symbol to express the extreme ridiculousness of a society that cannot accommodate the disabled body by abstracting these accommodation issues onto an inhuman, vampiric figure. Huff's narrative asks us if, as a society, the only "person" that a blind woman can "come out" to and be herself around is actually not a person at all, but a vampire, what does this suggest about us as a society and our ability to make space comfortable for everyone regardless of bodily composition or type?

Notes

1. Teiresias was a blind prophet in classical Greek mythology. He is unable to physically see, but is capable of expanded insight and visions about the world around him. He is most noted for his role in the play *Oedipus Tyrannos* by Sophokles where he is able to see the truth of Oedipus' situation that others ignore or suppress. See also Euripides' *Bacchae* and Sophokles' *Antigone.*

2. This is the subject of my current research and will be expanded upon in future papers and in my dissertation.

3. Isabel Brittain (2004) refers to the failure of many authors who write about disability in seeing the possibility of a character to live a fulfilling life with a disability. She notes that this often causes the impulse to equate a happy ending with a cure.

Works Cited

Auerbach, Nina. *Our Vampires, Ourselves.* Chicago: University of Chicago Press. 1995. Print.
Brittain, Isabel. "An Examination into the Portrayal of Deaf Characters and Deaf Issues

in Picture Books for Children." *Disability Studies Quarterly* 24.1 (2004). Web. 10 Jan. 2012.

Cohen, Jeffrey Jerome, ed. "Monster Culture: Seven Theses." *Monster Theory: Reading Culture*. Minneapolis: University of Minnesota Press, 1996. 3–25. Print

———. "Preface: In a Time of Monsters." *Monster Theory: Reading Culture*. Ed. Jeffrey Jerome Cohen. Minneapolis: University of Minnesota Press, 1996. vii–xiii. Print.

Dossa, Parin. "Racialized Bodies, Disabling Worlds 'They [Service Providers] Always Saw Me as a Client, Not as a Worker.'" *Social Science & Medicine* 60.11 (2005): 2527–2536. Web. 10 Jan. 2012.

Goffman, Erving. *Stigma: Notes on the Management of Spoiled Identity*. New York: Simon & Schuster, 1963. Print.

Huff, Tanya. Blood Books [series]. New York: Daw, 1991–2008. Print.

———. *Blood Pact*. New York: Daw, 1993. Print.

———. *Blood Price*. New York: Daw, 1991. Print.

Linton, Simi. *Claiming Disability: Knowledge and Identity*. New York: New York University Press, 1998. Print.

Michalko, Rod. *The Difference That Disability Makes*. Philadelphia: Temple University Press, 2002. Print.

———. *The Mystery of the Eye and the Shadow of Blindness*. Toronto: University of Toronto Press, 1998. Print.

Mittman, Asa. "Introduction: The Impact of Monsters and Monster Studies" *The Ashgate Research Companion to Monsters and the Monstrous*. Ed. Mittman and Peter J. Dendle. Burlington, VT: Ashgate, 2012. 1–14. Print.

Titchkosky, Tanya. *Disability, Self, and Society*. Toronto: University of Toronto Press, 2003. Print.

———. *Reading and Writing Disability Differently: The Textured Life of Embodiment*. Toronto: University of Toronto Press, 2007. Print.

Youngs, Deborah, and Simon Harris. "Demonizing the Night in Medieval Europe: A Temporal Monstrosity?" *The Monstrous Middle Ages*. Ed. Bettina Bildhauer and Robert Mills. Toronto: University of Toronto Press, 2003. 134–54. Print

Media Expressions

Scott Pilgrim vs. the Megacity

Chester N. Scoville

ACCSFF '13

The reception in Toronto of the *Scott Pilgrim* comics (2004–2010), written and illustrated by Bryan Lee O'Malley, and of the film *Scott Pilgrim vs. the World* (2010), directed by Edgar Wright, was enthusiastic and widely publicized. For the first time, Torontonians were told, their city was about to be portrayed as itself in a major Hollywood action blockbuster; the local landscape, which all too often has been dressed up as New York or Chicago for American film productions, was about to appear as itself, with its own distinctive landmarks and identity. Finally, Toronto was about to make its debut in the movies as, in the words of both the comic and the film, "one of the world's great cities." Although Toronto has been the subject and setting for many stories, fictional and otherwise, it does not frequently remember this fact; the city's "ongoing struggle to recover from its cultural amnesia" (Harris 31) has typically been unsuccessful. Here at last, it seemed, was an opportunity for all the myth-making power of Hollywood to break through the city's fog of memory and establish a genuinely iconic Toronto story. That *Scott Pilgrim* did not succeed in doing so (except problematically and very partially) is a reflection on the way in which local events can catch up unexpectedly to a city's self-image, and to the way in which that self-image manifests in fiction.

For those who are unfamiliar with the narrative, a brief précis may be in order. The world of *Scott Pilgrim* is largely that of contemporary Toronto; although in both comics and film some events take place elsewhere (especially in flashbacks), it is Toronto that dominates the main narrative. The titular character, an aimless and rather feckless recent graduate of the University of

Toronto, drifts through downtown life with his friends, also recent graduates, playing in mediocre rock bands, working at minimum-wage jobs when employed at all, and having rather shallow romantic relationships along the way. Eventually, a mysterious young woman named Ramona appears in Scott's dreams and later in real life. Instantly infatuated, Scott finds that to win Ramona he must defeat her seven evil exes in a series of increasingly fantastical duels, which operate using both the mechanics and the narrative build-up of an old-fashioned video game, culminating with a challenge against the final "boss" villain, the wealthy and powerful Gideon Graves. Along the way, some of Toronto's most distinctive landmarks, from Casa Loma to Honest Ed's and from Lee's Palace to the Toronto Reference Library, new establishments such as Sonic Boom Music and old clubs such as the Rockit, as well as such familiar sights as archetypically Torontonian downtown houses and Toronto Transit Commission (TTC) vehicles, all become magically transformed into the sites of fantastic battles and adventures. Surely, here was a narrative to give modern Toronto, at last, its own distinctive local myth and hero to match, for example, London's Sherlock Holmes or New York's myriad Marvel superheroes.[1]

The way in which this did and did not happen may tell us something about the nature of audience response and discourse communities in urban fantasy. Although both the comics and the film are well regarded critically and have large numbers of loyal fans both in Toronto and elsewhere, they are also curiously tied to a local cultural turning point—what one might call the Scott Pilgrim Event. That event represented a potential turn in the *Zeitgeist* of the city, a moment when a mythic possibility tied to these texts opened up. It was a moment, however, in which that possibility was declined, for reasons that were both comprehensible and in some ways fortunate.

The opening of this mythic possibility was not unique either to *Scott Pilgrim* or to Toronto; rather, it is common to the sub-genre (or, as some writers would say, the mode) of urban fantasy. As such, it arises both from realities common to the modern urban experience and from tropes common to urban fantasies in general; it also arises, equally, from realities and tropes that exist specifically and locally.

Urban experiences *per se* are of course so variegated that generalizations about them are necessarily simplifications, yet for our purposes a few common points are crucial. First, as Raymond Williams argues in "The Metropolis and the Emergence of Modernism," in the modern city "small groups in any form of divergence or dissent could find some kind of foothold" (qtd. in Irvine 203); that is to say, in a modern Western city one common experience is being part of a subculture or a scene—and often several—that both fosters and invites the creation of new identities. Additionally, as Jane Jacobs notes, the basic everyday experience of the city—that which most clearly distinguishes it from the small town or suburb—is the normal and constant interactions, large and small, with strangers. People whom one has never met before and may never encounter again are part of the living fabric of the urban environment (Jacobs 30). Such variety and frequency of encounter make the urban identity especially capable of reinvention; rather than being necessarily rooted vertically, in long historical heritage, the urban identity can be formed horizontally, out of the chance encounters and shifting contexts of present experiences.

One does not have to live in Toronto to recognize these experiences; they are common to modern cities in general. Yet, modern Toronto is a particularly vivid example of the way in which modern cities are created of subcultures, scenes, and localities, given its self-image as the "city of neighborhoods" and its famously multicultural demographics; the city's official motto, "Diversity Our Strength," recognizes this reality and makes it a conscious civic virtue. A hero like Scott Pilgrim, drifting through urban life at random, finding his purpose as he goes, seems ideal for such a place.

With regard to generalized urban fantasy tropes, we may consider Farah Mendlesohn's observation that, in immersive fantasy, the reader is invited to participate imaginatively in the same fantastic world as the characters; in other words, in such a fantasy the invitation to a potentially shared mythic experience and identity is held out to the reader. Mendlesohn writes:

> The immersive fantasy is a fantasy set in a world built so that it functions on all levels as a complete world. In order to do this, the world must act as if it is impervious to external influence; this immunity is most essential in its relationship with the reader. The immersive fantasy must take no quarter: it must assume that the reader is as much a part of the world as are those being read about [59].

While Mendlesohn's observations about immersion do not apply solely to urban fantasy, they do provide a useful description of how urban fantasy can work. If a fantasy set in a bizarre alien city such as China Miéville's New Crobuzon—to give one of Mendlesohn's own examples—can operate in such a way as to conceptualize the implied reader as an inhabitant of its own world, then how much more direct may this process be with regard to a fantasy set in something like a real, recognizable place, and most especially when that place is the actual reader's own home? Similarly, Attebery says of this latter mode of narrative, "the inevitable falling-into-place of fantasy governs a world that seems continuous with the reader's [real-world] experience" (133), at least when the narrative is successful, an important point.

Between these observations, and keeping in mind Mendlesohn's *caveat* that her study is intended as non-prescriptive, we have a fair theoretical framework for the Scott Pilgrim Event: that point when filmgoers, especially Torontonians, were invited to find a mythic home in a fantastic hipster Toronto (if the term "Scott Pilgrim Event" sounds overly portentous, so was the event itself in some ways).

We should take a brief moment here to address the word "hipster," a deeply problematic but necessary term. Given the ever-shifting definition of the word, it may not really be possible to identify an actual group of people to whom it certainly pertains at any given moment; rather, insofar as the word "hipster" represents anything, it usually seems to represent not any actually-existing people but rather a shifting, ambivalent, often pejorative, marker in various social discourses. It is notable that the most prominent uses of the word in *Scott Pilgrim* itself are derogatory: e.g. Knives Chau, Scott's ex-girlfriend, refers to her rival Ramona Flowers as a "fat-ass hipster chick" (2.103); Matthew Patel, the first evil ex, is accompanied by a cadre of "demon hipster chicks" (1.152); in the film Scott dispatches his nemesis Gideon's sword-wielding goons to the accompaniment of a tune named "All Hipsters Must Die." That said, we must use the term here because social discourses are precisely the present issue, and because it proved to be important to the way people, especially in media, reacted to the Scott Pilgrim Event.

To understand the local context for that event, a reminder of some of Toronto's recent cultural background may be in order, as they relate to the narratives in question. Both Bryan Lee O'Malley's graphic novels and Edgar Wright's film adaptation are specific in time, place, and demographic. Set almost completely in downtown Toronto (notably the Annex and Wychwood neighborhoods) during the David Miller era,[2] the books and film, via the activities of Scott and his friends, celebrate at least the lower tier of the youthful, cool, creative way of life that, as Edward Keenan notes in *Some Great Idea*, dominated much of the city's self-image as seen from the center of downtown at that time. Keenan describes

> an avalanche of cultural activity that was creating excitement in a thousand small and large, and variously interconnected, ways.... There was [among other things] the Wavelength music series and the monthly Vazaleen, a queer dance party, which together gave birth to a Toronto music scene that produced acts like Feist, the Constantines, Broken Social Scene, Metric and the Hidden Cameras [67].

Scott Pilgrim pays tribute to this real-world creative scene in numerous ways; it is, indeed, inextricable from it. Both the film and the books embed themselves into the Toronto music scene not only via Scott's fictional band Sex Bob-Omb but also by the appearance of such clubs as the now defunct Rockit and the still existing Lee's Palace. The film's indie rock soundtrack, although international in scope, prominently features both the Broken Social Scene song "Anthems for a Seventeen-Year-Old Girl" and, especially, the Metric song "Black Sheep," which the film transforms into a song performed by the fictional band The Clash At Demonhead. The song as performed in the film vividly demonstrates the levels of influence of the actual Toronto rock scene upon the fictional rock scene of the narrative: it uses Metric's original instrumental track, but on top of that track it replaces singer Emily Haines's vocals with those of actress Brie Larson, who plays the band's lead singer, Scott's ex-girlfriend Envy Adams—a character whom O'Malley had originally based visually upon Haines herself (Martens). A character visually based on a singer then replaces the singer in a fictionalized version of a real song as still performed by that singer's band.

There are other such examples, but the point here is that the adventures of Scott Pilgrim represent the translation of the creative real-world activity of a specific time and place into the realm of the fantastic. *Scott Pilgrim vs. the World* marks the mythologizing of the cool Annex scene, the transformation of Toronto indie rock, as well as games and alt-comics (and even such stereotypically downtown things as veganism), into the stuff of adventure, romance, superpowers, and magic. Nearly all of the major events in both comics and film are connected in some way to this music scene, culminating in Scott and Gideon's final showdown in Gideon's new rock club, the (fictional) Chaos Theatre.

This creative scene and other scenes like it, not incidentally, have had important effects on urbanism, especially in the work of the Toronto-based writer Richard Florida. In the Canadian edition of *Who's Your City?* Florida cites the same indie rock scene as one of the markers of the innovation and resilience of Toronto (127–9, 221). In an interview with *The Grid* more recently, Florida opined that the ideal next mayor of Toronto would be "[s]omebody who looks and acts like Jian Ghomeshi," the CBC personality and former member of the vocal group Moxy Früvous. It is fairly clear from these and other sources that the image of the indie pop hipster is, within certain discourses, still very much a part of Toronto's self-image.

Accordingly, when the film was in pre-release, the local media discourse regarding it was often elaborately enthusiastic. The film was spoken of in the press as Toronto's long-awaited movie debut as itself (Rayner); its pre-release publicity led to much local popular enthusiasm. As of this writing there is still, for example, an active local Scott Pilgrim Cosplay group, more than three years after the film's release. Local events still feature it; for one randomly-chosen example, in November 2013 the Gamercamp Festival was offering "an inside peek at Scott Pilgrim's Toronto" as one of its highlights (Jax). A librarian present at 2013's Academic Conference on Canadian Science Fiction and Fantasy told me between sessions, additionally, that during the run-up to the film's release in 2010, she and her colleagues could barely keep copies of the graphic novels on the shelves, so enthusiastic were the local teenagers about the story of Scott and his friends. At the end of 2010, John Semly wrote this in *Torontoist*:

> *Scott Pilgrim*'s Toronto seems lived in: a space demarcated by the distance its dorky hipsters can cover on foot or, if they can scrounge up the fare, red-and-white TTC bus. *Pilgrim*'s Toronto is alive, organic, multi-dimensional.... The film's plucky but reluctant hero ... seems to stand in for Toronto as a whole.... Watching him, it's hard not to feel twitches of civic pride, especially when he routs Jason Schwartzman's smirking paragon of New York cool ... the film gave Toronto something which may help us compete with the other Gothams and Metropolises of the world: our very own superhero [Semly].

The terms in which Semly describes Toronto and its relationship to its new avatar/superhero are similar in some ways to the personification of Toronto conjured up at the end of Erik Rutherford's essay "Toronto: A City in Our Image," published in the 2005 collection *uTOpia*, long before most people had ever heard of Scott Pilgrim:

> Toronto is a young man, just out of university.... When you praise him, he doesn't believe you; when you criticize him, his pride is wounded. He's still a little inexperienced, poorly dressed, a touch diffident ... though he doesn't yet know the best way to achieve glory, he makes you feel he will [21].

It could almost be a portrait of Scott Pilgrim himself. Rutherford's personified Toronto is overall both more energetic than Scott often is and more outwardly conventional (Rutherford adds that his young male Toronto-avatar studied commerce in university, for example, though the humanities were, Rutherford continues, a stronger subject for him). Yet the image of Toronto as a very young man with potential for glory is still there, and still striking.

Most importantly, both the comics and the film are decidedly about the city of Toronto itself, and about its notorious collective self-anxiety in relation to other cities. For example, the New York-Toronto polarity that Semly specifically references is apparent in numerous episodes. Scott's fight with Todd Ingram, Ramona's third evil ex and the bassist for The Clash At Demonhead, breaks out explicitly in this context. In O'Malley's book, Scott becomes enraged and attacks because of the way in which Envy Adams taunts Ramona for her experiences in New York (3.27–28), while in Wright's film, Scott's anger is triggered by Todd's snide remark, "Fun? In *Toronto*?" Similarly, Scott's battle with Lucas Lee, the second evil ex, takes place near Casa Loma, one of Toronto's most distinctive landmarks but one that is often disguised as other locations during film shoots; the film makes this especially clear at the moment when Lucas hurls Scott through a matte backdrop of a New York–like skyline, revealing Toronto's CN Tower looming momentarily through the rip.

Consistently, Toronto is both celebrated and mocked through the use of some of its most recognizable landmarks: for example, the fight between Ramona and Knives (2.138–158) takes place in the Metro Reference Library, a location that Ramona calls "unbelievable" but which she then proceeds partially to destroy, breaking off a piece of public art to defend herself against her attacker. Most strikingly, perhaps, part of the fight between Scott and Todd takes place (in the comics) in Honest Ed's, the iconic but garish discount retailer that Scott and Todd inadvertently cause to implode under the weight of its own "stark existential horror" (3.68, 76–77). Scott's always-critical friend Julie Powers describes the ambience of Honest Ed's as resembling "how, when a baby is first born, it just *cries* at the sheer horror of being alive" (3.66), a statement that may be genuinely comprehensible only to those who are familiar with the real place itself: a reflection both of humorous fondness and of something very much like contempt. Yet those twin reactions themselves are familiar, I would posit, to nearly any Torontonian as a way of encountering their own city.

Even the most straightforward words of praise for Toronto, as "one of the world's great cities" (1.87), is rendered problematic in that the phrase is that of Scott's arch-enemy, the New York mogul Gideon Graves, whose upscale and glitzy Chaos Theatre is, in the comics at least, obviously located on the northwest corner of Queen and Bathurst Streets (6.93), in a building that, to locals, is recognizably the real location of The Meeting Place, a charitable drop-in center for poor and homeless Torontonians, and one that is named after one of the traditionally-understood aboriginal meanings of Toronto's own name. Insofar as Gideon notices Toronto, it is as a place to be colonized, gentrified, and Americanized; Scott therefore becomes the unlikely defender of the city both against outside menace and against its own "world-class" ambitions, against both its typically Canadian fear of American takeover and its "greatest desire … to be any place other than itself" (Harris 19).

One might think that, given all this, the adoption of Scott as a natural avatar of the city at that time would have been relatively obvious. Yet despite the hype (and, in some quarters, the hope), that did not happen. Of course, the film turned out to be a commercial failure on the American market, for various reasons, but that need not have stopped it from being the local myth that it seemed destined to become. Its subsequent status as cult classic might have been more than enough.

In fact, however, despite their many virtues and their intensely local identity, both the film and the comics presented to Toronto a highly problematic vision of itself, for historical and political reasons. Ever since the forced amalgamation in 1997 of the old City of Toronto and its former inner suburbs into the new *megacity* of Toronto, the character of the entity known as "Toronto" has been uncertain and often angrily contested, so that any attempt to mythologize it at this stage was bound to run into difficulty. The specific aspects of Toronto depicted in the film and comics found themselves in for a particularly rough local ride, however, at the very moment of the film's release. Scott Pilgrim, by way of his personal qualities and (especially) his downtown persona, suddenly appeared to be everything that the megacity of Toronto was turning against in 2010.

The year of Scott Pilgrim was also, for example, the year of the Toronto G20, the aftermath of which revealed deep hostility to the very parts of town that Scott Pilgrim represented. The riot that smashed up Yonge Street, the subsequent mass arrest of (nearly all innocent) people in the downtown core and the all-too-commonly heard response, "you should have stayed at home if you didn't want to be arrested instead of going downtown," as if *nobody really lives* in Toronto's downtown, all added up to a stinging city-wide vituperation of the very parts of the city that the film attempts to mythologize as emblematic of the whole. As Harris notes (19) of the city's literary history and Tossell remarks (67–68) of its politics, loathing of Toronto, especially its downtown core, is not merely a characteristic found elsewhere in Canada; it is often strongest in Toronto itself.

The year 2010 marked, also, the election of Rob Ford to the mayoralty in late October, in a resoundingly official-seeming rejection of the downtown identity. Although Ford has recently become a notorious figure of derision and mockery around the world, at the time of his election he represented something quite different locally: a suburban and blue-collar uprising, a rejection of the very idea that the creative downtown scene was or should be emblematic of the whole city. As Keenan puts it, Ford's victory speech on election night at the Toronto Congress Centre

> was [at] a venue in an industrial park in an offstage area of Toronto far from the walkable neighborhoods and landmark buildings that together add up to the psychological entity of Toronto.... It is no accident that it was here, in the uncelebrated suburban fringe of Toronto, that Ford kicked off his campaign for mayor, and here that he celebrated his victory [106].

This new political reality clashed directly with the mythic possibilities of Scott Pilgrim as they had been anticipated; though writers such as Semly declared, as we have seen, that Scott Pilgrim's Toronto seemed to represent "the city as a whole," in fact the urban locations depicted in the narrative are to be found almost entirely within a few neighborhoods surrounding the University of Toronto's downtown campus; the main orbit of its story encompasses perhaps ten to fifteen square kilometers within a total urban area of well over six hundred and thirty. In the election of 2010, those other areas expressed their presence in no uncertain political and cultural terms.

Additionally, as O'Malley himself later observed on his blog, *Scott Pilgrim* is excessively and surprisingly monocultural for such a multicultural city as Toronto, a fact that he personally came to regret. His statement on this topic is worth quoting at some length (all formatting, punctuation, etc. are O'Malley's own):

> I think it sucks that Scott Pilgrim came out so white!!!!!!!!!!!
>
> I am mixed (white + korean) and grew up being told that race didn't matter—that race was kinda over. As with many things you're told as a kid, it took me many years to realize that it wasn't really true.... It was kinda wishful thinking on the part of my parents, who were in a mixed relationship. I mean, I wish it was true, we all wish it was true, but it's not true.
>
> I did grow up in an extremely white environment. In northern ontario during the time I was growing up it was really just white people and Native / First Nations people. i moved to a bigger town in high school and i think my school had like 3 black kids and 4 asian kids or something. later in high school and in college I hung out with asian kids a lot, but White Canadian Culture was like 99 percent of everything around us.
>
> so anyway, I guess what I'm saying is, what I knew in the first 20 years of my life was white people and a little bit of asian people and so that's what I put in Scott Pilgrim. I had an unexamined non-attitude towards race and I didn't think about it until years later.
>
> Honestly, when i saw the Scott Pilgrim movie it was kind of appalling to see just how white it was—to not even really see myself represented on the screen.... At least in the comic they were just cartoons. You can project yourself into a simple drawing of a person so easily; race seems to matter less [O'Malley, untitled blog post].

O'Malley is, in this post, responding to a question on the topic raised by a fan, and his rueful observations about *Scott Pilgrim*'s whiteness are accurate: with the exception of Knives, all of the central characters are white, a fact that also, increasingly, reflects the makeup of downtown Toronto, but certainly not that of the city as a whole (Hulchanski 10). The only significant non-white characters apart from Knives herself—that is, the only characters who act in ways that importantly advance the narrative—are her father (who appears in the comics but not the film), Matthew Patel, and the Katayanagi Twins, all of whom appear solely as antagonists for Scott to defeat and have little character development of their own.

Nor, arguably, do the Scott Pilgrim books even reflect downtown Toronto itself particularly well or accurately, in, for example, the queer-positive nature of downtown Toronto's demographics and culture—and this despite the major presence of Wallace Wells, Scott's gay roommate and best friend. This character's prominence, Ryan Lizardi argues, does not change or challenge the basic heteronormativity of the narrative; rather, the text as a whole "ends up reaffirming hegemonic gender roles and heteronormativity under the guise of a hip, politically correct perspective" (2) as Wallace's queerness is played largely for comedy, and as manifestations of queer sexuality in the narrative are depicted as inherently embarrassing and somewhat shameful, while straight sexuality per se is not.

These contextual events and inherent limitations seem to indicate that, insofar as we are talking about local discourses, *Scott Pilgrim* may succeed as a fully participatory, fantastic immersion primarily for a fairly specific demographic (and of course can be, and is, enjoyed by people beyond that demographic), but that it cannot claim to represent the city as a whole, or even come close to doing so. It may be an immersive Toronto fantasy by design, and it has certainly been regarded that way on some occasions, but it is simply not nearly broad enough to encompass the variegated city that it represents.

Of course, O'Malley's original series did not have such ambitions as to become the avatar of its setting; it was Hollywood and the surrounding hype that created such an expectation. Yet despite its limitations, one cannot help but wonder at the fatal coincidence of the film's timing: that it made its grand debut just as local conditions for easy immersion in its fantasy world were about to be radically, even violently undermined. As such the Scott Pilgrim Event raises, but does not answer, a generic question regarding immersive fantasy, particularly when it is urban fantasy: what happens when a city, largely (but not exclusively) for contextual reasons, rejects a narration's invitation to the fantastic that defines the genre?

Formally, it would seem that *Scott Pilgrim* fits Mendlesohn's conception of immersion very well; additionally, it seems to agree with Attebery's description of what fantasy in contemporary settings is supposed to do. It sets itself in a world that is recognizable to the local reader yet clearly a fantastic version thereof, and it does so in striking visual detail. Within the recognizable city, the narrative maps out fantastic adventures, as we have seen, that not only take place against Toronto as a backdrop but are utterly reliant on its character as urban space.

For readers and film-watchers, but especially for Torontonians, this experience is potentially immersive in at least two ways: first, it allows them to map their own lived memories of those places and experiences upon the fantastic versions of them; and second, it allows them the reverse process, of mapping the fantastic versions upon the real ones. The former process would be experienced while reading or viewing the text, while the latter would be experienced afterwards, as memory of the text transforms and "makes strange" the experience of the everyday. Aesthetically, it seems to fill the bill.

Politically, however, the story is different. While it may be the case that there are individual readers that experience this immersive process unproblematically, it is at least for now the case that the overall discourse and identity of the city has grown in a rather different direction. Toronto has been offered a superhero and a myth, yet, despite claims and hopes to the contrary, it has, as a whole and for the time being, rejected this potentially iconic narrative rather than embraced it, as it so often has before with other narratives. In short: in the conflict of Scott Pilgrim vs. the Megacity, the megacity won—and perhaps that is after all for the best.

Notes

1. Coincidentally, at almost the exact moment that *Scott Pilgrim vs. the World* hit the cinemas in North America, the BBC's series *Sherlock*, reimagining Holmes and Watson in present-day London, began displaying a similarly vivid re-imagining of that city—particularly in the debut episode, "A Study in Pink." A mere two years later, Joss Whedon's film of *The Avengers* re-imagined post 9/11 New York City in a surprisingly bold way for a commercial blockbuster. Cities have been fertile grounds for such re-imaginings of late.

2. Mel Lastman was mayor from 1997 to 2003, Miller from 2003 to 2010. From the TTC cash fares mentioned after Scott's fight with Matthew Patel ($2.25 in the book vol. 1 p. 159, and $2.75 in the film), we can place the time of the story as roughly 2001–2005, and 2006–2010 respectively. Volume 1 was published in 2004 and the film released in 2010; they are therefore exactly contemporary with the story they tell, and both within the Miller era. However, since the fight takes place at the Rockit, a club that closed in 2005, the film is taking some chronological license. A convenient chart of TTC fares over time can be found in Barr, noted in the Works Cited. Thanks to Edward Keenan for pointing me to this article.

Works Cited

Armstrong, Christopher, and H. V. Nelles. *The Revenge of the Methodist Bicycle Company: Sunday Streetcars and Municipal Reform in Toronto, 1888–1897*. Toronto: Peter Martin, 1977. Print.

Attebery, Brian. *Strategies of Fantasy*. Bloomington: Indiana University Press, 1992. Print.

Barr, Andrew. "Graphic: The TTC Fare Hike, and Fare Hikes Over the Years." *National Post*, 15 December 2011. Web. 29 May 2013. <http://news.nationalpost.com/2011/12/15/graphic-the-ttc-fare-hike-and-fares-over-the-years/>

Florida, Richard. *Who's Your City? How the Creative Economy Is Making Where to Live the Most Important Decision of Your Life*. Canadian ed. Toronto: Vintage, 2009. Print.

Harris, Amy Lavender. *Imagining Toronto*. Toronto: Mansfield, 2010. Print.

Hulchanski, J David. *The Three Cities within Toronto: Income Polarization Among*

Toronto's Neighborhoods, 1970–2005. Toronto: Cities Centre, University of Toronto Press, 2010. Print.

Irvine, Alexander C. "Urban Fantasy." *The Cambridge Companion to Fantasy Literature*. Ed. Edward James and Farah Mendlesohn. Cambridge: Cambridge University Press, 2012. 200–13. Print.

Jacobs, Jane. *The Death and Life of Great American Cities*. 1961. New York: Vintage, 1992. Print.

Jax, Aubrey. "Weekend Events in Toronto, November 1–3, 2013." *BlogTO*. 1 November 2013. Web. 17 November 2013. <http://www.blogto.com/radar/2013/11/weekend_events_in_toronto_november_1-3_2013/>

Keenan, Edward. *Some Great Idea: Good Neighborhoods, Crazy Politics and the Invention of Toronto*. Toronto: Coach House, 2013. Print.

Kupperman, Steve. "Scott Pilgrim vs. Reality: A Fan's Camera Captures Scott Pilgrim's Stomping Grounds." *Torontoist*, 25 Jan. 2012. Web. 11 May 2013.

Lizardi, Ryan. "Scott Pilgrim vs. Hegemony: Nostalgia, Remediation, and Heteronormativity." *Journal of Graphic Novels and Comics*, 7 Dec. 2012. Web. 14 Nov. 2013. <http://dx.doi.org/10.1080/21504857.2012.747974>

Martens, Todd. "Track-by-Track: Beck, Nigel Godrich, Emily Haines, Bryan Lee O'Malley & Edgar Wright Dissect the 'Scott Pilgrim' Music." *Los Angeles Times*, 14 August 2010. Web. 29 May 2013. <http://latimesblogs.latimes.com/music_blog/2010/08/beck-nigel-godrich-emily-haines-bryan-lee-omalley-edgar-wright-dissect-the-scott-pilgrim-soundtrack.html>

Mendlesohn, Farah. *Rhetorics of Fantasy*. Middletown, CT: Wesleyan University Press, 2008. Print.

O'Malley, Bryan Lee. *Scott Pilgrim*. 6 vols. Portland, OR: Oni, 2004–10. Print.

_____. Untitled blog post. *Radiomaru*. 25 June 2013. Web. 14 November 2013. <http://radiomaru.tumblr.com/post/53857149606/q-this-isnt-meant-to-be-an-insult-or-a-rant-or>

Rayner, Ben. "Toronto Finally Gets to Play Itself." *Toronto Star*, 8 August 2009. Web. 14 November 2013. <http://www.thestar.com/news/insight/2009/08/08/toronto_finally_gets_to_play_itself.html>

Rutherford, Erik. "Toronto: A City in Our Image." *uTOpia: Towards a New Toronto*. Ed. Jason McBride and Alana Wilcox. Toronto: Coach House, 2005. 16–21. Print.

Scott Pilgrim vs. the World. Dir. Edgar Wright. Perf. Michael Cera, Mary Elizabeth Winstead, Kieran Culkin, Chris Evans, Anna Kendrick, Alison Pill, Brandon Routh, Jason Schwartzman. Universal, 2010. Film.

Semly, John. "2010 Hero: Scott Pilgrim." *Torontoist*, 20 Dec. 2010. Web. 11 May 2013.

Tossell, Ivor. *The Gift of Ford: How Toronto's Unlikeliest Man Became Its Most Notorious Mayor*. Toronto: Random House, 2012. E-book.

From "Space Oddity" to Canadian Reality

Isabelle Fournier

ACCSFF '13

According to Robert J. Sawyer, "Science fiction is always about the time in which it was written, and not about the time in which it is set" (Sawyer). Although I would certainly agree with this great Canadian science fiction writer, this concept does not apply to music lyrics. Once books are printed, their content is difficult to modify over time. Songs, however, can potentially be adapted or changed with every performance, or with any new rendition by the original performer or different artists. This article will show how David Bowie's song "Space Oddity" has evolved with time and context as it was recorded by different people. To achieve this result, I will first briefly reflect on Bowie's various interpretations of "Space Oddity" before comparing the original song with two French translations: one by Gérard Palaprat produced in France in 1971, and another by the Québécois Lucien Midnight from 2008. Apart from Midnight, another Canadian recently made his own special rendition of "Space Oddity": in May 2013 astronaut Chris Hadfield recorded the song aboard the International Space Station to celebrate his return to Earth, thus providing the first music video made in space. An analysis of all four versions provide an exceptional laboratory for exploring not only the differences in these two flavors of French (France and Quebec), but also the different perceptions of science and science fiction in England, France, and Canada. First, I will start by exploring the European English and French versions, before turning to the two Canadian renditions.

David Bowie, England, 1969

A demo of "Space Oddity" was recorded by David Bowie in March 1969, but it was hastily re-recorded in June of the same year, just in time for the song to be broadcast by the BBC for its news coverage of the Apollo 11 moon landing on July 20 (Doggett 57). Several critics have noted how Bowie took advantage of the topicality; the song was rush-released only a few days before the first men were to set foot on the moon. Bowie had his own vision at the time, and he said, "I want it to be the first anthem of the moon. Play it as they hoist the flag and all that" (qtd. in Doggett 57). However, because of the rather odd ending to the story of the song, BBC radio carefully waited until Apollo 11 had safely landed back on Earth to play it again after the first broadcast on July 20.

In only a few lines, the song tells the story of a young astronaut during his first exciting and mesmerizing trip to space. The take-off seems problem-free. The lyrics reflect the communication between mission control and the astronaut, with the official countdown, and series of clear-cut directives. However, once in outer space, something goes awry, potentially some kind of technical difficulty. The song ends on all communication being interrupted and ground control desperately trying to contact Major Tom, while he looks down at our planet, forever drifting into space.

Bowie himself recorded numerous alternative versions of "Space Oddity." The lyrics per se did not change. However the instrumentation has progressed from the first demo in the Bee Gees style used for the *Love You Till Tuesday* film in early 1969, to the use of Stylophone and futuristic electro sound in June 1969, to an adaptation by Ivan Mogol sung in Italian by Bowie ("*Ragazzo Solo, Ragazza Sola*"), and finally a stripped-down acoustic version with only guitar, drum, and piano in 1980 (Pegg 148–49). Instrumentation can change the feeling of a song, and played live, songs can become theatrical performances. André Gaulin noted that if a prose work requires a public, a song needs one even more "*à cause de sa fugacité, de son instantanéité*" (because of its ephemerality and instantaneousness). A song can change with every live delivery, and the plasticity and malleability of the instrumentation and vocal interpretation can modify the emotion and impression conveyed to the listener.

The reading of the lyrics' meaning can change with the addition of new elements. A decade after the original version of "Space Oddity" was written and performed, Bowie reused the same fictional protagonist in another song, and we hear back from Major Tom after losing track of him in space. Recorded in 1980, "Ashes to Ashes" refers to the astronaut with various hints and calling him by name twice. This song could be the object of an entire study in itself, but for my current analysis the important idea from the lyrics is that Bowie calls his character a "junkie," which could give a totally different view on "Space Oddity." Various critics have since read "Space Oddity" as a man high on drugs, but other than the "pills" and the reference to "floating" in space there is very little in the lyrics to establish a direct connection with drugs. I believe that the substance abuse idea came to Bowie after the fact, while looking back at his life experience after surviving the 1970s, and not when he originally wrote the song. Therefore, for the current study, I have chosen to discard this interpretation in favor of a more science-oriented analysis. In fact, several lines in the song do point to a more straightforward science-fictional interpretation, in accordance with the belief of the time. For example, the use of some NASA terminology gives a sense of scientific reality to the song. The mindset in the 1960s was quite different, somewhat more naïve, with lingering images of spacemen, new frontiers, and colonizing the moon.

The theme of an astronaut stranded in space was already present in science-fiction literature and movies at the time Bowie wrote "Space Oddity," an example being the short story "Kaleidoscope" found in Ray Bradbury's 1951 collection *The Illustrated Man* (1951). But most importantly, Stanley Kubrick and Arthur C. Clarke's science-fiction movie *2001: A Space Odyssey* was released the previous year. In the movie, HAL, the ship's computer, threatens and betrays the crew. Bowie recognized the movie as a major influence for the song: "I related to the sense of isolation," he explained (qtd. in Doggett 59). Peter Doggett says that "The scenario [of the song] represented a central theme of the existential literature (Camus, Sartre, Genet) that Bowie had devoured in recent years: an individual's alienation from society, and from himself. Like the astronauts on the Moon, Major Tom could look back at Earth and reflect on its perilous, insignificant place in the heavens" (59–60).

Moreover, barely a few weeks before Bowie wrote his lyrics, three American astronauts, Frank Borman, Jim Lovell, and William Anders, were the first men to orbit the moon on December 24, 1968. The same day they held a live broadcast during which were presented several pictures of the moon and Earth they had taken earlier that day (NASA). One of them, now known as the famous *Earthrise* photo, was taken by Anders, who later commented in an interview on NASA TV, "There are basically two messages that came to me. One of them is that the planet is quite fragile [and] Earth is really small. We're not the center of the universe; we're way out in left field on a tiny dust mote" (qtd. in Atkinson). This picture immediately became a symbol of human fragility, and of its insignificance in the universe. Like this picture, Major Tom looking at our home world from space reminds us of the vulnerability of the planet and of humankind, and of the alienation of our species.

Ken McLeod goes even further by saying that the "lyrics warn of the dangers of technological nihilism and alienation in an increasingly dehumanized world" (397). "The publicity image of spaceman at work is of an automaton rather than a human being," Bowie said in July 1969. "My Major Tom is nothing if not a human being" (qtd. in Doggett 58). And "Tom" being a fairly common name, it can be seen as representing all humans. James Perone suggests that

> The genius of Bowie's lyrics is that Major Tom can so easily be understood as a literal character and as a metaphor for those people who are blissfully unaware of the world as it is, or either because they do not make the effort to observe, or because through no fault of their own, they are unable to interpret the world around them. Major Tom is the first of Bowie's famous alienated characters [11].

Bowie tells us in "Space Oddity" that life on the moon or in space is just as hollow as it is on Earth.

The vocabulary of radio transmission is somewhat misused by Bowie. For example, in the first line, "ground control" is used instead of the more official name Mission Control Center used by NASA, and there is the odd combination of a military rank "Major" associated with a first name, "Tom." These "mistakes" reminds us that it is a work of fiction. As Bowie himself reminded people in November of 1969, "It's only a pop song, after all," and added, "I suppose it is an antidote to space fever, really" (qtd. in Doggett 57).

In 1969, the idea that humans would walk on the moon was so overwhelming that the accomplishment of American astronauts Neil Armstrong and Buzz Aldrin was acknowledged as our species' greatest feat. Yet after the glory of Apollo 11, and following the near disaster of Apollo 13, "manned trips to the Moon failed to hold the American imagination, or … justify the staggering expense" (58), Doggett said. In 1972, the Apollo missions were cancelled. Space had been conquered, but to no great avail. Space fever was subsiding as Bowie seems to have anticipated with his song.

Later on, Major Tom, the science-fictional character created by Bowie, took on a life of his own, and made an appearance in many other songs, for example "Rocket" by Def Leppard. Many artists paid tribute to Bowie and his protagonist. The most notable piece is probably Peter Schilling's commercially successful "Major Tom (Coming Home)" which he originally performed in German, and then adapted in English (both versions were released in 1983). This homage to Bowie's work could also be the subject of its own analysis since there were numerous remixes by Schilling himself and covers by other artists, including one adaptation in French by Belgian singer Plastic Bertrand at the end of 1983, which was also a commercial success. If Schilling's version had the astronaut return home after an extensive stay in space,

Bertrand alters Schilling's lyrics and offers a different vision under the title "Major Tom (s'en allait de la Terre)": Major Tom chooses to stay far from Earth, where he sees only egocentricity and great danger of nuclear threat. Less commercially successful but still interesting to note, moreover in the context of Canadian reality, is the song "Mrs. Major Tom" written by Canadian artist K.I.A. (Kirby Ian Andersen) in 2003, in which we hear Major Tom's wife's side of the story as she is expectantly hoping for her husband's recovery. The now legendary character has travelled far in popular culture. Let us now return to analyze in more depth the French translations of the original song, starting with the European French version.

Gérard Palaprat, France, 1971

Recorded in 1971, "*Un homme a disparu dans le ciel*" is Gérard Palaprat's interpretation of Bowie's hit. The lyrics were actually translated / adapted into French by Boris Bergman. In the 1960s, 1970s, and 1980s translating English songs into French was fairly common practice, and Bergman is well known for a number of musical translations (both from and into French) and original compositions throughout his career. Palaprat was then a young singer whose popularity in France was quickly growing. The song appeared on his album *Fais-moi un signe* and did not achieve any particular success.

When we look at only the written lyrics of "*Un homme a disparu dans le ciel*," without the musical and vocal performance, Bowie's song is hardly recognizable. Bergman's changes add new elements to the original song, for example it talks about a man painting rainbows, and an old willow tree in front of a house, and stars are metaphorically seen as pearls of oblivion ("perles d'oubli"). A different flavor of poetic than the original, with images of rainbows, night sky, languishing kings, and an old familiar neighborhood, this version is more reminiscent of a child dreaming of the stars, also reflected by another interesting difference: while Bowie's Major Tom sends his love to his wife, the final words of Palaprat's astronaut are for his "*mère.*" In other words, the astronaut's wife from Bowie's version becomes a child's mother in Palaprat's.

The title itself is also quite different. In the original title, which is a pun on Kubrick's "Space Odyssey," the word "oddity" can refer to someone or something strange, peculiar or unusual. The title "Space Oddity" does not reappear in Bowie's lyrics. So it could refer either to the fact that something unusual happens while the astronaut spends time in space or the simple idea that someone being in space is in itself peculiar. The French title plainly indicates "*un homme*" (a man) disappeared in space, without specifying whom. As a matter of fact, there is absolutely no reference to "Major Tom" in the song. The first line of Bowie's song shows that the communication is between Ground Control and the astronaut; in Palaprat's version, communication is instead between the "*tour de contrôle*" (control tower) and the "*fusée*" (rocket). Nonetheless, using both the word "*fusée*" in lieu of the person and the indefinite expression "*un homme*" in the title, without any reference to a name nor a military rank, is not a bad translation strategy to represent the previously mentioned sense of dehumanization perceived in Bowie's song.

Another reference in the French lyrics reads differently from the original: instead of having the newspaper comment on the news, Palaprat refers only to the idea that people on "*la radio*" who would like to hear from the astronaut. In *Imagining Outer Space,* Alexander Geppert notes numerous "astral sub-themes" including "the intricate commerce/media/public triangle" in "Space Oddity," which is partially lost with Palaprat because of the ambiguity over the word "radio." Are we still talking about commercial radio stations, which would be more similar to Bowie's newspapers, or simply mission control radio? The countdown to lift-off remains, but this time is in Russian instead of English. There could be different reasons for this, one being that Bergman was of Russian origin. Another possibility was to mark the ten year anniversary of the first human to journey in outer space by the Russian cosmonaut Yuri Gagarin.

Other losses are the reference to the religious/spiritual aspect of this spatial-transcendence towards the heavens and God in the original, and more down-to-the-earth scientific concepts like the "protein pills" and the "helmet." Overall, only the clear references to the "tin can" and the radio communication between Earth and the rocket closely match the original. If overall the song tells a similar story, several "scenes" have been modified.

When we listen to the song, Palaprat's voice goes between speaking and singing within a "tin can," and the sound quality brings us back to the original. If the lyrics seem erroneous or freely adapted at first glance, the musical ambiance of the recording is appropriate. Musically speaking it is a fine adaptation, and the feeling conveyed by the song, even though the lyrics have been modified, is overall well preserved.

The question that remains is: Why would the version made in France be more evocative of kids dreaming of the stars? Well, only NASA could make a moon landing relatively boring and so scientific that it became dehumanizing and alienating as we have seen with Bowie. Assigned to cover the Apollo missions by *Life* magazine, American novelist Norman Mailer noted "how all metaphysical concerns about the mission were masked in scientific sterility designed to excise emotions from the quest" (qtd. in Doggett 58). Palaprat and Bergman, as the dreaming young men they were at the time, clearly had a more romantic and childlike view of space exploration.

Lucien Midnight, Québec (Canada), 2008

And now we will leap forward almost forty years in time, and move to a different continent altogether: North America. What would prompt a Montréal musician and singer who usually sings in English under the name Frank Fuller to record a French cover of Bowie's hit on his only French album, *Champion des choses en bois*, in 2008 under the pseudonym Lucien Midnight? If translation of songs was popular in the 1970s and 1980s, in more recent years they tend to be far less frequent, even frowned upon in Québec, as the province is trying to define its cultural identity by distancing itself from Anglophone culture. Yet, "Space Oddity" is not only a British English song, the lyrics also talk about space exploration, which at the time was generally associated with NASA and American culture, precisely the Anglophone culture Québec is trying to protect itself against. And, before going any further, let us add a side note on Midnight's French pseudonym: the name comes from the long narrative poem "Old Angel Midnight" by American novelist and poet Jack Kerouac (whose parents were both French-Canadians), and it aptly reflects Fuller's mood for his French album. In contrast to the dreamer Palaprat was, Fuller is known for his rather melancholic, occasionally dark music, so for him this song is no real break from previous trends. He can write "dark" humorous songs. Compared to the Palaprat/Bergman version, Midnight's lyrics are closer to a faithful translation, but done in colloquial Québécois speech, with cruder words. His flavor of poetry contrasts with the European French version, and contains a funny touch, without falling into parody mode.

The title "Major Tom" makes the song easy to associate with the original, and avoids the problem of translating "oddity" in French, the same way Bowie's Italian version was given the title "*Ragazzo Solo, Ragazza Sola*" (Lonely Boy, Lonely Girl), and Palaprat's title was "*Un homme a disparu dans le ciel*." The pun on Kubrick's movie does not translate well in Italian nor French, and the word oddity itself is hard to render in the language of Molière. Midnight incorporates Québec particularisms in his lyrics. For example, Midnight has replaced the astronaut's helmet by a different type of hat associated with winter in Québec's folklore, a "*casque de poil*." The cold helmet has humorously been replaced by a warmer *fur hat* to fight the coldness of the outer space! In this version, the media aspect is respected with a reference to the astronaut's journey making the TV news also expressing the idea that the early astronauts had become popular figures, celebrities that people wanted to hear about. When Bowie wrote this song in the 1960s astronauts were regarded as heroes. But people quickly got bored with the space race and space exploration: who, except for a few science (fiction) geeks, can name any of the other ten American astronauts who walked on the Moon after Aldrin and Armstrong's landmark expedition? Who can name the people currently aboard the ISS? Over the last few decades space exploration has become so commonplace for younger generations that people barely pay attention to what is going on any more.

As mentioned, the French-Canadian lyrics are written in slang. Midnight frequently uses English words mixed into French sentences. Yet he does not necessarily keep the original's English words, for example: "*le* countdown," "*la* clutch," "*ton* starter" (instead of Bowie's "countdown," "engines on," and "ignition"). Midnight uses words more frequently associated with car mechanics than rocket science. In Québec, mechanical and construction words are frequently abusively borrowed from the English language and used instead of their correct French equivalents. On the album version, the lift off countdown in the song is in English, a language Midnight is comfortable with; which reminds us that Québec is always the little French player surrounded by a sea of English influence. I suspect the song was not meant to be released for radio (because of the coarse language), but more for him to play on stage. When Midnight performed "Major Tom" in Québec City in 2009, alone with his keyboard, the countdown was replaced by a beautiful musical bridge (Midnight, *YouTube*). Again, the acoustic simplicity of the performance can change the fleeting impression left by the song.

Using swear words is also common practice in informal language in Québec to express one's feelings, and Midnight's language tends to be colorful. In "Major Tom" he uses a wide variety of typical Québécois expressions including some that are considered profanities, for example "*un peu* fucké" (feeling "fucked up"), "*en* calvaire" and "*en* ostie." Moreover, Midnight uses the expression "*ma blonde*" to designate the astronaut's loved one. Indeed, if the astronaut's *wife* from Bowie's song had been replaced by his *mother* by Palaprat/Bergman, this time it is replaced by his "*blonde*," a word meaning "girlfriend" commonly used in Québec, but not in other French-speaking countries.

On his album, Midnight's version of the song stops short compared to the original, concluding right after the line expressing his love for his girlfriend, without the frantic reply "she knows." In contrast to Bowie's version, Midnight's lyrics contain no direct reference to a ship malfunction, which indicates it is the astronaut's decision to stay in space, after feeling disconnected from human reality. This is confirmed by the penultimate line in which Major Tom indicates his desire to stay in space for the rest of his life. Instead, Midnight has chosen a rather dark and radical way to express the ship malfunction, and to end the song. For his finale, Midnight used the actual voice recording of Steve Nesbitt from NASA's official message announcing the Space Shuttle *Challenger* disaster in January 1986: "We have a report from the Flight Dynamics Officer that the vehicle has exploded. The flight director confirms that. We are looking at checking with recovery forces to see what can be done at this point" (qtd. in Midnight).

Dreaming of reaching the stars is one thing, but the goal was not achieved without numerous accidents and unfortunate deaths. With his song Bowie anticipated problems associated with space exploration. Midnight has found a different way to express some of the dreaded reality that can occur when something goes wrong in space.

Chris Hadfield, International Space Station, May 2013

Like many others, Canadian astronaut Chris Hadfield was first inspired as a child to become an astronaut by the Apollo moon landing presented on TV in 1969. As noted by journalist Janet Davidson, "Canada had no astronaut program, and no Canadian could realistically expect to follow in the American footsteps Neil Armstrong had planted as the first man on the Moon in that steamy summer of 1969." In 1992, at a time where space exploration was mainly dominated by Americans, Hadfield was selected to become one of four new members of the Canadian Astronauts Corps, which to date counts a total of only twelve people. His space career over the following two decades counts a number of notable achievements including flying two NASA space shuttle flights, being the first Canadian to operate the Canadarm in orbit, executing two spacewalks, and being the first Canadian to float freely in space. More recently he became the first Canadian to be Commander of the International Space Station (ISS).

As the name indicates, the *International* Space Station is a collaborative effort between several nations, including two countries which were previously competing over the Space Race (1957–1975): the United States and the Soviet Union. In 1993 NASA and the Russian Federal Space Agency (FKA) agreed to join forces to collaborate on what would become the ISS, a project which also involves the European, the Japanese and the Canadian Space Agencies. The ISS is currently maintained and supplied by an international team of astronauts. From the time Bowie wrote the song during the years of the Space

Race to the time Hadfield recorded his own rendition of "Space Oddity" with his acoustic guitar aboard the ISS, space exploration has become an endeavor based on international cooperation, instead of competition.

The music video for Hadfield's version of "Space Oddity" went viral on *YouTube* with over 20 million hits, and made news coverage world-wide. With Bowie's permission, Hadfield modified the lyrics to reflect his own personal experience, to make it relevant to the time and place where he was when he recorded the song. Several variations were noted in his version. For example, Hadfield nicely replaced the "protein pills" which are an outdated science fiction concept since the first Apollo flights' crew members complained about the poor quality of the food. Most changes reflect how Hadfield was not about to depart from Earth, but was soon to be leaving the ISS to come back home. For his return trip to Earth, he travelled aboard the Russian spacecraft Soyuz, as he mentions in his version of the song. So the new lyrics simply reflect the astronaut's real journey. Hadfield knew he was likely spending his last few days in space, and he was making the most of it (he has since announced his retirement from NASA). As a result he modified Bowie's overlook of the moon with words expressing his final glance at the Earth from above, while in the video he can be seen floating in his version of a "tin can" orbiting our planet.

I mentioned earlier the line in which Major Tom expressed his love for his wife. Hadfield's version is far more prosaic, referring to his professional experience only, and stating that as commander, *he* knows (instead of "she knows"). Even though Hadfield is married, he has chosen a less romantic approach to the song to focus more on his current reality, using his well-deserved title of commander, an achievement he can be proud of. The astronaut in Bowie's version might have felt insecure, apprehensive, and astonished during his adventure, but the commander of the ISS is a calm and confident experienced astronaut.

Quite certainly Hadfield did not want to end up marooned in space like Major Tom, so he also modified the previous gloomy ending into something more positive. He nicely substituted Bowie's two lines which indicate the ship malfunctioning with words communicating the fast approaching end of his final journey in outer space. Hadfield seems content and satisfied to have had the opportunity to realize his own dream.

Despite the change in context, both Canadians (Hadfield and Midnight) end their version on the same contemplative note as Bowie did, with the astronauts mesmerized by their experience in outer space and their global overview of our blue marble. The main difference is that Hadfield lives to tell the tale. The ending of the song is worth noting and comparing by way of conclusion. In Bowie's story, the astronaut knows he has (voluntarily or involuntarily) lost control of his ship, and of his life. The astronaut is perceiving the world as sorrowful and full of problems he cannot solve. There is nothing *he* can do. No longer will he return to Earth and influence people, and all communication is cut between the astronaut and the rest of humanity. Midnight's gloomy interpretation also expresses the astronaut's disenchantment with the entire planet, and humankind's alleged technological and scientific progresses. For him, heaven is better than Earth, and he no longer cares what might happen to the rest of the world and the people left behind. Hadfield's version reveals that there might be nothing left for him to do aboard the ISS (he has performed his duty as an astronaut and commander of the ISS), yet he does not give up on humans and comes back to Earth ... with a more optimistic version of "Space Oddity" to share with people.

Hadfield is obviously a man of science. He firmly believes in space exploration, and in the various scientific experiments he conducted during his 5-month stay aboard the ISS. He also tried to make his daily life aboard the station accessible to the general public. During his time in space, on top of recording the video for his version of "Space Oddity" he took beautiful pictures of Earth, and made short videos explaining how to live in a weightless environment which were then posted on YouTube, Facebook, and Twitter. In Fall of 2013 he also published a book, *An Astronaut's Guide to Life on Earth: What Going to Space Taught Me About Ingenuity, Determination, and Being Prepared for Anything* and his pictures were featured in *Earth, Spirit of Place: Featuring the Photographs of Chris Hadfield*. Through arts and social media, Hadfield takes away the dehumanization and alienation elements of Bowie's song and of space exploration. This also reflects the pragmatism and forwardness of the Canadian view, in contrast with the more gloomy and nihilistic European view. Hadfield's rendition of "Space Oddity" took the fictional element out of the science fiction scenario of the original song, to make it a scientific reality.

Works Cited

Atkinson, Nancy. "Apollo 8 Astronaut Bill Anders Reflects on *Earthrise* Picture." *Universe Today*, 22 April 2008. Web. 3 March 2014
Bertrand, Plastic. "Major Tom *(s'en allait de la Terre)*." RKM/WEA, 1983. LP.
Bowie, David. "Ashes to Ashes." *Scary Monsters (and Super Creeps)*. RCA, 1980. LP.
_____. "Ragazzo Solo, Ragazza Sola." Adapted by Ivan Mogol. Philips (UK). 1969. LP.
_____. "Space Oddity." Philips (UK), 1969. LP.
Bradbury, Ray. "Kaleidoscope." *The Illustrated Man*. Garden City, N.Y: Doubleday, 1951. 28–39. Print.
Davidson, Janet. "Chris Hadfield Ready for 'Surreal' Space Station Odyssey: Astronaut

in Quarantine Before Blasting Off in Russian Capsule." *CBC News*. CBC, 7 December 2012. Web. 3 March 2014

Def Leppard. "Rocket." *Hysteria*. Prod. Robert John "Mutt" Lange. Phonogram, 1987. Audiocassette.

Doggett, Peter. *The Man Who Sold the World: David Bowie and the 1970s*. New York: HarperCollins, 2012. Print.

Gaulin, André. "*La chanson comme genre*." *Québec Français*, 46 (Mai 1982): 37–39. Print.

Geppert, Alexander C. T. *Imagining Outer Space: European Astroculture in the Twentieth Century*. New York: Palgrave Macmillan, 2012. Print.

Hadfield, Chris. "Space Oddity." Online video clip. *YouTube*, 12 May 2013. Web. 3 March 2014.

K.I.A. "Mrs. Major Tom." *Adieu, Shinjuku Zulu*. Neuphoria Recordings, 2003. MP3.

Love You Till Tuesday. Dir. Malcolm J. Thomson. Perf. David Bowie. Rec. 1969. Polygram,1984. Film.

McLeod, Ken. "Music." *The Routledge Companion to Science Fiction*. Ed. Mark Bould, Andrew M. Butler, Adam Roberts, and Sherryl Vint. New York: Routledge, 2011, 393–402. Print.

Midnight, Lucien. "Major Tom." *Champion des choses en bois*. Independent recording, 2008. MP3.

_____. "Major Tom." Online video clip. *YouTube*, 17 July 2009. Web. 12 Nov. 2013.

NASA Administrator. *Earthrise*. Image Gallery. NASA website. NASA. Last Updated: 28 July 2013. Web. 12 Nov. 2013.

Palaprat, Gérard. "*Un homme a disparu dans le ciel*." Adapted by Boris Bergman. *Fais-moi un signe*. AZ, 1971. LP.

Pegg, Nicholas. *The Complete David Bowie*. London: Reynolds & Hearn, 2004. Print.

Perone, James E. *The Words and Music of David Bowie*. Westport, CT: Praeger, 2007. Print.

Sawyer, Robert J. Personal Interview with Herb Kauderer, at Confluence: The Annual Literary Sci-Fi/F/H Conference in Pittsburgh, PA, July 2011.

Schilling, Peter. "Major Tom (Coming Home)." Elektra, 1983. LP.

2001: A Space Odyssey. Screenplay by Stanley Kubrick and Arthur C. Clarke. Dir. Stanley Kubrick. Perf. Keir Dullea, Gary Lockwood, and William Sylvester. Metro-Goldwyn-Mayer, 1968. Film

From Monstrous Mommies to Hunting Heroines: The Evolution of Women on *Supernatural*

Lisa Macklem

ACCSFF '13

Women on the television series *Supernatural* (2005 to the present [renewed for 2014/15]) have had a hard go of it. Initially, women were cast in maternal or victim roles or as monsters. Creed points out that "[a]s with all other stereotypes of the feminine, from virgin to whore, she is defined in terms of her sexuality. The phrase 'monstrous-feminine' emphasizes the importance of gender in the construction of her monstrosity" (3). As the show developed, however, there was an attempt to create stronger, recurring roles for women. Fan resistance spelled the doom of many female characters initially, especially those cast primarily as love-interests for the male main characters, Sam and Dean Winchester. In fact, even the possibility of a woman's becoming a love interest could spark immediate and rabid fan hatred. Interestingly, the one female character who was universally loved, Mary Winchester, the main characters' mother, evolved from a seemingly passive victim to a kick-ass hunter in her own right over the course of five seasons as her hitherto unknown past came to light. Arguably, the acceptance of Mary's past helped to pave the way for more strong female characters such as Sheriff Jody Mills and Charlie Bradley. Spigel points out that "audiences 'decode' media according to their own social backgrounds and identities" ("Introduction" 9). The women in *Supernatural* are constructed both from without, by the fandom, and from within, by the television and horror stereotypes. The fandom influenced the show to such an extent that the show actually incorporated a female fan, Becky, into the *Supernatural* universe. Rosinsky notes the split in feminist criticism, particularly in speculative fiction, of whether the female identity is constructed from within or from outside of the individual. Judith Butler asserts that "[t]he view that gender is performative sought to show that what we take to be an internal essence of gender is manufactured through a sustained set of acts" (xv). *Supernatural*'s construction of women moves from a highly patriarchal and "traditional" view of women to a more nuanced and complex construction in part both because of and despite of its largely female fanbase.

A recent amateur survey on Tumbler indicated that 93 percent of the *Supernatural* fans surveyed were women, while 4 percent were male and 4 percent self-identified as other. The same survey indicated that 87 percent of those responding were under the age of 24 (Non Timebo Mala on Tumblr http://destiels-impala.tumblr.com/results). Ratings news for the eighth season (2012/13) indicates that *Supernatural* had the largest gains in the 18–49 demographic of any show on network television, indicating that the age data of the survey done on Tumblr may be inaccurate at least as far as overall viewership is concerned. The important point here is that whether or not the demographic information is accurate for all viewers, it does point to the gender of fans who are actively engaging with each other on the Internet and who are consequently the fans most likely to have an influence on the production as "active" fans. Another place that "active" fans can meet each other and interact with the stars of the show and even at times those involved in production is fan conventions. While male attendance at *Supernatural* conventions appears to be on the rise, the vast majority of those in attendance are female.[1] The age demographic skews higher than that found on Tumblr, but that could be attributable to the cost of attending conventions. Online fans are engaged on many levels with the show, and because they are already engaged on a more active level than casual viewers, these are the fans most likely to have an increased interaction with the show's producers. Showrunners oversee every aspect of the writing of the show, from hiring the writers to negotiating with networks and studios over notes to seeing the scripts through production as well as interacting with fans. Phalen and Osellame point out that "Ultimately, the showrunner is responsible for the tone of the writers' room and for the script that comes from it" (13). Michael Newman recognizes that the showrunner needs to balance concerns of studios, networks, and advertisers by attracting and maintaining an audience through the ebb and flow of the television season. Caldwell points out that these pressures may see the showrunner stifle the creativity that comes out of pitch sessions with writers to satisfy corporate demands (60). There is pressure from above to cultivate a relationship with the fans. Andrejevic points out that "the more the boundary between the 'offstage' site of production and that of consumption is eroded, the greater the sense of participation-based loyalty" (31). Deery points out that in the past, "direct audience influence has been largely restricted and largely under producer control" (168). However, more recently, according to Deery, "the Web enables private reactions to become public and acquire currency and weight" (168). Showrunners Eric Kripke and Sera Gamble have been candid about admitting to reading online forums and taking an informal gauge of the audience reception of the show through those interactions. Gamble states that the thing that is "unique about the show *Supernatural* is the quality of the fanbase. We have always been in a pretty direct dialogue with our fans *through* the show" (emphasis added).

The way viewers interact with television has changed remarkably in the last decade, and this is evident in the recently completed five-year study by Zubernis and Larsen on *Supernatural* fandom and identity. They concluded that the "relationship between fans and the creative side, as well as the human representations of the fannish objects themselves, are increasingly reciprocal" (14). Zubernis and Larsen's study focused on the relationship itself and not how that relationship affects the production of the television show itself. Victor Costello and Barbara Moore in their 2007 study also observe that fandoms have a new-found power with the advent of the Internet to connect individual fans with one another: "Where pre-internet fandom was largely decentralized and limited in mass, inhibiting the collective bargaining power of individuals and geographically dispersed fan consortiums, online fan communities have the potential to produce unified centers of resistance to influence the global industries of cultural production" (140). Fans are beginning to understand their own power in the greater scheme of the industry. Catherine Johnson examines the rise of cult television as a way for marginal networks to gain loyal audiences and compete with the larger networks' higher ratings. She sees this strategy as having changed since the inception of cult television in the 1960s:

> cult television and fan audiences are no longer understood by the industry as marginal, atypical, or simply irrelevant. As the example of *Lost* demonstrates, the networks appeal to the "fan" in all viewers, encouraging fan activity and loyalty as a part of television spectatorship in an era when multi-media participation is increasingly becoming the norm [Johnson 144].

Fans have a greater influence and producers and writers have a greater awareness of them than ever before. Jeremy Butler points out that the growing interest in media production studies places more emphasis on how the industry encodes the text with meaning. Furthermore, Jeremy Butler points out that one of the major aspects "of the current global economy to interest political economists is the rise of digital technologies and networking and their impact upon media economics" (409–10). *Supernatural* is on the CW, the fifth U.S. network.[2] As such, it does not have the pressure to have the same ratings as a show on say NBC or ABC, but it does still have to bring in enough revenue to finance the production and justify remaining on the air. As a "cult" show, with a small, but fiercely loyal fan base, *Supernatural* is able to derive a significant portion of its revenue through alternate streams such as foreign distribution, DVD/Blu-Ray sales, and merchandise. All of these are good reasons to remain sensitive to audience reaction and reception of characters.

Supernatural has been on the air since 2005, in its ninth season at the time of writing, and even in that time, attitudes towards women have arguably changed, but it is important to take a brief look at how far women's roles on television have changed—or not changed. Television has moved from the Mrs. Cleavers to the Kate Becketts. Jeffrey Brown points out that "our depiction of women in the media is so grounded in eroticism and objectification it is difficult to conceive of them in different terms" (13). Brown points to the action heroine as having the potential to "function as progressive role models" (14). *Supernatural* first aired on the WB network, the network that also gave television audiences *Buffy the Vampire Slayer*, arguably one of the strongest female action heroes to date. *Supernatural* would seem to have a natural, cultural space for the action heroine in the guise of female hunters, yet there has been great resistance to the introduction of female hunters on the show. Mothers and mother figures tend to be the most well-received, and this is likely an aspect of identification on the part of the 18–49 year old largely female demographic. Science fiction and fantasy tend to offer better roles for women—ostensibly because they are most often set in the future, the past, or an alternate reality, such as Captain Janeaway on *Star Trek Voyager* (1995–2001), Xena on *Xena, Warrior Princess* (1995–2001), or Buffy on *Buffy the Vampire Slayer* (1997–2003). These shows featured women in lead roles. *Supernatural* only featured two women as regular cast members and both only in season three. Stuller was inspired by Xena and Buffy to look for modern day superwomen role models in the tradition of Wonder Woman. She devised a four part criterion for superwomen characters: narrative that draws on mythology, an element of the fantastic, a uniquely identifiable skill or power, and a mission that benefits the greater good (5–7). Interestingly, while one would not immediately think of many of the female characters on *Supernatural* as *super*women, many of them do fit these criteria. Mary Winchester is but one example: she is an integral part of the mythology of the show as its matriarch; she appears as a ghost to save her sons in "Home" (1.09)[3]; she is a trained hunter; and the hunter code is hunting things, saving people—all the while without ruining the general public's innocence in regards to the evil surrounding them.

How women are portrayed on *Supernatural* is a product of a number of influences. In some ways it grows out of the patriarchal vision generally embodied on television. It is also important to realize that the writers' room itself on *Supernatural* is the product of a largely patriarchal system. In addition, that writers' room has been almost entirely populated by men. At most there have been three women writers on any given season, even when Sera Gamble was the showrunner. I would, however, contest the accusations of outright misogyny on the part of the writers. The discussion of misogyny among the writers has been an on-going one. Most recently, Misha Collins, who plays Castiel on the show, said at a fan convention that he is disturbed by the level of misogyny displayed by the show (Superwiki). Collins is known for making outrageous and often tongue-in-cheek remarks at conventions, and this comment arguably falls into that category. The high death toll of women can be more realistically explained by turning to horror conventions and tropes in general. Horror as a genre is more stuck in a rigid and stereotypical rut when it comes to the portrayal of women than perhaps any other genre.

Kawin provides a useful gloss on horror: "As a genre, the horror film is defined by its recurring elements (such as undeath, witches, or gross, bloody violence), by its attitudes toward those elements (such as that transgressing limits is dangerous), and by its goal: to frighten and revolt the audience" (4). Creed identifies some of the major female stereotypes found in horror: "archaic mother, monstrous womb, vampire, possessed monster, *femme castratrice*, witch, castrating mother" (151). Short criticizes the assumption of Creed and other critics "that the genre's main audience is male and [their use of] psychoanalytic principles to argue that its representation of women either reiterates male fears surrounding sexual difference, or anxiety about female power in general" (2). Short identifies ambiguities in the stereotypes identified by Creed and others and sees these as "recoverable spaces, providing textual openings by which to reinterpret meanings and debate possibilities" (172). Other highly recognizable tropes for women in horror include the virgin (often for sacrifice), the tramp/seductress (interestingly, also often for sacrifice), medium or seer, the screamer, and the damsel in distress. How then, do the women of *Supernatural* fit into these various categories and tropes? How do they compare to others on television and in horror, and what kind of response has the audience had, and what was the response of the writers to that reception, especially in the case of recurring characters?

The mother is a particularly strong trope in *Supernatural* and drives a great deal of the plot. The entire entry of the Winchester brothers and their father into the world of "hunting things, saving people" is initiated by the death of Mary Winchester, the mother of Dean and Sam and the wife of John. The series begins with her death in the "Pilot" (1.01) and for much of the first season, the episodes begin with a flashback to her death. Mary begins as the quintessential sacrifice, right down to the white nightie that is her only costume until the end of season two. In the first season, she is destroyed by fire not once but twice in the course of trying to save her youngest son. Her real purpose is as victim, generating the revenge motive for both her husband and her sons.

The "Pilot" (1.01) contains two virginal sacrifices which bookend the episode. Immediately after the scene of Mary's death, the first person the viewer meets in the present is Jessica Moore, also dressed in white, but as a naughty nurse for Halloween. The mother figure is juxtaposed with the femme fatale or stereotypical sexy blond of horror movies. The link to Mary is completed by the camera panning to a shot on the mantel of Mary and John. The audience quickly learns that Jessica is the most important woman in Sam Winchester's life as she has been his only support and girlfriend while he has been at Stanford. We next see her later that night being protected by Sam from a supposedly dangerous intruder who turns out to be his brother. In this scene, her status as innocent (though still seductress) is emphasized by her wearing a Smurf t-shirt. The episode ends with a bookend of the opening scene when Jessica is sacrificed by fire in a white nightie just as Mary was. Jessica's death becomes the impetus for Sam to rejoin the hunting life. Because his mother died when he was still a baby, her death had not affected him in the same way it had Dean and John, but Jessica's death generated the anger necessary to set Sam on the same road of vengeance as his father. Jessica's character is never given the opportunity to develop the way Mary's is in the show. Neither Jessica nor Mary has ever represented a point of contention between the fans and producers. Most often fan rejection of a female character is due to that character coming between the brothers. In some ways, the fans themselves mother the characters on the show and are very protective of them.

Mary is able to become a recurring character because of the supernatural element of the show. In an alternate reality in "What Is and What Should Never Be" (2.20), Dean experiences a world in which Mary is alive. Dean's life is very much shaped by the loss of his mother. In the season one episode "Dead in the Water" (1.03), Dean tells Lucas that he tries to be brave because that is what his mother would have wanted. Sam learns, along with the viewer, that for some time after his mother died, Dean did not speak. In the "Pilot" (1.01) and in flashback in "A Very Supernatural Christmas" (3.08), Dean becomes angry when Sam does not afford their mother's memory sufficient respect. Creed explains that the "archaic mother is the parthenogenetic mother, the mother as primordial abyss, the point of origin and of end" (17). Mothers and their absence is a central theme for the show. Dean is protective of Mary in "What Is and What Should Never Be" (2.20), which also features a return of Jessica in this alternative reality. Both brothers are in successful and happy relationships, in this alternate reality, but their relationship with each other is strained. There is a recurring theme in the series that anything that comes between the brothers is suspect and likely evil. This almost perfect world has been created in Dean's mind by the Djinn who is slowly draining the life out of him. Dean's perfect world includes his mother, a fiancé for Sam, and a girlfriend who is both beautiful and understanding for Dean. Dean's perfect world is horrific to the fan who wants nothing to come between the brothers or between the fan and her fantasy. Mary is the one person in this fantasy world who brings the brothers together. In "Dark Side of the Moon" (5.16), in a scene from his past, Dean is protective of Mary even as a child and comforts her when she and John are briefly separated. Yet, in this same episode, Mary is used against Dean by Zachariah the angel as he uses her image to taunt Dean, and she becomes the castrating mother.

Mothers are frequently seen as victims in the show. In the first season alone, single mothers or women in mothering roles need help or rescuing in 9 of the 22 episodes. Women are central victims in 19 of those 22 episodes. The season three episode "The Kids Are Alright" (3.02) centers on mothers whose children are being taken by changelings. Central to the episode is an old love interest of Dean's, Lisa Braedon. Dean actually wonders whether her son Ben could be his child. She tells him no, but there is continuing speculation that she may have lied about it. A demon taunts Dean that Ben is his son in the Braedons' last appearance on the show in season six's episode, "Let It Bleed" (6.21). Interestingly, both the episode that created Lisa and the last one she appears in were written by Sera Gamble, and in season six, Gamble's first season as showrunner, Lisa Braedon emerges as a recurring character and as a love interest for Dean. Ultimately, her storyline comes to a close because of an on-going resistance on the part of fans to either of the brothers having a love interest. This fan resistance may be due in part to the similar resistance among many fans to what is viewed as a "Mary-Sue," a female character used in fan fiction to place the author inside her own fiction: in this case Gamble. While fans are protective of the characters, in fiction, fans have little interest in casting themselves in the mother role: "Mary-Sues" in most fan fiction are almost always love interests for the brothers. How fans view the show itself may also be linked to how they view it in fan fiction. *Super-*

natural is the second most popular show on fanfiction.net, second only to *Glee* in the number of stories posted about it. While this chapter is not about fan fiction, it is still important to note the influence that medium has over fans and their reception of storylines. Fans who style themselves as writers are more likely to feel they should have a say over the writing of the show and the shape of the storyline.

Any relationship that comes between the brothers has met with fan resistance. In season eight, even Dean's friendship with Benny was a source of contention among fans. Regardless of the cause, this fan push back began in the hiatus between seasons one and two, when it was discovered that a recurring character in season two would be Jo Harvelle. Jo was touted as a kickass hunter in her own right and a love interest for Dean. Over the hiatus, fan reaction to this possibility was extremely heated and negative. Superwiki reports that Jo was initially named Alex and was "heavily rejected by fans" when the character first appeared on the show's IMDb page in June 2006 ("Fandom Chronicle: 2006"). In July, new sides for the character were leaked and the character had been completely re-written, ostensibly in response to the fan reaction. In contrast, Ellen Harvelle, Jo's mother, and another mother figure for the brothers, was extremely well received. By the end of the season, Jo had disappeared, but Ellen makes a final appearance to help in the final showdown in "All Hell Breaks Loose Part 2" (2.22). However, in that final showdown, she does become a victim who needs to be saved. Ultimately, in season five's "Abandon All Hope" (5.10), Jo and Ellen are given heroes' deaths in the course of saving the brothers. Looking once more to fan fiction, one of the most popular types of stories on fanfiction.net is hurt/comfort. Who better to provide succor for the characters than a mother figure? While fans may fantasize about being the woman in the characters' lives, many of them are in the age demographic to be mothers and therefore can identify with that role. Mothers are acceptable female characters but female characters are not acceptable when they pose any kind of a challenge to the male characters' prowess or the relationship between the two brothers.

Mary's characterization as passive victim is revisited in season one in the episode "Home" (1.09), when she saves her sons, but even more significantly in season four's "In the Beginning" (4.03), when Dean travels back in time and learns that his mother and her family were, in fact, hunters. Even Mary's mother, Deanna, after whom Dean is named, is an effective hunter, even displaying those skills in the kitchen while cutting up fruit salad. Young Mary is seen again in season five's "The Song Remains the Same" (5.13). In this trip back in time, she once again plays a strong, competent character who is able to contribute to the safety of the group on an equal level with her sons, and in fact, more effectively than John, their father, who was not a hunter until after his wife's death. Fan reaction to learning about Mary's past was mixed but primarily positive. The revelation of her past also caused a reassessment of her actions in the "Pilot" (1.01). With a hunter's knowledge, and knowing that she had made a deal with Azazel, the Yellow-Eyed Demon in "In the Beginning" (4.03), did she know what she was getting into when she stepped into that nursery? Was she, in fact, attempting to save her family instead of simply being a passive sacrifice? These are questions that have never been definitively answered.

Creed argues that the "central characteristic of the archaic mother is her total dedication to the generative, procreative principle. She is the mother who conceives all by herself, the original parent, the godhead of all fertility and the origin of procreation. She is outside of morality and the law" (27). The archaic mother is one of the monstrous-feminine archetypes that Creed describes along with the monstrous womb. Neither of these descriptors particularly captures Mary, but they do describe Eve, the mother of all monsters who appears in season six, in "Like a Virgin" (6.12). Eve appears from out of a fiery abyss in a white nightdress in a mirrored, negative image of Mary and Jessica's deaths. When Eve wants to try to persuade Dean and Sam, she assumes the guise of Mary, their own mother, in the episode "Mommy Dearest" (6.19). In another odd twist on the mother/child dynamic, it is Dean who names her newest offspring "Jefferson Starships." Ultimately, Dean is the one to kill her.

Because *Supernatural* is a horror show at its heart, and because the central characters have dedicated their lives to killing monsters, they necessarily do kill rather a lot of women in gruesome ways. However, the show is not completely simplistic in its depiction of female monsters or female horror tropes either. Vampires are depicted as both male and female. In "Dead Man's Blood" (1.20), Kate and Luther are the two vampire leaders. Luther is killed, but while Kate is held captive and tortured, she ultimately escapes. In "Bloodlust" (2.03), it is the male hunter Gordon who turns out to be the monster, not the female vampire Lenore who has trained herself to live on animal blood and is the leader of her nest, directing the male vampires. Similarly, werewolves in the show are seen as both male and female. In season two's "Heart" (2.17), Madison is clearly a victim when she is bitten. Sam falls in love with her and ultimately she asks him to kill her to prevent her from hurting anyone else. In point of fact, in contrast to the usual vagina dentata of horror, Sam has the penis of death as almost every woman he sleeps with ends up dead. Amelia from season eight and Dr. Roberts from season four's "Sex and Violence" (4.14) are notable exceptions. Even though Madison is a victim and a monster, she is still given the dignity of determining her own fate. In season eight's "Bitten" (8.04), the case once more revolves around werewolves. In this case, Kate is bitten by Brian and ultimately kills him. She tells Dean and Sam via video that she promises never to hurt anyone ever again, and they decide to let her live unless she becomes violent.

Possession is another way that women can become monstrous. Creed explains that "Possession becomes the excuse for legitimizing a display of aberrant feminine behavior which is depicted as depraved, monstrous, abject—and perversely appealing" (31). Creed goes on to describe the monstrous female as being beautiful on the outside to hide a truly evil nature inside, reinforcing that notion from Judith Butler about the performativity of the feminine: being a woman requires that the woman adopt a role. Two prominent demons recur on the show, and both appear in multiple, but always beautiful guises. Meg first appears in season one's "Scarecrow" (1.11) and her last appearance is in season eight's "Goodbye Stranger" (8.17). Meg moves from purely evil to an ally of the brothers and a potential love interest for Castiel. In season two's episode "Born Under a Bad Sign" (2.14), Meg possesses Sam. While possessed, Sam displays no overtly feminine traits nor is he weakened in any way. Meg is discovered simply because both Dean and Bobby know Sam well enough to sense that he is not himself. At the end of the episode, Dean does tease Sam: "Dude. You like full on had a girl inside you for like a whole week. That's pretty naughty." Dean characteristically makes a sexual joke about it, but the reality is that it takes the combined efforts of Dean and Bobby to defeat Meg and get her out of Sam. It would be easy for Meg as a stereotypical horror figure to have had a static arc, but she is seen to evolve over the course of the series. She learns from her defeats and disappointments to die by redeeming herself and saving the Winchesters, or at least allowing them to escape from Crowley. It is a testament to the strength of the character that it takes the King of Hell himself to ultimately defeat and kill her. Interestingly, Meg was always a favorite among fans, once again because she did not pose a threat as a romantic interest. Even though she was a formidable foe, the brothers always managed to defeat her as well.

Positive reception can be linked to the characters not posing a threat to the brothers as a romantic interest or as being "better" than the brothers unless, like Meg, she is a villain. Villains, of course, must be worthy of the brothers and therefore pose a challenge. In addition, villains bring the brothers closer as they must work together to defeat the common enemy. Jo's fate was sealed the minute she disarmed Dean in her first scene. Both Bela Talbot and the demon Ruby were introduced as regulars in season three. Once again, as before season two, there was a massive fan outcry. Michael Ausiello of TVGuide.com, interviewed Kripke after "fans ... inundated [Ausiello] with hundreds of angry e-mails." According to Ausiello, fans were concerned that "In a bid to broaden the serial thriller's appeal, CW brass [were] forcing producers to bimbofy the show, hence the two new lady killers." In that interview, Kripke makes the following, very revealing statement:

> First of all, I love our fans. I love them to death. I love how passionate they are. But they tend to worry unnecessarily. They tend to get stressed before they have a chance to judge the finished product. We are so conscious and aware of our fans. We're making the show for the fans; we're not making the show for the network. We would never do anything to betray them. I'm not saying we're perfect. I'm not saying we don't make mistakes. But we're very conscious and aware. And when we *do* make mistakes, we course-correct.

Kripke definitively states that the writers' room and the production are influenced by fan feedback. In this instance, it would appear to be to the detriment of the portrayal of women. Both Bela and Ruby begin the season as strong, independent women. Bela was an independent business woman who bought and sold supernatural artifacts to the highest bidder. She was projected to be a potential love interest for Dean, as Ruby was destined for Sam. In an interesting twist early in the season, Bela is the one to objectify Dean in "Red Sky at Morning" (3.06) and tells him they should have "angry sex." Her fate was sealed with the audience when she outsmarted the brothers on several occasions. Later in the season, when it became clear the audience was not accepting her, Sam is the one to have a sex dream about her in "Dream a Little Dream" (3.10). This returns the male gaze back to objectifying the woman (Mulvey). Ruby, unlike the other recurring demon, Meg, was universally disliked. The character was downgraded to recurring and recast for season four but did become a romantic interest for Sam. She meets her end violently, literally between the two brothers as Sam holds her and Dean stabs her. Interestingly, Kripke wrote and directed "Lucifer Rising" (4.22) and would have both written and blocked the scene. Ruby's death can be seen as a way of appeasing fans who had been in an uproar over the character coming between the brothers. Bela was, no doubt, a victim of fan backlash, but Ruby appears to have been the character Kripke was asking fans not to worry about in the interview with Ausiello. Ruby was destined to play a significant role within the overall mytharc of seasons three and four.

Two other popular characters who also fill a traditional horror stereotype are Pamela Barnes and Missouri Mosley who are both seers/psychics. Karin Beeler points out that "Women of vision in television and film articulate a resistance to patriarchal attitudes, but also suggest the need to subvert the polarization of men and women and the polarization of science or reason with the inner world of visionary, mystical experience" (1). In addition, Beeler states that "Historically and in myth, women have often been linked to 'the home' (Campbell, *The Power of Myth* 153) environment and to inner strength or intuition (e.g., women's intuition)" (3). Missouri actually appears in the episode "Home" (1.09). Initially, the character was supposed to fill the role that Bobby Singer filled in the season one finale, but they could not get the actress who had gone on to book bigger and better (that is, more lucrative) things. Singer, of course, went on to fill a surrogate father role, so it is likely that Missouri would have filled a surrogate mother role. She facilitates the connection between the boys and their mother in the episode, further underscoring her maternal role. They visit Pamela at her home initially in the season four episode "Lazarus Rising" (4.01), and she is the one to tie them to their bodies—another form of home—in "Death Takes a Holiday" (4.15). Pamela's literal vision is taken from her when she looks upon the true form of Castiel the angel, yet she is still able to use her heightened senses to "see," and this even extends to being able to sense her environment to physically battle a demon, though she loses the fight and is killed.

Season five saw the introduction of Sheriff Jody Mills—another mother and initially a victim in "Dead Men Don't Wear Plaid" (5.15). However, she manages to help save her town, Bobby, and Dean. Mills would go on to become a romantic interest for Bobby, which was strongly supported by the fandom. She also develops into a support system of sorts for the brothers, providing help on a few cases, most notably in season seven's "Time After Time" (7.12). In this episode, she acts as a support system, bringing Sam Bobby's research material and helping him go through it to rescue Dean from the past. She also acts as a mother figure, even admonishing Sam to go to bed or she will use her Mom-voice. Mills had the role of mother taken away from her when her child is killed (twice) in "Dead Men Don't Wear Plaid" (5.15). Pairing her with Bobby makes her place as surrogate mother very clear, even though there was some fan speculation about Jody and Sam having a romantic possibility when they share a bottle of Scotch in "Time After Time" (7.12). Rhodes dispelled this possibility at subsequent fan conventions. Conventions are one way that fans can get clarity on storylines and plot developments. The information garnered at these conventions is generally shared widely through YouTube videos and fans blogging about their experiences. Rhodes' popularity at fan conventions is likely a contributing factor to the character appearing again in the last episode of season eight, "Sacrifice" (8.23). That episode continued the storyline begun in "Clip Show" (8.22) that saw Crowley threatening to kill everyone the brothers had ever saved. Mills also features in "Rock and a Hard Place" (9.08) in season nine when she calls the brothers in to investigate what looks like a supernatural case. It turns out that Vesta, the Roman goddess of the hearth, is sacrificing "virgins" who used to be sacrificed in her name to ensure a good harvest. Jody once again helps Sam rescue Dean when he is captured. The links to losing one's virginity, a rite of passage for any child, and to the hearth/home theme once again mark Mills as a mother figure. However, she is able to step in and actually be the one who is stabbed by the goddess and save both brothers without negative backlash from fans. This acceptance has been bestowed on few female characters.

"Clip Show" (8.22) saw the return of Sarah Blake from season one's episode "Provenance" (1.19). Blake represents the one love interest introduced for the brothers (in this case Sam) who the fans were willing to embrace and yet the writers killed her. Blake had been characterized as a strong character, able to accept what the brothers do and even help them with the case in season one. For most of season one, Sam is seen mourning the loss of Jessica. Fans embraced Sarah because she represented Sam's ability to love again and demonstrated that he had started to move out of the grieving process. Fan attachment would have been somewhat weaker in season one, and therefore, fans were more willing to accept the introduction of a love interest. In season eight, however, Sarah has moved on with her life and is primarily depicted as the typical female victim. She represents the normal life that Sam has always yearned for and which he tried to have again with Amelia at the beginning of season eight. Sarah's death symbolizes the death of that dream. In addition, the writers brought back a character that would be sure to garner the most sympathy from fans, heightening the horror element by playing on the writers' knowledge of fans.

Perhaps the strongest character introduced to date is Charlie Bradbury. She has extraordinary computer skills, which make her a valuable ally for the brothers and the target of season seven's major antagonist, Dick Roman, the leviathan, in "The Girl With the Dungeons and Dragons Tattoo" (7.20). She helps them defeat Roman in the episode but is injured and needs to be rescued in the end. She is next seen in "LARP and the Real Girl" (8.11) in which she is Live Action Role Playing, but she is not the victim; she is the Queen of Moondor and gets to be the one to save the damsel in distress. In "Pac-Man Fever" (8.20), she has learned all about the hunting life and is clearly like a little sister to the brothers—Dean refers to her as the "little sister he never wanted." In the episode, she gets to appear as a Lara Croft type and is instrumental in solving the case. Even though she is captured by the Djinn and cast in the victim role so is Dean. She demonstrates that her researching skills rival those of Sam. Fan reception for Charlie has been very strong, in part because she is played by Felicia Day, but to a large extent because the character is self-identified as gay. She poses no threat to the viewers of a love interest for either brother. In "Slumber Party" (9.04), Charlie demonstrates that she is becoming a hunter in her own right, and by the end of the episode, she has once again saved the brothers, this time from the Wicked Witch. She is last seen entering Oz with Dorothy Gale, who it turns out is also a hunter. Charlie is also seen to be a fan herself as she amply displays by her participation in fan practices. Charlie's pop culture references, much like Dean's, clearly identify her as "one of us," and this facilitates her acceptance.

Charlie begins as a victim but quickly becomes an ally before evolving into a hunter in her own right. The show has featured other female hunters, but the majority of them appear for only one episode. Most are seen to be capable like Reisa in "The End" (5.04), Tamara in "The Magnificent Seven" (3.01), or Olivia Lowry in "Are You There God? It's Me, Dean Winchester" (4.02). Most of them are single. Olivia and Annie Hawkins in "Of Grave Importance" (7.19) are both living an existence similar to the loner/outsider existence of the male hunters. Some like Tamara or Gwen Campbell ("Exile on Main Street" [6.01], "Two and a Half Men" [6.02], "Family Matters" [6.07], and "…And Then There Were None" [6.16]) are part of a family unit. In the end, most of them meet similar fates to the male hunters on the show who also appear as victims in need of saving. One example is Lee Chambers in "Adventures in Babysitting" (7.11). Interestingly, this episode also introduces his daughter Krissy who is being raised in much the same way as Dean and Sam were. Dean is determined to save her from the hunting life even though she proves herself to be a competent hunter and is even instrumental in helping to save Sam and Dean in addition to her father. In her second appearance on the show, after her father has been killed, in "Freaks and Geeks" (8.18), it becomes clear that Krissy will very likely continue in the hunting life.

One of the most significant female characters to emerge in the series is Becky Rosen. Becky Rosen is a fangirl of the *Supernatural* novels in the series which the prophet Chuck has written. She is a direct result of the writers' perception of fans. In her first appearance in "Sympathy for the Devil" (5.01), written by Kripke, she is contacted by Chuck (Kripke's stand in in the show) to help the brothers. She is seen writing wincest and cannot stop touching Sam when she does meet the brothers. She expresses disappointment in Dean and is clearly identified as a "Sam-girl." Initial fan reaction was resistant as she was seen as a monster who exposed fan practice and who lusted after Sam. However, her second appearance in "The Real Ghostbusters" (5.09) is more sympathetic. She also transfers her love interest to Chuck in that episode. Her final appearance in "Season Seven: Time for a Wedding" (7.08), however, forever tagged her as a stalker willing to go to any lengths to secure the object of her desire. Once again, fans were confused and unhappy with this portrayal. As Gamble who was showrunner at the time was under fire for two lackluster seasons, this shift in Becky's portrayal could be seen as a way of speaking back to the fans. Sam essentially tells Becky to "get a life" much as William Shatner famously told fans of *Star Trek*. Shatner came to regret that remark as he came to understand the passion fans had for *Star Trek* and also the level of understanding they brought to their consideration of the show (Jenkins 10). Perhaps this final portrayal of Becky might be an indication that Gamble had come to regret the level of input that fans had achieved: there may be no clearer indication of the influence fans have had on the storyline than the fans themselves being incorporated into the story itself. However, in "Slumber Party" (9.04), showrunner Jeremy Carver revisits Becky. While she does not appear in the episode, Charlie mentions her as having been the one to upload all of the *Supernatural* novels onto the Internet. Once again, Becky is seen as a valuable resource. Rather than looking annoyed at the mention of her name, Sam, in particular, looks a little embarrassed and uncomfortable, much more in keeping with his initial response to Becky, so there seems to be a softening toward the character from the writers.

Some of the more recent successful female characters have been the monsters. The primary villain in season eight is arguably Naomi, the angel who has taken over the running of Heaven. She tortures other angels to bend them to her will. The writers characterize her, as they have the other angels in "administrative" positions, as a stereotypical emotionless white-collar worker. Rather than being a nurturing leader for the angels, Naomi has taken on this male stereotype. Naomi falls into the performative trap described by Judith Butler. When she finally realizes that Metatron means to destroy Heaven, she tries to help the brothers and confesses her deceptions. Interestingly, it is while she is trying to help prevent Sam's death that Naomi finally breaks down crying and we see real emotion from her.

Another villain introduced in season eight is Abaddon, a Knight of Hell, who is determined to take over Hell from Crowley. She first appears in "As Time Goes By" (8.12) when she follows Henry Winchester to the present from 1958. She was modeled after Lauren Bacall, according to writer Adam Glass (Superwiki). While she is incredibly sexual, she is also the equal of any of the male villains on the show and has dominated those around her through force and her intellect. Abaddon is able to embrace her feminine persona while still remaining the equal of any of the male characters.

Supernatural's portrayal of women is hampered by the show's being steeped in the tropes of the horror genre. Women inevitably fill stereotypical roles as victims and monsters. Its cult status and active fanbase allow for a greater interaction between fans and producers in coding characters, however.

Through the seasons of the show portrayals of women have become stronger and more positive. The subject of female characters is an active site of discourse between fans and producers. While the close relationship and ongoing dialogue between fans and producers has led to greater creativity in some areas of the show, in many ways this dialogue has hampered producers' creativity with respect to the portrayal of women.

Notes

1. This conclusion is based on the author's own attendance at and observation of roughly 20 conventions between 2009 and 2013.

2. The CW is the fifth largest network in the United States and was formed in 2006 by a merger between the WB network and UPN. It is jointly owned by CBS and Time Warner. *Supernatural* is produced by Warner Bros. Studio (Gray, especially Table 3.1, 84).

3. References to the series will be by title as well as by season and episode number (e.g. "Pilot" 1.01).

Works Cited

Andrejevic, Mark. "Watching Television Without Pity: The Productivity of Online Fans." *Television & New Media* 9.1 (January 2008): 24–46. Web. 5 Feb. 2013.

Ausiello, Michael. "Supernatural Exec: 'We Won't Be One Tree Hill with Monsters!'" TVGuide.com. 21 July 21 2007. Web. 15 Aug. 2013.

Beeler, Karin. *Seers, Witches and Psychics on Screen*. Jefferson, NC: McFarland, 2008. Print.

Brown, Jeffrey A. *Dangerous Curves: Action Heroines, Gender, Fetishism, and Popular Culture*. Jackson: University Press of Mississippi, 2011. Print.

Buffy the Vampire Slayer. Exec. Prod. Josh Whedon. WB; UPN. 1997–2003. Television.

Butler, Jeremy G. *Television: Critical Methods and Applications*. 4th ed. New York: Routledge, 2012. Print.

Butler, Judith. *Gender Trouble*. New York: Routledge, 1999. Print.

Caldwell, John. "Convergence Television: Aggregating Form and Repurposing Content in the Culture of Conglomeration." *Television After TV: Essays on a Medium in Transition*. Ed. Lynn Spigel and Jan Olsson. Durham: Duke University Press, 2004. 41–74. Print.

Costello, Victor, and Barbara Moore. "Cultural Outlaws: An Examination of Audience Activity and Online Television Fandom." *Television & New Media* 8.2 (2007): 124–43. Web. 15 Nov. 2013.

Creed, Barbara. *The Monstrous-Feminine: Film, Feminism, Psychoanalysis*. New York: Routledge, 1993. Print.

Deery, June. "TV.com: Participatory Viewing on the Web." *Journal of Popular Culture* 37.2 (2003): 161–83. Print.

Gamble, Sera. "Commentary for 'The French Mistake.'" *Supernatural: The Complete Sixth Season*. Warner Bros., 2011. Blu-Ray.

Gray, Jonathan. *Television Entertainment*. New York: Routledge, 2008. Print.

Jenkins, Henry. *Textual Poachers: Television Fans and Participatory Culture*. Rev. ed. New York: Routledge, 2013. Print.

Johnson, Derek. "Fan-tagonism: Factions, Institutions, and Constitutive Hegemonies of Fandom." *Fandom: Identities and Communities in a Mediated World*. Ed. Jonathan

Gray, Cornel Sandvoss, and C. Lee Harrington. New York: New York University Press, 2007. 285–300. Print.
Kawin, Bruce F. *Horror and the Horror Film*. London: Anthem Press, 2012. Print.
Kripke, Eric. *Supernatural*. Warner Bros. 2005–2013. Television.
Newman, Michael. "From Beats to Arcs: Toward a Poetics of Television Narrative." *Velvet Light Trap* 58 (2006): 16–28. Web. 10 Nov. 2013.
Phalen, Patricia, and Julia Osellame. "Writing Hollywood: Rooms with a Point of View." *Journal of Broadcasting & Electronic Media* 56.1 (March 2012): 3–20. Web. 10 Aug. 2013.
Rosinsky, Natalie M. *Feminist Futures: Contemporary Women's Speculative Fiction*. Ann Arbor, MI: UMI Research Press, 1982. Print.
Short, Sue. *Misfit Sisters: Screen Horror as Female Rites of Passage*. New York: Palgrave Macmillan, 2006. Print.
Spigel, Lynn. "Introduction." *Television After TV: Essays on a Medium in Transition*. Ed. Lynn Spigel and Jan Olsson. Duke University Press, 2004. 1–34. Print.
_____, and Jan Olsson, eds. *Television After TV: Essays on a Medium in Transition*. Durham: Duke University Press, 2004. Print.
Star Trek: Voyager. Exec. Prod. Rick Berman, Michael Piller, and Jeri Taylor. UPN. 1995–2001. Television.
Stuller, Jennifer K. *Ink-Stained Amazons and Cinematic Warriors: Superwomen in Modern Mythology*. London: I.B.Tauris, 2010. Print.
Supernatural: Season 1–8. Exec. Prod. Eric Kripke et al. Warner Bros., 2013. Blu-Ray.
Superwiki. *Supernatural Wiki*. Est June 2006. http://www.supernaturalwiki.com/index.php?title=Super-wiki. Web.
Xena, Warrior Princess. Dir. Robert Tapert. Syndicated. 1995–2001. Television.
Zubernis, Lynn, and Katherine Larsen. *Fandom at the Crossroads: Celebration, Shame and Fan/Producer Relationships*. Newcastle Upon Tyne, UK: Cambridge Scholars Publishing, 2012. Print.

About the Contributors

Cat **Ashton** is a doctoral candidate at York University. She did her M.A. in interdisciplinary studies and her B.A. in creative writing, both also at York. Her work focuses on the mythic dimensions of fantastic literature.

Tammy **Dasti** received a B.A. from McMaster University, where she wrote an undergraduate thesis on the changes to the modern vampire myth. She earned an M.A. from Wilfrid Laurier University and a Ph.D. at the University of Bristol, UK. Her doctoral thesis examined the influence of Catholicism on the work of Anne Rice.

Maude **Deschênes-Pradet** is a Ph.D. student in French studies at the University of Sherbrooke. She intends to develop geocritical tools adapted to the study of invented places in literature, under the direction of professor Christiane Lahaie.

Isabelle **Fournier** is a Ph.D. student in French literature at the University at Buffalo, and an adjunct professor at Brock University. She is writing her dissertation on French-Canadian science fiction. She has a B.A. and an M.A. in translation with well over ten years of experience in the field.

Dominick **Grace** is an associate professor of English at Brescia University College in London, Ontario. He is co-editor with Eric Hoffman of *Dave Sim: Conversations*, *Chester Brown: Conversations*, and *Seth: Conversations*, and author of *The Science Fiction of Phyllis Gotlieb: A Critical Reading*, forthcoming from McFarland.

Adam **Guzkowski** is an instructor in science fiction literature at Seneca College in Toronto, Ontario, and in women's studies and feminist research at Western University in London, Ontario. He is also a Ph.D. candidate in Canadian studies at Trent University in Peterborough, Ontario, where his dissertation work focuses on Canadian science fiction and fantasy literature.

Brecken **Hancock**'s poetry, essays, interviews, and reviews have appeared in *Riddle Fence*, *Event*, *CV2*, *Grain*, *The Fiddlehead*, and *Studies in Canadian Literature*. She is reviews editor for *Arc Poetry Magazine* and interviews editor for *Canadian Women in the Literary Arts*.

About the Contributors

Veronica **Hollinger** is a professor of cultural studies at Trent University in Ontario. She is a long-time co-editor of the journal *Science Fiction Studies* and co-editor of several scholarly collections, the most recent of which is *Parabolas of Science Fiction* (Wesleyan University Press, 2013).

Michael **Kaler** is a Toronto-based musician and scholar. He holds doctorates in religious studies and ethnomusicology, and his research work has focused around the artistic expression of the quest for transcendence, in the contexts of early Egyptian heterodox Christianity and improvised music (particularly the work of the Grateful Dead).

Lisa **Macklem** is a Ph.D. candidate in law at the University of Western Ontario. Lisa holds both a J.D. and an LL.M., and her M.A. thesis in media studies was on the fan/producer relationship as evidenced by *Supernatural*. She has presented at numerous conferences on *Supernatural* and fan works, as well as on copyright.

David **Milman** is a Ph.D. candidate at York University. He earned an M.A. in English literature and a B.A. honors degree in English literature. His interests revolve around the fields of occidental philosophy, cybernetics, and contemporary fiction.

Derek **Newman-Stille** is a Ph.D. candidate at Trent University. His research examines the representation of disability in Canadian Speculative Fiction, with a particular interest in the ascription of images of disability upon monstrous protagonists. He has given papers at the past three Academic Conference on Canadian Science Fiction and Fantasy sessions as well as other conferences in the field.

Robert **Runté** is an associate professor at the University of Lethbridge and senior editor with Five Rivers Publishing. In 1989, his *NCF Guide to Canadian Science Fiction* won an Aurora Award; he won a second Aurora in 1990. In 1994 he was honored as Fan Guest at the 52nd WorldCon, and in 1996 he co-edited (with Yves Meyard) the *Tesseracts*[5] anthology. The essay published herein won an Aurora Award in 2014.

Chester N. **Scoville** is a lecturer in the Department of English and Drama at the University of Toronto Mississauga. He writes and teaches in the fields of fantasy fiction, medieval drama and literature, narrative, and rhetoric. He is also editing an anthology of rhetoric.

Clare **Wall** is a Ph.D. candidate at York University in Toronto studying contemporary posthuman bodies. She received her B.A. honors in English from York University and completed an M.A. in English from McMaster University. She has presented research on posthuman subjects, contemporary speculative fiction, and the portrayal of gender and otherness in science fiction and fantasy.

Allan **Weiss** is an associate professor of English and humanities at York University in Toronto, and author of approximately two dozens short stories, both mainstream and fantastic. He has published and presented numerous papers on Canadian literature, especially Canadian science fiction and fantasy.

Index

alienation 20
Anderson, Poul 84–85, 91
April, Jean-Pierre 7
Armstrong, Kelley 10, 173–83
Astounding/Analog 17, 22, 25
Atwood, Margaret 2, 8, 17, 28, 141
Aurora Awards 18

Ballard, J.G. 35–36
Beagle, Peter S. 117
Bell, John 7
Bewitched (TV series) 173
Botte, Jim 1
Bowie, David 212
Bradbury, Ray 111
Brown, Dan 84
Bugnet, Georges 4
Bull, Emma 117
Bullock, Michael 6
Bundoran Press 29
Burroughs, Edgar Rice 36–37

Callaghan, Morley 3
Campbell, John W., Jr. 9, 16–17, 20, 22, 25–28, 55–65
Canadia (radio program) 21
Canadian Broadcasting Corporation (CBC) 20
Canvention 18
Card, Orson Scott 30
Carnell, Ted 22
Carpenter, John 55-
Centennius, Ralph 4
Champetier, Joel 7
Charmed (TV series) 173, 182
Choyce, Lesley 7
Clarke, Arthur C. 17
Clarke, J. Brian 17
Clute, John 2
Colombo, John Robert 7–8, 17–20

colonialism and postcolonialism in Canadian SF 95–104, 166–67, 170–71, 178–79, 181
Coney, Michael G. 17
Cooper, Susan 111
The Craft (TV series) 173
Crowley, John 117

Datlow, Ellen 117
De Bergerac, Cyrano 17
De Gaspe, 4
Delany, Samuel R. 35–36, 39
De Lint, Charles 2, 10, 112–18
De Mille, James 4
De Quincey, Thomas 9, 44–46, 50–54
Derrida, Jacques 37, 44–45, 53
De Sade, Marquis 120–21, 129
Dick, Philip K. 84, 91, 92n12
Dickson, Gordon R. 17
Dorsey, Candas Jane 22
Ducornet, Rikki 7, 10, 120-
Duncan, Dave 17, 21, 31

Eco, Umberto 141, 144n2
Edge Publishing 29
environment in Canadian SF 22, 68–79, 111–18

fandom 7, 55–56, 224–39
Findley, Timothy 8
Fitting, Peter 2
Five Rivers Publishing 29
Freud, Sigmund 120, 125–29, 171
Further Perspectives on the Canadian Fantastic 8

Gadallah, Leslie 23, 26–27
Gagnon, Maurice 6
Galbraith, John 4
Garner, Alan 111

243

Gedge, Pauline 17
gender in SF 10, 37–38, 140, 173–83
George, Henry 4
Gibson, William 2, 8–9, 17, 45-, 53–54, 70
Godfrey, Ellen 7
The Good Witch (TV series) 173
Gotlieb, Phyllis 5, 17, 23
Green, Robert 6
Green, Terence M. 17
Grenier, Armand 5
Grove, Frederick Philip 6

Hadfield, Chris 212, 220–22
Hargreaves, H.A. 5, 17, 22–26
Harrison, Kim 173
Hartwell, David G. 7
Harvey, Jean-Charles 5
Heaps, Leo 6
Heinlein, Robert A. 16
Hekkanen, Ernest 7
Hemon, Louis 5
Hesse, Hermann 85
Hodgins, Jack 7
Hoffman, Alice 173, 182
Holden, Helene 6
Hopkinson, Nalo 2, 8, 10, 95-, 146–58
Horeck, Brian 163–67, 171
Howard, Robert E. 111
Huff, Tanya 2, 10, 186–97
Hughes, Matthew 17
The Hunger Games (book and film series) 31

Jung, Carl 85, 92n5

Kant, Immanuel 9, 50–53
Kay, Guy Gavriel 2, 18, 28–29, 32
Ketterer, David 3, 8
Kilian, Crawford 17
King, Stephen 8
Kirkpatrick, David 24

Lackey, Mercedes 117
Larlabestier, Justine 37–38
Laurence, Margaret 3
Lawrence, W.H.C. 4
Llewellyn, Edward 17
Lucas, George 8

MacLennan, Hugh 3, 8
Manguel, Alberto 17
Manning, Laurence 5
Mantley, John 6
Martin, George R.R. 30
The Matrix (film series) 84
McCormack, Eric 8
Melville, Herman 91–92

Mercer, Rick 19
Merril, Judith 17
Merril Collection 1
Midnight, Lucien 212, 218–21
Mieville, China 202
Miller, Elizabeth 2
Moloney, Susan 161–63, 171
Morris, William 109
multiculturalism in Canadian SF 24, 29, 95–104, 146–57

nationalism and national identity 4–5, 18–19
Nelson, Frederick 4
The New Wave 38
New Worlds 22
Norton, Andre 16
Nourse, Alan E. 15

O'Hagan, Howard 6
O'Malley, Bryan Lee 11, 200–10
On Spec (magazine) 18

Palaprat, Gérard 212, 216–18
Paquin, Ubald 5
Pedley, Hugh 5–6
Perspectives on the Canadian Fantastic 8
Poe, Edgar Allan 5, 35
politics in Canadian SF 5, 19–20
posthumanism in SF 67–79
Powe, Bruce 6

Ransom, Amy J. 8
regionalism 3, 159–71
Reid, Siàn 1
religion in SF 4, 81–93, 120–30
Requiem/Solaris 7
Robinson, Spider 17
Rochon, Esther 10, 131–44
Rooke, Leon 17
Rowe, Michael 167–71
Runte, Robert 1–3, 8–9, 11

Sabrina, the Teenage Witch (TV series) 173
Saunders, Charles 7
Sawyer, Robert J. 7. 29, 212
Schroeder, Andreas 6
Schroeder, Karl 2
Science Fiction Studies 35–36
Sernine, Daniel 7
Shelley, Mary 34, 36
Shetterley, Will 117
Star Trek (TV and film series) 8
Star Wars (film series) 8
Stewart, Sean 17
Stockton, Paul 24

Index

Supernatural (TV show) 11, 224–39
Suvin, Darko 39–40
surrealism 3

Tardivel, Jules-Paul 4
Tesseracts (anthology series) 18
Thériault, Yves 6
Tolkien, J.R.R. 109–12
Twain, Mark 35
Tycho Books 29

United States and Canadian SF 24, 26, 110–12
Updike, John 173

Van Vogt, A.E. 5, 17, 28
Verne, Jules 5, 131
Vonarburg, Elisabeth 7

Walcott, Rinaldo 149–51, 155–56,
Watts, Peter 2, 8–9, 55–57, 62–65, 67–79
Weiner, Andrew 17
Weintraub, William 6
Wells, H.G. 5, 17
Wiener, Norbert 44–54
Willer, Jim 6
Willett, Edward 17
Williams, Lynda 31–32
Willis, Connie 38
Wilson, Robert Charles 2, 7–9, 17, 81–94
Windling, Terri 117
Wolf, Casey 26
Wright, Edgar 203
Wyl, Jean Michel 6

Yates, J. Michael 6